Timothy Silence

The Foundling Hospital for Wit

Intended for the Reception and Preservation of such Brats of Wit and Humour

whose Parents Chuse to Drop Them

Timothy Silence

The Foundling Hospital for Wit
Intended for the Reception and Preservation of such Brats of Wit and Humour whose Parents Chuse to Drop Them

ISBN/EAN: 9783744794657

Printed in Europe, USA, Canada, Australia, Japan

Cover: Foto ©Thomas Meinert / pixelio.de

More available books at **www.hansebooks.com**

THE
Foundling Hospital
FOR
W I T.

INTENDED

For the Reception and Preservation of such Brats of WIT and HUMOUR, whose Parents chuse to drop them.

CONTAINING

All the SATIRES, ODES, BALLADS, EPIGRAMS, &c. that have been wrote since the Change of the Ministry, many of which have never before been printed.

Number I.   To be continued Occasionally.

———————*Poetica furgit*
Tempeſtas.———   JUVENAL.

LONDON: Printed 1743.
Reprinted for W. WEBB, near St. Paul's.
M DCC LXIII.

THE
ROYAL CHARTER
OF
Apollo *and the* Muses,

FOR

Establishing an HOSPITAL for the Reception and Preservation of such Brats of WIT and HUMOUR whose Parents chuse to drop them.

Apollo, *God of Wit, Father of Light, King of Parnassus, and all the Territories thereunto belonging*; *to all to whom these Presents shall come, Greeting.*

WHEREAS our Trusty and Well-beloved Subject *Samuel Silence*, Gentleman, in Behalf of great Numbers of *Mental Infants* daily exposed to Destruction, has, by his Petition, humbly represented unto us, that many Persons of WIT and HUMOUR of both Sexes, being sensible of the frequent Murders committed on these beautiful Infants by the inhuman Custom of exposing them to perish and starve in the common News Papers, or to be bury'd and suffocated

suffocated in Dunghils of Trash in the Monthly Magazines, have, by Instruments in Writing, declared their Intentions to contribute liberally towards the erecting and supporting an Hospital for the Reception and Preservation of such exposed and deserted Productions, as soon as We should be graciously pleased to grant our Letters Patent for that good Purpose.

We, taking the Premisses into our Royal Consideration, and being desirous to promote so good and laudable an Establishent, are graciously pleased to gratify the Petitioner in his Request.

Know ye therefore, that We, of our especial Grace, certain Knowledge, and mere Motion, have willed, ordained, constituted, and appointed, and by these Presents do will, ordain, constitute and appoint, our aforesaid trusty and well-beloved Subject *Samuel Silence*, Esq; his Heirs, Executors, Administrators, and Assigns, to be the sole Director, Proprietor, and Governor of this our *Hospital*, intituled and known by the Name of THE FOUNDLING HOSPITAL FOR WIT.

And our Will and Pleasure is, that the said *Samuel Silience* shall, on or before the 25th Day of *March*, in the Year 1743, publish the first Number of this our Pamphlet, intituled, the *Foundling Hospital for Wit*, and so shall continue from Time to Time, once in 3 or 4 Months, or oftener, as new Materials shall come in, and he shall see Occasion, to publish a Number of the said Pamphlet, at the Price of One Shilling.

And

[iii]

And for the Encouragement of all such well-disposed Persons as are willing to become Contributors to this laudable Design, by purchasing this our Pamphlet, *be it further enacted*, that it shall be printed with a neat Letter, on a handsome Paper, and in the size of this our first Pamphlet.

We will moreover, that our said trusty and well-beloved *Samuel Silence*, Esq; shall have full and sole Power to refuse whatever Brats he shall think proper, particularly such as shall be judged infected with any dangerous Distemper, as also all mishapen, weak, or sickly Productions, neither such as are untoward, wicked, and licentious: forasmuch as the Admission of such might tend to the Disgrace of our *Hospital*, and change what was intended as a Nursery for spritely and beautiful Infants, into an Infirmary for Invalids.

Provided always, and be it further enacted, by the Authority aforesaid, that the said *Samuel Silence* shall preserve an inviolable Secrecy, as his Name betokeneth, not only with regard to the Names and Places of Abode of the Parents of such Offspring as he chuseth to admit, but also of those whom he refuseth: Nay, it shall not be lawful for him, on any Pretence whatsoever, so much as to enquire after them.

We will moreover, for the sake of such modest Parents as would dispose of their Issue privately, that Letters directed for *Samuel Silence*, Esq; to be left at *Brown's* Coffee-House in *Spring Gardens*, shall be carefully delivered, and all proper Care

taken

taken of their Contents gratis. And if it requires immediate Publication, it shall be done with the utmost Expedition.

And as this noble Foundation is intended for the general Benefit of all our loving Subjects, 𝕺ur 𝖂ill and 𝕻leasure is, that the Offspring of all Parties shall be received and cherished, let who will be its Father, and no Cause shall be deem'd sufficient to exclude it, except, as aforesaid, that of Sickness or Deformity.

𝕬nd finally we will, for the universal Encouragement of all our loving Subjects, in the delightful Occupation of begetting Children, that whether their Offspring shall speak in the musical and sublime Language of Rhime, or in the plain and natural Cadence of Prose; whether they shall appear in the finer Dress of Epistles, Satires, Odes, Songs, and Epigrams; or in the plain and modest Garb of Letters and Essays, they shall be equally fitted with an Apartment in this our *Hospital*, and as carefully attended and provided for, as if they were under the Eye of their own dear Parents.

THE
Foundling Hospital
FOR
W I T.

Verses occasioned by a Quarrel betwixt Mr. F—ld—g and Mrs. Cl--ve, *on his intending her the Part of a Bawd, in his new Play called* The Wedding Day.

Bawd! a Bawd! where is this scoundrel Poet?
Fine Work indeed! By G--d the Town shall know it.
F--ld--g who heard, and saw her Passion rise,
Thus answer'd calmly: Prithee C--ve be wise,
The Part will suit your Humour, Taste, and Size.
Ye lye! ye lye! ungrateful as thou art,
My matchless Talents claim the Lady's Part;
And all who judge, by Jesus G--d, agree,
None ever play'd the gay Coquet like me.
   Thus said and swore the celebrated *Nell*;
Now judge her Genius: is she *Bawd*, or *Belle*?

[2]

An Epitaph upon the Political Memory of W——
P———— E—— *of* B——, *who died to Fame on*
July 15, 1742.

P——y, no Friend to Truth! in Fraud sincere,
   In Act unfaithful, and from Honour clear;
Who broke his Promise, serv'd his private Ends;
Who gain'd a Title, and who lost all Friends:
Dishonour'd by himself, by none approv'd;
Curs'd, scorn'd, and hated ev'n by th'ose he lov'd.

On hearing the Death of Cardinal Fleury *confirm'd, an* Old *and* Great *Friend of his thus cry'd in Raptures:*

Pardon, *Old Friend*, if at thy Death
   A sudden Joy prevails;
'Tis not that you've resign'd your Breath,
   But that you CAN'T TELL TALES.

A SONG.

THE Man so silly
   To think he's able,
To back a Filly
   When old and feeble;
    Sighing,
    Toying,
    Grunting,
    Mounting,
Scarce after all to his Saddle can rise.
And when upon her
   At last he's got,
Headstrong she's gone, or
   Frisky and hot;
   Sudden she plunges,
   Capers and lunges,
Off he is flung, and away Filly flies.

But the clever
  Jolly brisk Rider,
While you live ever,
  Mount her, he'll guide her:
    Freaking,
    Squeaking,
    Neighing,
    Playing,
Sweetly she moves to his Pleasure and Ease:
  Walk, Trot, or Gallop,
  Yet quite in Hand,
  And with her Tail up,
  At your Command,
  Freely she'll set up,
Tit up, a tit up, as long as you please.

To Mr. Thomson, *Author of the Poem on the Four Seasons, on Occasion of the Part which that Gentleman took in the Concert, and for promoting Mr.* Dennis's *Benefit Night, given him by the Players, when he was very old, very poor, and short-liv'd.*

WHILST I reflect thee o'er, methinks I find
    Thy various Seasons in the Author's Mind!
Spring, in thy flow'ry Fancy, spreads her Hues;
And, like thy soft Compassion, sheds her Dews.
Summer's hot Strength in thy Expression glows;
And o'er thy Page a beamy Ripeness throws.
Autumn's rich Fruits th'instructed Reader gains,
Who tastes the meaning Purpose of thy Strains.
Winter—but that—no Semblance takes from thee,
That hoary Season's Type was drawn from me.
Shatter'd by Time's bleak Storms I withering lay,
Leafless, and whitening in a cold Decay.
Yet shall my propless Ivy—pale—and bent,
Bless the short Sun-shine, which thy Pity lent.

DENNIS.

An EPIGRAM.

DEEP, deep in S——'s blund'ring Head,
　　The new Gin Project funk:
O happy Project! fage, he cry'd,
　　Let all the Realm be drunk.

'Gainft univerfal Hate and Scorn,
　　This Scheme my fole Defence is,
For when I've beggar'd half the Realm,
　　'Tis Time to drown their Senfes.

An Account of the Hampfhire Wonder, *or* Groaning Tree, *from a Gentleman of that County to a Courtier in* London.

WHILE publick Robbers fafter breed,
　　Than *Hatchet*, or than *Hemp* can rid;
While P—rs and P—ts, with fuch Fellows,
Combine to rob the Block and Gallows;
And injur'd *Tyburn* fadly grieves,
It can't come at thefe *mighty Thieves*;
The Gallows' Wrongs an *Elm* bemoans,
And vents its Grief in louder Groans.
Spreading his Limbs, as if the Tree
Defir'd they all might *Gibbets* be,
Whereon to tye up Knaves at Helm
From ever ftaining Boards of *Elm*:
For Boards of C--nc--l, Boards of *Trade*,
May of light *Elm* be often made.
　We now expect that *Britifh* Oak,
Will foon complain; 'tis made a Joke:
Saw'd, hack'd, and hew'd, and fent to Sea,
To bully *Britain's* Enemy:

When

When all the while, 'tis made their Sport;
For are not *Britain's* Foes at C---rt?
  In short, if thus your Friends go on,
'Tis well if any *Stock* or *Stone*,
Their Stations keep, or *only groan*.

A CASE, *supposed to be true.*

TWO Heroes went, we thought to fight;
  One, tho' he knew it not, did right:
And warm with Zeal for *Britain's* Glory,
Must live recorded fair in Story.

The other knew his *whole Command*,
Yet to our Conquests put a Stand,
And sacrific'd to *Spain's* Ambition,
Because he acted by *Commission*.

Did *V-——-n*, or did *W-——-th* well?
The *First*, if *Englishmen* may tell.
By *Courtiers* be the Judgment past,
They to a Man will say, the *Last*.

But what will People say abroad,
If *Worth* to Honour's not the Road?
If at St. *J—'s* Folks inherit,
For *Crimes Applause*, *Neglect* for Merit?

An EPIGRAM.

SIR *Thomas* of *Wentworth*, inflexibly good,
  Had long *Ministerial Power* withstood:
At length thro' Ambition, an *Earl* he was made;
So first lost his *Friends*, and then lost his *Head*.
O *Pulteney!* consider, like his thy *Condition*,
How great and how glorious thy long *Opposition:*
Thou art now made an *Earl*, have a Care of thy *Head*,
Our *Pyms* and our *Hampdens* are not all of 'em dead.

The

The OLD COACHMAN: *A New* BALLAD.

WISE *Caleb* and *C-r-t*, two Birds of a Feather,
Went down to a Feast at *N—s* together:
No matter what Wines, or what choice of good Chear,
'Tis enough that the Coachman has his Dole or Beer.
Derry down, down, high derry down.

Coming home, as the Liquor work'd up in his Pate,
This Coachman drove on at a damnable rate:
Poor *C--f--t*, in Terror, and fear'd all the while,
Cry'd, "Stop! Let me out! Is the Dog an *Argyle?*"
Derry down, &c.

But he soon was convinc'd of his Error; for, lo,
John stopt short in the Dirt, and no farther would go.
When *C--r--t* saw this, he observ'd with a Laugh;
"This Coachman, I find, is your own, my Lord
 B--b." *Derry down,* &c.

Now the Peers quit their Coach in a pitiful Plight,
Deep in Mire, and in Rain, and without any Light;
Not a Path to pursue, nor to guide them a Friend;
What Course shall they take then, and how will
 this end? *Derry down,* &c.

Lo! Chance, the great Mistress of human Affairs,
Who governs in Councils, and conquers in Wars;
Strait with Grief at their Case (for the Goddess well
 knew,
That these were her Creatures, and Votaries true:)
Derry down, &c.

This Chance brought a Passenger quick to their Aid.
Honest Friend, can you drive?---What should ail
 me? he said,
For many a bad Season, through many a bad Way,
Old *Or-f d* I've driven, without stop or stay.
Derry down, &c.

He

He was once overturn'd, I confess, but not hurt:
Quoth the Peers, it was we help'd him out of the Dirt.
This Boon for thy Master, then prithee requite,
Take us up, or else here we must wander all Night.
     Derry down, &c.

He took them both up, and thro' thick and thro' thin
Drove away for St. *James's*, and brought them safe in.
Learn hence, honest *Britons*, in spite of your Pains,
That *Or-f-d*, old Coachman, still governs the Reins.
    Derry down, down, high derry down.

The COUNTRY GIRL; an ODE.

THE Country Girl that's well inclin'd
 To love, when the young 'Squire grows kind,
  Doubts between Joy and Ruin;
Now will, and now will not comply,
To Raptures now her Pulse beats high,
  And now she fears undoing.

But when the Lover with his Pray'rs,
His Oaths, his Sighs, his Vows and Tears,
  Holds out the profer'd Treasure;
She quite forgets her Fear and Shame,
And quits her Virtue and good Name
  For Profit mixt with Pleasure.

So virtuous P———, who had long
By Speech, by Pamphlet, and by Song,
  Held Patriotism's Steerage,
Yields to Ambition mixt with Gain,
A Treasury gets for *Il———y V—c*,
  And for himself a Peerage.

Tho' with joint Lives and Debts before,
H———y's Estate was covered o'er,
  This *Irish* Place repairs it;
Unless that Story should be true,
That he receives but half his Due,
  And the new C———ss shares it.

            'Tis

'Tis said, besides, that t'other H——y
Pays half the Fees of Secretary
    To B——'s ennobled Doxy;
If so—good Use of Pow'r she makes,
The Treasury of each Kingdom takes,
    And holds them both by Proxy.

Whilst her dear L——d obeys his Summons,
And leaves the noisy H——e of C———s,
    Amongst the L——s to nod;
Where, if he's better than of old,
His Hands perhaps a Stick may hold,
    But never more a Rod.

Unheard of, let him slumber there,
As innocent as any P——r,
    As prompt for any Job?
For now he's popular no more,
Has lost the Power he had before,
    And his best Friends, the Mob.

Their Fav'rites shou'dn't soar so high,
They fail him when too near the Sky,
    Like *Icarus's* Wings;
And Popularity is such,
As still is ruined by the Touch
    Of gracious giving Kings.

Here then, O B——h! thy Empire ends
A——le shall with his Tory Friends
    Soon better Days restore;
For *Enoch's* Fate and thine are one,
Like him *translated*, thou art gone
    Ne'er to be heard of more.

A New

A New ODE.

To a great Number of Great Men, *newly made.*
Jam nova Progenies.

By the Author of THE COUNTRY MAID.

SEE, a new Progeny descends
From Heav'n, of *Britain's* truest Friends.
   Oh, Muse! attend my Call!
To one of these direct thy Flight,
Or, to be sure that we are right,
   Direct it to them all.

Oh *Clio!* these are Golden Times;
I shall get Money for my Rhymes,
   And thou no more go tatter'd:
Make haste then, lead the Way, begin;
For here are People just come in
   Who never yet were flatter'd.

But first to C——r——t fain you'd sing;
Indeed he's nearest to the K——,
   Yet careless how you use him:
Give him, I beg, no labour'd Lays;
He will but *promise,* if you praise,
   And *laugh* if you abuse him.

Then (but there's a vast Space betwixt)
The new made E. of B——h comes next,
   Stiff in his popular Pride:
His Step, his Gait, describe the Man;
They paint him better than I can,
   Waddling from Side to Side.

Each Hour a different Face he wears,
Now in a Fury, now in Tears,
   Now Laughing, now in Sorrow;
Now he'll command, and now obey,
Bellows for Liberty To-day,
   And roars for Pow'r To-morrow.

At Noon the Tories had him tight,
With ſtaunched Whigs he ſupp'd at Night,
    Each Party try'd to've won him;
But he himſelf did ſo divide,
Shuffled and cut from Side to Side,
    That now both Parties ſhun him.

[*Wilmington*] See yon old, dull, important Lord,
Who at the long'd-for Money-Board
    Sits firſt, but does not lead:
His younger Brethren all Things make;
So that the Treaſury's like a Snake,
    And the Tail moves the Head.

Why did you croſs God's good Intent?
He made you for a Pr—ſi—nt;
    Back to that Station go:
Nor longer act this Farce of Power,
We know you miſs'd the Thing before,
    And have not got it now.

See valiant *C—m*, valorous *S—r*,
Britain's two Thunderbolts of War,
    Now ſtrike my raviſh'd Eye:
But, oh! their Strength and Spirits flown,
They, like their conquering Swords, are grown
    Ruſty with lying by.

Dear *Bat*, I'm glad you've got a Place,
And ſince Things thus have chang'd their Face,
    You'll give Oppoſing o'er:
'Tis comfortable to be in,
And think what a damn'd while you've been,
    Like *Peter*, at the Door.

See who comes next—I kiſs thy Hands,
But not in Flattery, *S—l S—s*; [*Sandys*]
    For ſince you are in Power,
That gives you Knowledge, Judgment, Parts,
The Courtier's Wiles, the Stateſman's Arts,
    none before. When

When great impending Dangers shook
Its State, old *Rome* Dictators took
    Judiciously from Plough:
So they (but at a Pinch thou knowest)
To make the Highest of the Lowest,
    Th' Exchequer gave to you.

When in your Hands the Seals you found,
Did it not make your Brains go round?
    Did it not turn your Head?
I fancy (but you hate a Joke)
You felt as *Nell* did when she 'woke
    In Lady *Loverule*'s Bed.

See H—y V—e in Pomp appear,
And since he's made V—e T—r,
    Grown taller by some Inches:
See *Tw*———— follow *C*————*t*'s Call;
See *Hanoverian G*————*r*, and all
    The black Funereal *F*—*s*.

And see with that important Face
Beranger's Clerk to take his Place,
    Into the T—-—y come;
With Pride and Meanness act thy Part,
Thou look'st the very Thing thou art,
    Thou *Burgeois Gentilhomme*.

Oh, my poor Country! is this all
You've gain'd by the long-labour'd Fall
    Of *Wa*l*p*·*le* and his Tools?
He was a Knave indeed---what then?
He'd Parts---but this new Set of Men
    A'n't only Knaves, but Fools.

More Changes, better Times this Isle
Demands; oh! *Chesterfield*, *Argyle*,
    To bleeding *Britain* bring 'em:
Unite all Hearts, appease each Storm,
'Tis yours such Actions to perform,
    My Pride shall be to sing 'em.

The

The CAPUCIN. *A New* BALLAD.

To the Tune of *Ye Commons and Peers.*

Ecce iterum Crispinus, *& est mihi sæpe vocandus.*

WHO at *Paris* has been,
　　Has a *Mendicant* seen,
Who for Charity follows to dun you;
　　Offer him what you will,
　　He refuses it still,
For he'as sworn that he'll never take Money.

　　But near him there stands,
　　With two open Hands,
A Creature that follows for Hire;
　　Any Gifts that you make,
　　He'll readily take;
And at Night he accounts with the Fryar.

　　So the great E— of B——
　　Has sworn in his Wrath,
That he'll never accept of a Place;
　　Neither Chancellor he,
　　Nor Treasurer will be,
And refuses the Seals and the Mace.

　　But near him * a Crowd
　　Stand bellowing aloud,
For all that two Courts can afford;
　　And 'tis very well known,
　　That for them what is done,
Is the same as if done for my Lord.

---

* *A Crowd.* Here every intelligent Reader will immediately have in his Thoughts eight or ten of the ablest Men and greatest Genius's in this Kingdom; such as, H. V——, H. F——se, L—d L——l, Mr. Hoo···r. Mr. S——l S——s, Mr. B——tle, Mr. G——, Sir J. R——t, &c. &c. &c. &c.

But

But I'm told, noble Peer,
Lest these Things should take Air,
And with Dirt all Mankind should upbraid ye,
That you try a new Way,
('Tis as safe I dare say)
And make them account with my Lady.

But indeed this won't do,
And the World will see through,
And your *Virtue* (I fear) will bespatter:
Then mind what I send,
For I'm so far your Friend,
That I'm sure you can't say that I flatter.

There's my good Lord of *G----r*
I'n't a quarter come o'er,
And I fancy you'll find he wants Zeal;
If he don't come plum in,
And vote through Thick and Thin,
Turn him out, and be made Privy Seal.

Don't slight this Advice,
Nor affect to be nice,
Laugh at Oaths that obstruct your great Ends:
For an Oath's but a Joke,
To one that has broke
Through all Honour and Tyes with his Friends.

Go to *C---t--t* and *P-e-lham*,
You'll still go on, tell them,
All honest Mens Hopes to defeat;
To crown your Disgrace,
They'd give you this Place,
And your Character will be compleat.

An

An ODE, Humbly inscribed to the Right
Honourable W—— E--- of B----.

Neque enim lex justior ulla,
Quam necis artifices arte perire sua.
Parcius junctas quatiunt fenestras
Ictibus crebris juvenes protervi :
Nec tibi somnos adimunt : amatque
  Janua limen.
    &c. &c. &c. HOR. Lib. 1. Od. xxv.

GREAT E--- of B---, your Reign is o'er;
The Tories trust your Word no more,
  The Whigs no longer fear ye;
Your Gates are seldom now unbarr'd,
No Crowds of Coaches fill your Yard,
  And scarce a Soul comes near ye.

Few now aspire at your good Graces,
Scarce any sue to you for Places,
  Or come with their Petition,
To tell how well they have deserv'd,
How long, how steadily they starv'd,
  For you in Opposition.

Expect to see that Tribe no more,
Since all Mankind perceive that Pow'r
  Is lodg'd in other Hands:
Sooner to C---t---t now they'll go,
Or ev'n (though that's excessive low)
  To W---lm---n and S---s.

With your *obedient* Wife retire,
And sitting silent by the Fire,
  A sullen *tete à tete,*
Think over all you've done or said,
And curse the Hour that you were made
  Unprofitably great.

With

With Vapours there, and Spleen o'ercast,
Reflect on all your Actions past,
   With Sorrow and Contrition:
And there enjoy the Thoughts that rise
From disappointed Avarice,
   From frustrated Ambition.

There soon you'll loudly, but in vain,
Of your deserting Friends complain,
   That visit you no more;
But in this Country 'tis a Truth,
As known as that Love follows Youth,
   That Friendship follows Pow'r.

Such is the Calm of your Retreat!
You through the Dregs of Life must sweat
   Beneath this heavy Load;
And I'll attend you, as I've done,
Only to help Reflexion on,
   With now and then an Ode.

The STATESMAN.

Quem virum, aut heroa, lyra, vel acri
Tibia sumes celebrare, Clio?
Quem deum? &c.   HOR. Lib. I. Ode XII.

WHAT Statesman, what Hero, what King,
   Whose Name thro' the Island is spread,
Will you chuse, O my *Clio*, to sing,
   Of all the great Living or Dead?

Go, my Muse, from this Place to *Japan*
   In search of a Topic for Rhyme:
The great E---- of *B--h* is the Man,
   Who deserves to employ your whole Time.

But, howe'er, as the Subject is nice,
   And perhaps you're unfurnish'd with Matter;
May it please you to take my Advice,
   That you may'nt be suspected to flatter.

When you touch on his L----p's high Birth,
  Speak *Latin*, as if you were tipsy:
Say, we all are the Sons of the Earth,
  Et genus non fecimus ipsi.

Proclaim him as rich as a *Jew*;
  Yet attempt not to reckon his Bounties.
You may say, he is married; that's true:
  Yet speak not a Word of his C----ss.

Leave a Blank here and there in each Page,
  To enroll the fair Deeds of his Youth!
When you mention the Acts of his Age,
  Leave a Blank for his Honour and Truth!

Say, he made a great M-------h change Hands:
  He spake --- and the Minister fell.
Say, he made a great Statesman of S---ds;
  (Oh that he had taught him to spell!)

Then enlarge on his Cunning and Wit::
  Say, how he harangu'd at the *Fountain:*
Say, how the old Patriots were bit,
  And a Mouse was produc'd by a Mountain.

Then say, how he mark'd the new Year,
  By encreasing our Taxes, and Stocks:
Then say, how he chang'd to a P---r,
  Fit Companions for *E----be* and *F--x.*

A New ODE.

Quis multa gracilis te Puer in rosa
Perfusus liquidis urget adoribus
  Grato, Pyrrha, sub antro?   HOR. Od. 5. Lib. 1.

WHAT (good L--d B---) prim Patriot now,
  With courtly Graces woes thee?
And from St. *Stephen's* C----l to
  The H--- of L--ds pursues thee?

How

How gay and debonnair your're grown
  How pleas'd with what is paſt!
Your Title has your Judgment ſhewn,
  And choice of Friends your Taſte.

With ſparkling Wits to entertain
  Yourſelf and your good C———ſs,
You've hit on ſweet-lip'd H———y V———
  And high-bred H—y F———ſt.

But to direct th' Affairs of State,
  What Geniuſes you've taken!
Their Talents, like their Virtues, great!
  Or all the World's miſtaken.

The Taſk was ſomething hard, 'tis true,
  Which you had on your Hands,
So, to pleaſe P—— and People too,
  You wiſely pitch'd on S———s.

O *Britain!* never any thing
  Could ſo exactly hit you:
His Mien and Manners charm'd the K—,
  His Parts amaz'd the City.

But to make all Things of a Piece,
  And end as you begun;
To find a Genius ſuch as his,
  What was there to be done?

O where—where were they to be found?
  Such Stars but rare appear!
Dart not their Rays on every Ground,
  Gild ev'ry Hemiſphere.

But you with aſtronomick Eyes,
  Not *Tycho Brahe's* more true,
From far ſpy'd ſome bright Orbs ariſe,
  And brought them to our View.

D   Sir

Sir *J—n*'s clear Head, and Sense profound,
  Blaz'd out in P———t ;
G———n, for Eloquence renown'd,
  To grace the C———t you sent.
To these congenial Souls you join'd
  Some more, as choice and proper,
Bright *B—tle* ! Darling of Mankind !
  Good L———k——— and sage H———r.

Such Virtue and such Wisdom shone,
  In ev'ry chosen Spirit !
All Men at least this Truth must own,
  Your nice Regard to Merit !
What Pray'rs and Praise to you belong,
  For this blest Reformation !
Thou Joy of ev'ry Heart and Tongue !
  Thou Saviour of the Nation !

O *W———le, W——le,* blush for Shame,
  With all your Tools around you !
Does not each glorious Patriot-Name,
  Quite dazzle and confound you ?
Had you sought out this Patriot Race,
  Triumphant still you'd been ;
By only putting them in Place,
  You had yourself kept in.

LABOUR in VAIN.
A SONG an Hundred Years Old.
To the Tune of MOLLY MOGG.

YE Patriots, who twenty long Years
  Have struggled our Rights to maintain :
View the End of your Labours and Fears,
  And see them all ended in Vain !
                                Behold !

Behold ! in the Front ſtands your Hero,
    Behind him his Patriot Train :
Hear him rail at a Tyrant and *Nero*;
    Yet his railing all ended in Vain.

Then ſee him attack a Convention,
    And calling for Vengeance on *Spain* :
What Pity ſuch noble Contention
    And Spirit ſhould end all in Vain !

That the Place-Bill he got for the Nation,
    Was only a Shadow, is plain :
For now 'tis a clear Demonſtration,
    The Subſtance is ended in Vain.

His bloody and horrible Vow,
    Which once gave the Courtiers ſuch Pain,
No longer alarums them now,
    For his Threats are all ended in Vain.

What though the Committee have found,
    That O——d's a Traitor in Grain ;
Yet wiſer than they may compound,
    And Juſtice be ended in Vain.

How certain would be our Undoing,
    Should the People their wiſhes obtain ?
Then to ſave us from danger of Ruin,
    He has ended our Wiſhes in Vain.

Then let us give Thanks and be glad,
    That he knew how our Paſſion to rein,
And wiſely prevented the Bad,
    By ending the Good all in Vain.

About *Brutus* let *Rome* diſagree,
    We won't from our Praiſes refrain ;
Our *Brutus* has more Cauſe than he
    To declare even Virtue in Vain.

Three Thousand five Hundred a Year,
      He valu'd it not of a Grain ;
His Scorn of such Filth is most clear,
      Since that too he ended in Vain.

Corruption he hates like a Toad,
      And calls it the National Bane,
Yet damn'd T——s, his Virtue to load,
      Say, that all is not ended in Vain.

He rejects all employments and Places,
      And thinks ev'ry Pension a Stain :
Yet T——s, with their damn'd sly Faces,
      Say, that all is not ended in Vain.

In spite of his Caution and Care,
      To avoid the Appearance of Gain,
Say those Tories, his Wife has a Share,
      And all is not ended in Vain.

The Patriots are Come: or, a Doctor for a Crazy Constitution. A new BALLAD.
    To the Tune of, *Derry down.*

OH! *E-g-d* attend, while thy Fate I deplore,
    Rehearsing the Schemes and the Conduct of Pow'r ;
And since only of those who have Power, I sing ;
I'm sure none can think that I hint at the ———
                              Derry down.

From the time his S-n made him Old *Robin* depose,
All the Power of a—— he was well known to lose ;
But, of all but the Name and the Badges bereft,
Like Old Women his Paraphernalia are left.
                              Derry down.

To tell how he shook in St. *J—s's* for Fear,
When first the new M----rs bully'd him there,

Makes my Blood boil with Rage to reflect what a
   Thing
They made of a Man we obey as a ----
                              Derry down.

Whom they pleas'd they put in, whom they pleas'd
   they put out,
And just like a Top they all lash'd him about;
Whilst he like a Top with a murmuring Noise,
Seem'd to grumble, but turn'd to these rude lashing
   Boys.   *Derry down.*

At last *C*---- arriving, thus spoke to his Grief,
If you'll make me your Doctor, I'll bring you
   Relief;
You see to your Closet familiar I come,
And seem like my Wife in the Circle at Home.
                              Derry down.

Quoth the ----, my good L---d, perhaps you've
   been told,
That I us'd to abuse you a little of old;
But now bring whom you will, and eke turn away,
Let me and my Money and *W---d--n* stay.
                              Derry down.

For you and *W--d--n*, I freely consent,
But as for your Money, I must have it spent:
I have promis'd your S--n (nay no Frowns) shall
   have some,
Nor think 'tis for nothing we Patriots are come.
                              Derry down.

But howe'er little---- since I find you're so good,
Thus stooping below your high Courage and Blood:
Put yourself in my Hands, and I'll do what I can,
To make you look yet like a ---- and a Man---
                              Derry down.

At the A--l--y and your T--y Board,
To save one single Man, you shan't say a Word;
                                        For

For by G--d all your Rubbish from both you shall shoot,
W--p--'s Cyphers entire, and G--ry's to boot.
Derry down.

And to guard P--es Ears, as all St--f--n take Care,
So long as yours are, not one Man shall come near :
For of all your old Crew, we'll leave only those
Whom we know never dare to say boh ! to a Goose.
Derry down.

So your Friend booby G--n I'll e'en let you keep,
Awake he can't hurt, and is still half asleep ;
Nor ever was dangerous, but to Woman kind,
And his Body's as Impotent now as his Mind.
Derry down.

There's another C—t Booby, at once hot and dull,
Your pious Pimp S--z, a mean H--r Fool,
For your Card-play at Night he too shall remain,
With virtuous and sober, and wise D----ne.
Derry down.

And for your C--t Nob-s who can't write or read,
As of such Titl'd Cyphers all C--ts stand in need ;
Who like P—t *Swisses* vote and fight for their Pay :
They're as good as a new Set, to cry yea and nay.
Derry down.

Tho' N--'s as false as he's silly, I know,
By betraying old *Robin* to me long ago,
As well as all those who employ'd him before,
Yet I'll leave him in Place, but I'll leave him no Pow'r.
Derry down.

For granting his Heart is as black as his Hat,
With no more Truth in this, than there's Sense beneath that ;
Yet as he's a C---d, he'll shake when I frown ;
You call'd him once R--l, I'll treat him like one.
Derry down.

And since his Estate at *E---n's* he'll spend,
And beggar himself without making a Friend:
So whilst the extravagant F---l has a Souse,
As his Brains I can't fear, his Fortune I'll use.
        Derry down.

And as Miser *H---* with all *C---rs* will draw,
He too may remain, but shall stick to his Law;
For of F--gn Affairs, when he talks like a Fool,
I'll laugh in his Face, and cry out go to School.
        Derry down.

The Countess of *W--n,* like your old Nurse,
I'll trust at the T---y, not with its Purse,
For nothing by her I'm resolved shall be done,
She shall sit at that Board, as you sit on the T--e.
        Derry down.

Perhaps now you expect that I shou'd begin
To tell you the Men I design to bring in;
But we've not yet determined on all their Demands,
And you'll know soon enough when they come to
  kiss H--ds.   *Derry down.*

All that Weather-cock *P--y* shall ask we must grant,
For to make him a N--e for nothing, I want;
And to cheat such a Man demands all my Arts,
For tho' he's a Fool, he's a Fool with great Parts.
        Derry down.

And as popular *Clodius,* the *P---y* of *Rome,*
From a Noble, for Pow'r did Plebeian become:
So this *Clodius* to be a Patrician shall chuse,
Till what one got by changing the other shall lose.
        Derry down.

Thus flatter'd, and courted, and gaz'd at by all,
Like *Phaeton* rais'd for a Day, he shall fall,
Put the World in a Flame, and show he did strive
To get Reins in his Hand, tho' 'tis plain he can't
  drive.   *Derry down.*

For your F---gn Affairs, howe'er they turn out,
At leaſt I'll take care you ſhall make a great Rout;
Then cock your great Hat, ſtrut, bounce, and look bluff,
For tho' kick'd and cuff'd here, you ſhall there kick and cuff.   *Derry down.*

That *W—p—e* did nothing they all uſed to ſay,
So I'll do enough, but I'll make the Dogs pay:
Great Fl-ts I'll provide, great A-mies engage,
Whate'er Debts we make, or whate'er Wars we wage.   *Derry down.*

With Cordials like theſe, the M--'s new Gueſt
Reviv'd his ſunk Spirits, and gladden'd his Breaſt,
Till in Raptures he cry'd, my dear L-d you ſhall do
Whatever you will, give me T---ps to r---w.
              Derry down.

But, oh, my dear Country! ſince this is thy State,
Who is there loves thee, but weeps at thy Fate?
Since, in changing thy Maſters, thou'rt juſt like old *Rome*,
With Faction, Opp--ſſ-n and Sl-v-y thy Doom.
              Derry down.

For tho' you have made that Rogue *W--e* retire,
You're out of the Frying-pan into the Fire;
But ſince to the Proteſtant Line I'm a Friend,
I tremble to think where theſe Ch--ges may end.
              Derry down.

A BALLAD.

In Imitation of William *and* Margaret.

Addreſſed to the ———

'TWAS at the Hour, when guiltleſs Care
    Is lulled in ſoft Repoſe;
When nothing wakes, ſave fell *Deſpair,*
    Beſet with cureleſs Woes.

Inviting Sleep, lo! *William* lay,
   The Down he vainly prest:
Honour, alas! had soar'd away,
   And Shame had p ison'd Rest.

B--t---ia, with that stern Regard
   That conscious Worth puts on,
Before his frantick Eye appear'd,
   And pierc'd him with a Groan.

Her Cheek had lost its rosy Bloom,
   And languid roll'd her Eye:
This once cou'd brighten midnight Gloom,
   That shame the *Tyrian* Dye.

The Laurel Wreath, by Glory's Hand,
   Twin'd round her awful Brow,
As what her Grief and Rage disdain'd,
   She rent in Fury now.

Away she hurl'd her boasted Shield,
   Away her useless Spear:
What Joys to Slaves can Trophies yield?
   What Pride the Pomp of War?

Behold the dire Effects (she cry'd)
   Of *William's* perjur'd Troth!
Behold the Orphan, who rely'd
   On a false Guardian's Oath!

How couldst thou with a Lover's Zeal,
   My widow'd Cause espouse,
Yet quit that Cause thou serv'dst so well,
   In scorn of all thy Vows?

How couldst thou swear, Wealth, Titles, Pow'r,
   Thy Candour wou'd disclaim?
Yet barter, in an evil Hour,
   That Candour for a *Name?*

How couldst thou win my easy Heart
   A Patriot to believe?
How could I know, but by the Smart,
   A Patriot would deceive?
Bethink thee of thy broken Trust;
   Thy *Vows* to me unpaid!
Thy Honour humbled in the Dust;
   Thy Country's Weal betray'd!
For this may all my Vengeance fall
   On thy devoted Head!
Living, be thou the Scorn of all!
   The Curse of all when dead!

This said, while Thunder round her broke,
   She vanish'd into Air;
And *William's* Horror, while she spoke,
   Was follow'd by Despair.

The WIFE and the NURSE, *A New Ballad.*

VICE once with VIRTUE did engage,
   To win *Jove's* conqu'ring Son;
So, for th' *Alcides* of our Age,
   As strange a Fray begun.
His Wife and ancient Nurse between
   Arose this wond'rous Strife:
The froward Hag his Heart to win,
   Contended with his Wife.
His Wife, an Island Nymph most fair,
   Bore Plenty in her Hand;
A Crown adorns her Regal Hair,
   Her Graces Love command.
With modest Dignity she stood;
   Fast down her lovely Face
A Stream of swelling Sorrow flow'd,
   A righteous Cause to grace.

The

The tatter'd Nurse, of Aspect grum,
  Look'd prouder still than poor,
With lofty Airs inspir'd by Mum,
  The Queen of Beggars sure:

Mud was her Dwelling, lean her Plight,
  Her Life on Heaths she led;
With Wreaths of Turnip-tops bedight;
  Her Eyes were dull as Lead.

Yet thus the Caitiff, proud and poor,
  Our Hero Judge address'd,
" Thy Fondness all to me assure,
  " To me who loves thee best.

" I am thy aged Nurse, so kind,
  " Who ne'er did cross thy Will;
" Thy Wife to all thy Charms is blind,
  " Perverse and thwarting still.

" Give me her Cloaths, (continued she)
  " With thy Assistance soon
" Her costly Robe may shine on me,
  " On her my Rags be thrown.

" Seize on her Store of boasted Gold,
  " Which she with jealous Fear
" From thee still grudging would with-hold,
  " And trust it to my Care."

This caught the Judge's partial Ear.
  The Lady of the Isle
Spake next: " Thyself at least revere,
  " And spurn this Caitiff vile.

" With thine my Int'rest is the same,
  " For thee my Sailors toil;
" They for thy Safety, Pow'r, and Fame,
  " Enrich my spacious Isle.

" Think too upon thy solemn Vow,
  " When thou didst plight thy Love ;
" Thou cam'st to save me, wilt thou now
  " Thyself my Ruin prove ?

" How was I courted, how ador'd !
  " More happy as thy Bride ;
" For thee, my Safeguard, Love and Lord,
  " I slighted all beside.

" Do thou still act a Guardian's Part,
  " Nor be thy Love estrang'd ;
" Treat me but kindly, and my Heart
  " Shall e'er remain unchang'd.

" By thee abandon'd, must I bend
  " Beneath thy Nurse's Scorn ?
" No ; live with me thyself, and send
  " To her thy youngest born.

" Let not her Mud-built Walls thy Stay
  " Before my Tow'rs invite ;
" Do not beyond my Verdure gay,
  " In her brown Heaths delight.

" Do not her dingy Streams prefer
  " To all my Rivers clear ?
" Good Heavens ! looks Poverty in her
  " Than Wealth in me most fair ?

The Judge here lets his Fury out,
  Unable to contain ;
He frowns, and rolls his Eyes about ;
  And to his Wife began :

" If she be poor, I'll make her rich ;
  " Thy Treasure she shall hold :
" Thou art a low, mechanick B——h,
  " Besides a cursed Scold.

" My

"My Nurse is of imperial Race,
  "By Trade was never stain'd.
"What thou dost boast of, is Disgrace:
  "Nurse, thou thy Cause hast gain'd.

Polite and candid, thus the Judge:
  His Creatures watch his Call,
To raise (alas!) this dirty Drudge
  On his fair Consort's Fall.

Who first obeys th' unjust Decree,
  Regardless of his Fame,
To spoil and rob with cruel Glee
  That lovely Island Dame?

Hard by a ready Wight behold!
  Aspiring, rash, and wild;
Of Parts too keen to be controll'd
  By Wisdom's Dictates mild.

Still from the Midnight Goblet hot,
  He fires his turgid Brain,
With jarring Schemes, from Wine begot,
  To ravage Land and Main.

With these wild Embryo's, shapeless all,
  Without Head, Tail, or Limb,
He lures his Master to his Call,
  While both in Fancy swim.

He now receives th' absurd Command
  This beauteous Queen to spoil:
Ah! Deed unseemly for his Hand,
  A Native of her Isle.

He runs and strips her gracious Brows
  Of her Imperial Crown,
To dress the Hag, who quickly throws
  Her Turnip-Garland down:

Yet

Yet smiling greets the Queen, and swears
   He only means her Good,
That Exigencies of Affairs
   May want her Heart's best Blood.

Thus spoil'd, she sinks with Sorrow faint
   Before th'insulting Hag,
And, lest she publish her Complaint,
   Is menac'd with a Gag.

There lying, of her Cloaths she's stript,
   Her Money too, we're told,
Into the Judge's Hand was slipt,
   Ah! shameful Thirst of Gold.

Against APOLLO *Midas* old
   Gave Judgment; did he worse,
Than one who to his Wife, for Gold,
   Could thus prefer his Nurse?

Ah! yet recall her cruel Fate,
   Mistaken Judge, thy Friend
Here warns thee; Dangers soon or late
   On Avarice attend.

In thy Wife's Ruin yet behold
   Thou dost thyself destroy;
Then cease to barter Love for Gold,
   Which thou canst ne'er enjoy.

S———S and J———L. *A New Ballad.*

Obstupuit steteruntq; comæ. ——VIRG.

'TWAS at the silent solemn Hour,
   When Night and Morning meet,
In glided J———l's grimly Ghost,
   And stood at S———s's Feet.

His Face was like a Winter's Day,
   Clad in *November's* Frown;
And Clay-cold was his shrivel'd Hand,
   That held his tuck'd-up Gown.

S———s quak'd with Fear, th' Effect of Guilt,
   Whom thus the Shade bespoke;
And with a mournful, hollow Voice,
   The dreadful Silence broke.

The Night-Owl shrieks, the Raven croaks,
   The Midnight Bell now tolls;
Behold thy late departed Friend,
   The M———r of the R—lls.

And tho' by Death's prevailing Hand
   My Form may alter'd be;
Death cannot make so great a Change,
   As Times have wrought in thee.

Think of the Part you're acting, *S—ds*,
   And think where it will end;
Think you have made a thousand Foes,
   And have not gain'd one Friend.

Oft hast thou said, our Cause was good,
   Yet you that Cause forsook;
Oft against Places hast thou rail'd,
   And yet a Place you took.

'Gainst those how often hast thou spoke,
   With whom you now assent!
The Court how oft hast thou abus'd,
   And yet to Court you went!

How could you vote for War with *Spain*,
   Yet make that War to cease?
How could you weep for *England's* Debts,
   Yet make those Debts increase?

How could you swear your Country's Good
   Was all your Wish, or Fear?
And how could I, old doating Fool,
   Believe you was sincere?

Thou art the Cause why I appear,
   (From blisful Regions drawn)
Why teeming Graves cast up their Dead,
   And why the Church-yards yawn.

Is owing all to thee, thou Wretch!
   The Bill thou hast brought in
Opens this Mouth, tho' clos'd by Death,
   To thunder against Gin.

If of Good-nature any Spark
   Within thee thou canst find;
Regard the Message that I bring,
   Have Mercy on Mankind!

But oh! from thy relentless Heart
   The horrid Day I see,
When thy mean Hand shall overturn
   The Good design'd by me.

Riot and Slaughter once again
   Shall their Career begin,
And every Parish suckling Babe
   Again be nurs'd with Gin.

The Soldiers from each Cellar drunk
   Shall scatter Ruin far,
Gin shall intoxicate them, and
   Let slip those Dogs of War.

This proves thee, S———s, thy Country's Foe,
   And Desolation's Friend.
What can thy Project be in this?
   And what can be thy End?

Is it, that conscious of thy Worth,
    Thy Sense, thy Parts, thy Weight;
Thou know'st this Nation must be drunk
    Ere it can think thee Great?

Too high, poor Wren! has thou been borne
    On *P---y's* Eagle Wings.
Thou wert not form'd for great Affairs,
    Nor made to talk with Kings.

But where's thy Hate to Court and Pow'r,
    Thy Patriotism, *S---s*?
Think'st thou that Gown adorns thy Shape,
    That Purse becomes thy Hands?

As when the Fox upon the ground,
    A Tragic Mask espy'd,
Oh! what a specious Front is here!
    But where's the Brain? he cryed,

So thou a L---d of T---y
    And C---ll--r art made;
Sir *R--b--t-'s* Place, and Robe, and Seal,
    Thou hast; but where's his Head?

Thou'rt plac'd by far too high; in vain
    To keep your Post you strive;
In vain, like *Phaeton*, attempt
    A Chariot you can't drive.

Each Act you do betrays your Parts,
    And tends to your Undoing;
Each Speech you make your Dulness shews,
    And certifies your Ruin.

Think not like Oaks to stand on high,
    And brave the Storms that blow;
But like the Reed bend to the Earth,
    And, to be safe, be low.

Poor in thyself, each Party's Joke,
  Each trifling Songster's Sport,
P——m supports thee in the House,
  The E--l of B--h at Court.

These are the Men, that push thee on
  In thy own Nature's Spite;
So, like the Moon, if thou could'st shine,
  'Twould be by borrow'd Light.

But soft, I scent the Morning Air,
  The Glow-worm pales his Light,
Farewell, remember me, it cry'd,
  And vanish'd out of Sight.

S--s trembling rose, frighted to Death,
  Of Knowledge quite bereft,
And has, since that unhappy Night,
  Nor Sense nor Mem'ry left.

BRITANNIA's *Lamentation:* Or,

The BANKS *of the* THAMES.

To the Tune of Tweed's Side.

WHY, *Britannia,* thus senseless of Praise,
  On the Banks of thy *Thames* dost thou weep,
Whilst its Bosom thy Navy conveys
  To confound all thy Foes on the Deep?
Does not *Matthews* thy Glory advance,
  Where but late thou wast covered with Shame?
Does not *Spain,* with *Sicilia,* and *France,*
  Fly for Shelter, and shrink at thy Name?

Turn to valiant *Sardinia* thy Sight;
  None but C—— could rouse him to War,
He it was taught the *Croats* to fight,
  The *Sclavonian* he brought from afar.

He it was shook the Emperor's Throne;
   By his Counsels the *Daunbe* was past,
All the Wreaths won at *Lintz* are his own,
   And by him all *Bavaria* lies waste.

At his Nod, lo! each Enemy yields,
   Spain, and *France* their lost Armies shall mourn;
For from *Prague*, and fair *Italy's* Fields
   He has sworn not a Man shall return.
Then thy Praise while the *Moldaw* proclaims,
   And *Hungaria* is freed from her Foe,
Why, alas! should the Banks of the *Thames*
   Be the Seat of Repining and Woe?

Not at *Austria's* Success I repine,
   May she triumph (*Britannia* reply'd)
Tho' with Anguish my Head I decline,
   And lament on the *Thames'* fruitful Side!
May the *Moldaw* and *Danube's* wide Flood
   With the Shouts of her Victories sound,
And their Currents run Crimson with Blood,
   While the *French* are mow'd down to the Ground.

Thou, *Hungaria*, may'st bless thy kind Stars,
   And thy Captains experienc'd and brave;
Thou may'st thank thy undaunted Hussars,
   And thy valiant Train'd Bands of the *Saave:*
Yet had all thy Success and thy Fame
   Flow'd from C-----'s Courage and Art,
Would the Honour, exalting his Name,
   Heal the Canker which preys on my Heart?

For if Freedom and Virtue must smile
   Never more, where the Silver *Thames* flows,
What, alas! will avail this lost Isle,
   That *Hungaria* is freed from her Foes?
Has her Safety restored my dead Laws?
   Yet secur'd is my Birthright to me?
Tho' the *Gaul* from *Bohemia* withdraws,
   From Corruption have I been let free?

See! my Patriots around me defert,
  The Arch-Criminal fcreen'd without Shame;
Such Apoftates have taught my fad Heart,
  That e'en Virtue is now but a Name:
Yet amongft that fall'n Train there is one,
  There is one, I fhall ever deplore ---
What a Labour of Years is undone!
  What a Fall, ah! to rife never more!
He was once all my Glory and Pride,
  He alone my loft Rights could retrieve ----
But his Name now in Silence to hide,
  Is to him all the Boon I can give.
Then my Praife tho' *Bohemia* proclaims,
  And with Joy through the *Moldaw* may flow;
Still I weep, and the Banks of my *Thames*
  Are the Seat of Repining and Woe.

A Great Man's SPEECH in *Downing-ftreet*, againft the ENQUIRY.

To the Tune of Packington's Pound.

YE *old Whigs*, met here my new Honours to grace,
And keep it when got, (as we all muft, you know)
By now crying *Ay*, where we always cry'd *No*.
  Be this our great Plan!
  To fwear to a Man,
Things ne'er went fo well fince the World firft began.
  So farewel *Enquiry*; for *Orford* is flown
  Quite to *Arlington-ftreet*, and the Seals are my own.
Lord B-- could not leave me, in quitting the Field,
His Tongue for a Sword; but thank God I've a Shield;

Not

Not a Shield of *Professions, Vows, Tears, Double-dealing:*
But a *Front that won't blush, and a Heart above feeling.*
   All *England* shall see,
    I am arm'd Cap-a-pee,
Rage and Envy may pour their whole Quivers on [me.
 So farewel *Enquiry*, &c.

Romantic young Patriots may rant and declaim,
That, *in Place or out*, Honour still is the same;
But shew me what Honour *(in my high Condition)*
Would be for *Enquiry, the second Edition:*
   Be rather accurst
   Of *Vain Glory* the Thirst!
For we hardly knew how to get rid of the first.
 So farewel *Enquiry*, &c.

What time that Committee too forc'd me to waste!
The *Minutes* I often transcrib'd --- tho' in haste,
Nay the *Board*, for a Moment, sometimes I forsook,
But then, you may think, I could give but a Look:
   Yet when I had Leisure,
   What Friend to that Measure
Took *Notes* more than I, or in *Notes* took more Pleasure.
 So farewel *Enquiry*, &c.

In the House when this Question you come to debate,
You must fancy yourselves in a *Council of State,*
For *Councils of State* follow what is expedient,
And *Justice* is *there*, but a second Ingredient;
   Then *Justice* postpone,
   Home Affairs let alone,
Till *Austria* once more fill the Emperor's Throne.
 So farewel *Enquiry*, &c.

To Foreign Affairs I don't vastly pretend,
But I hear from *Lord B----*, my great Master and Friend,
           Lord

Lord C--- swears *France* is in such a Quandary,
For Peace she shall kneel to the *Queen of Hungary*,
    Or *Broglio* he'll nab,
    (*He's at War such a Dab*)
By seizing, *this Winter*, Franconia *and* Suabe.
  So farewel *Enquiry*, &c.

Indeed he was all, for a March, last *October*,
Each Night 'twas his Theme, and each Morning,
    quite sober,
Not *Maillebois* to follow, (for blest was the Day,
When *quiet* he march'd from *Westphalia* away!)
    But *Dunkirk* to storm,
    And when he was warm,
To push to *Versailles*, and beat up the *Gens d'arms*.
  So farewel *Enquiry*, &c.

The ------ too he counsel'd in Person to go,
In *Beauty's* fair Cause his high Prowess to show:
Beef-eaters, gay Lords, gallant Squires commanded,
The Train, which at *Calais* our *eighth Henry* landed;
    Harry too, Debonnair,
    Wou'd have dyed for the *Fair*,
As his *Arms* (cry the Wags) in the *Tower* declare.
  So farewell *Enquiry*, &c.

Some hinted, that may be 'twas rather too much,
To conquer *all France* without help from the
    Dutch:
But my *Lord*, in high Schemes not so easily bamm'd,
Swore the *Dutch shou'd come in*, ------ or the *Dutch*
    might be damn'd:
    That *Paris* with Ease,
    We may *jack* when we please;
Then fill'd up a *Bumper* to *George* and *Terese*.
  So farewel *Enquiry*, &c.

But mark his *cool Prudence*, how far from *Romance*!
Shou'd the *French*, he bethought him, be scar'd out
    of *France*   (As

(As who, but from *C---'s* bold Thunder must fly!)
They might meet in *Bavaria*, and help their *Ally*:
   Which hap'ly might end,
   In distressing our Friend,
For whom our *last Shilling* we'll joyfully spend.
 So farewel *Enquiry*, &c.

Yet of all the *round* Millions I *vow'd* to propose,
For *seven hundred thousand* to *Hanover* goes,
And tho', I'm aware, *Disaffection* may say
Hanoverians are meant *Civil List Debts* to pay;
   'Tis a Jacobite Lye:
   They are meant to supply
The want of *Dutch*, *Prussians*, and every *Ally*.
 So farewel *Enquiry*, &c.

Then to these *Hanoverians* what Praises are due?
While *Maillebois* was flying, they scorn'd to pursue,
Now to *Mentz* they will march, (so in War they
   delight)
Where the *Laws of their Country* forbid them to fight,
   And where is the Man,
   When he thinks of the *Ban*,
But had rather go fight against great *Kouli Kan?*
 So farewel, *Enquiry*, &c.

To *old standing Corps* who can grudge Levy-Money?
Or *Douceurs* to sweeten, far sweeter than Honey;
Contingent Expences, that can't be computed,
Things ne'er to be known, to be never refuted?
   Not to pay *all*, were hard:
   What has *Hanover* spar'd,
Field Pieces, Staffs, Hangmen, Prevôts or Life
   Guard?
 So farewel *Enquiry*, &c.

Shou'd you keep them ten Years—*till the Dutch
 are come in*,
You never shall pay *Levy-Money* again.

And when we to saving, *hereafter*, shall come,
Since we find them so cheap, make them *Guards* here at Home,
  For they love us so well,
  They'd quit *Bremen* and *Zell*
To help us, our turbulent Spirits to quell.
 So farewel *Enquiry*, &c.

Then be patient, *my Friends*, and expect the blest Hour,
When you may have *Places*, and I, perhaps, *Pow'r*;
And ah! without *Levies* don't doom me to live!
Tho' *your Levy-Money*, as yet, I can't give:
  But think, who shall stand
  Before my *Lord B---d*,
If e'er *Secret Service* should flow through my Hand.
 So farewel *Enquiry*; for *Orford* is flown,
 Quite to Arlington-street, and the Seals are my own.

Esq; Sandys's *Budget open'd, Or Drink and be D---d.*
A New BALLAD.
To the Tune of, A begging we will go,

ATTEND, my honest Brethren,
 Who late came into Place;
I'll tell you a new Project,
 To win our Master's Grace,
  As a Drinking we do go, &c.

An A-----y from H-----r
 We'll take into our Pay:
And *Britons* to support them
 Shall drink their Lives away,
  As a Drinking they do go &c.

From Statesmen to Excisemen,
 All Placemen may drink Wine:
But tatter'd 'Squires and Merchants
 Shall swill up Gin like Swine,
  When a Drinking they do go, &c.

And should old *England* perish,
   Why e'en let it be so;
For ev'ry Man she loses,
   We Turncoats lose a Foe.
         Then a Drinking they may go, &c.

'Tis true, when *Walpole* ruled,
   We bellow'd loud at Gin;
But now it is no Evil,
   For we are now come in.
         And a Drinking all shall go, &c.

No more shall sober *Britons*
   Pronounce us Fools and Knaves;
Their Note shall quickly alter,
   We'll make them drunken Slaves.
         And a Drinking they shall go, &c.

Behold what Shoals of Beggars
   Now crowd up ev'ry Door!
'Twill greatly ease the Poor's Rates,
   We'll poison all the Poor.
         While a Drinking they do go, &c.

The People all complain,
   That by Trade they nothing get;
Then let them sit and drink,
   They will drink us out of Debt.
         As a Drinking they do go, &c.

And should the War continue,
   What Cause have we to fear?
To licence Theft and Murder,
   Will raise a Fund next Year.
         So a Drinking we will go, &c.

Then welcome all my F———s,
   With black Funereal Face!

Ah, *Bat!* you had been welcome,
  If pledged by his Grace,
      As a Drinking we do go, &c.
And you cool foreign Statesman,
  Who drink both Night and Day,
Shall humble haughty *France*,
  Just as we our Debts shall pay,
      As a Drinking you do go, &c.
As for my honour'd Patron,
  The mighty Earl of *B—h*,
Since no Man courts his Favour,
  And no Man fears his Wrath,
      Now a Drinking he may go, &c.
Sir *Robert* was a V——n,
  But here comes *P———m*; Mum!
Your Servant Master *P———m*,
  Pray when will *Orford* come?
      That a Drinking we may go, &c.
Then fill a rosy Bumper,
  I'll send the Glass about;
Here's Health to all those in,
  Here's Death to all those out,
      As a Drinking they do go, &c.

A Newer ODE *than the Last.*

Ad Hominem———
Iterum, iterumq; movebo.

GReat E— of *B—h*,
    Be not in Wrath
At what the People say;
  Bob was abus'd,
  And roughly us'd,
Each Dog must have his Day.   'Tis

'Tis true, you are
A Man of War,
Of Courage ſtout, and try'd;
It was, we know,
But Word and Blow,
When Honour ſeem'd your Guide.

Lord *Fanny* once
Did play the Dunce,
And challeng'd you to fight;
But he ſo ſtood,
To loſe no Blood,
But had a dreadful Fright.

Poor Member *Ned*,
Said ſomething bad,
And wrote it down to *Y—k*;
Your Sword you drew,
And at him flew,
And fought like any *Turk*.

No Man ſo dread,
That wore a Head,
Durſt either ſpeak, or write,
Things to diſpraiſe
Your virtuous Ways,
But draw he muſt, and fight:

Tho' once ſo brave,
I'll call you K—,
And ſhow your Courage bound.
For if you dare
With me to war,
You muſt the Nation round.

Britannia's *Ghost* to the E— of B—.

WHILE *P——y*, seeking lost Repose,
    His downy Pillow prest,
Fresh Horrors in his Soul arose,
    And farther banish'd Rest.

For lo! *Britannia* by his Side,
    All ghastly, pale, and wan!
Thus in deep doleful Accent cry'd,
    " O base perfidious Man!

" How can'st thou hope that balmy Sleep
    " Should close thy guilty Eyes!
" Whilst all *Britannia's* Sons must weep
    " Her fall'n—thy Sacrifice!

" Long had she trusted to thine Aid
    " Against her Bosom-foe;
" Depending on the Vows you made,
    " To ward the fatal Blow.

" Hence the each Traitor had suppest,
    " Or boldly had defy'd;
" Till, leaning on her Guardian's Breast,
    " His treacherous Arms she spy'd.

" And art *Thou*, *P——y?* said she:—Fie!
    " *Thou!* of the Traitor-Crew?
" Nay then, brave *Cæsar*-like, I'll die,
    " Since *Brutus* lives in you.

" But oh! why must *Britannia* bleed,
    " To sate Ambition's Flame?
" Ah! Titles thence you'll gain indeed,
    " But gain with endless Shame.

" How can you e'er Atonement make
    " For all your broken Vows?
" Why—cancel your late grand Mistake;
    " —Her Int'rest re-espouse.   " So

[45]

"So shall her Genius yet revive;
    "—You barter Guilt for Fame:
"She shall revere you when alive;
    "When dead, adore your Name."

'Ah! no; he said; Too false I've prov'd,
    'Too fickle, vile a Thing,
'Ever to be sincerely lov'd,
    'By *Country*, *C—t*, or *K—g*.'

Hereat the Spectre disappear'd;
    But *Conscience*, in its Stead,
Dire-cursing Legions quickly rear'd
    Round his devoted Head.

Then to his Wife—he raving cry'd,
    'Thou Daughter of Perdition!
'*Britannia's* ruin'd by thy Pride;
    I'm damn'd for thy Ambition.'

A LAMENTABLE CASE,

Submitted to the Bath *Physicians.*

YE fam'd Physicians of this Place,
    Hear *Strephon's* and poor *Chloe's* Case,
    Nor think that I am joking;
When she would, he can not comply,
When he would drink, she's not a-dry;
    And is not this provoking?

At Night, when *Strephon* comes to rest,
Chloe receives him on her Breast,
    With fondly-folding Arms:
Down, down he hangs his drooping Head,
Falls fast asleep, and lies as dead,
    Neglecting all her Charms.   Reviving

Reviving when the Morn returns,
With rising Flames young *Strephon* burns,
    And fain, would fain be doing:
But *Chloe* now, asleep or sick,
Has no great Relish for the Trick,
    And sadly baulks his Wooing.
O cruel and disast'rous Case,
When in the critical Embrace
    That only one is burning!
Dear Doctors, set this Matter right,
Give *Strephon* Spirits over Night,
    Or *Chloe* in the Morning.

BROGLIO's *Breeches.*

WHEN erst the gallant *Koningsegg*
    (As in the News we've read from th'*Hague*)
    Had storm'd poor *Broglio's* Quarters;
A fierce *Hussar* seiz'd on the Chief,
As he was saving, with his Life,
    His Breeches and his Garters.
Disturbing a Marshal of *France* in the Night,
Is not *à la mode à Paris*, or polite.
    Who're you? quoth th'*Hussar:* Monsieur shook,
    Said, I'm his Excellency's Cook;
        No Follower of the Drum.
Houndsfoot! replies the *German* quick,
Begone with that; so with a Kick
        Salutes the Marshal's Bum.

Disgraceful! of War how capricious the Chance!
A *German Hussar* kicks a Marshal of *France*.
    But *Broglio*, say, wouldst not be glad,
    In spite of all thy Gasconade,

Sans

Sans Breeches or a Rag,
To be as fairly now difmift,
By fuch another kicking Jeft,
From young *Lorrain* and *Prague?*
Since thus one is drove to fo piteous a Taking,
Who the De'il would again go an Emperor-making?

A Receipt to make a P$\underline{ee}$R, occafioned by the Report of a Pr$\underline{o}$m$\underline{o}$t$\underline{io}$n.

TAKE a Man who by Nature's a true Son of Earth,
By Rapine enrich'd, tho' a Beggar by Birth;
Of Genius the loweft, ill bred and obfcene,
Of Morals moft wicked, moft nafty in Mien;
By none ever trufted, yet ever employ'd,
In Blunders moft fertile, of Merit quite void;
A Scold in the Senate, abroad a Buffoon;
The Scorn and the Jeft of all C$\underline{ou}$ts but his own:
A Slave to that Wealth which ne'er made him a Friend,
And proud of that Cunning which ne'er gain'd an End;
A Dupe in each Tr$\underline{ea}$ty, a *Swifs* in each Vote,
In Manners and Form a compleat *Hottentot:*
Such a one could you find, of all Men I'd commend him,
But be fure let the Curfe of each *Br-t--n* attend him.
Thus fitly prepar'd, add the Grace of a Th—ne,
The Folly of M—n—chs, and Screen of a Cr—n.
Take a Pr--ce for this purpofe without Ears or Eyes,
And a long Parchment P-t--t ftuft brimful of Lies;
Thefe mingled together a *Fiat* fhall pafs,
And a Thing ftrut a P—r, that before was an Afs.
      Probatum eft.

A Right

A Right Honourable DIALOGUE.

C. TO the *Earl*, says the *Countess*, What makes you so dull?
E. Because for your *Ladyship* I've play'd the Fool.
Co. For *Me*, do you say, Sir? Your *Lordship* you mean.
E. Ay,—Curse the damn'd *Title*, 'tis That gives me Spleen.
Co. You've no Sense of *Honour*, no Notions of Glory.
E. Yours are--*Polly W——e* should not *Rank* before ye. But more *Honour* We'd had, and been *happier* still, Had you been plain *Madam*, and I been plain *Will*.

Scotch *Taste on* Vista's.

OLD I——y, to shew a most elegant Taste
In improving his Gardens, purloin'd from the Waste;
And order'd his Gard'ner to open his Views,
By cutting a couple of grand Avenues.
With secret Delight, he saw the first View end
In his favorite Prospect, a Church—that was ruin'd:
But what should the next to his Lordship exhibit?
'Twas the terrible Sight of a Rogue on a Gibbet.
A View so ungrateful then taught him to muse on,
Full many a *C--mp--ll* had dy'd with his Shoes on,
All amaz'd and aghast, at the ominous Scene,
He order'd it strait to be shut up again
With a Clump of *Scots* Firs by Way of a Screen.

On Cibber's *Declaration that he will have the last Word with Mr.* Pope.

QUOTH *Cibber* to *Pope*, tho' in Verse you foreclose,
I'll have the last Word, for by G-d I'll write Prose.
Poor *Colly*, thy Reas'ning is none of the strongest,
For know the last Word is the Word that lasts longest.

CIBBER's Answer.

DEAR *Pope*, tho' you have, I have not the Temerity,
To think of surviving to talk to Posterity;
I said what I meant, and it is not absurd,
That with you, Mr. *Pope*, I will have the last Word.

The BUFFOON. *An Epigram.*

DON'T boast, prithee *Cibber*, so much of thy State,
That like *Pope* you are blest with the Smiles of the Great;
With both they converse, but for different Ends,
And 'tis easy to know their *Buffoons* from their *Friends*.

An Epigram, dropt in a Glass at a certain Ballot.

THY Horse, like thee, does Things by Halves;
  Thou, through Irresolution,
Hurt'st Friends and Foes, thyself and me,
  The K—g and Constitution.

On Admiral VERNON's *being presented with the Freedom of the City of* London.

ERE old *Rome's* City could corrupted be,
  Her Consuls *honest*, and her Tribunes *free*,
The greatest Name the Greatest could assume
Was, to be stil'd *Free Citizens of Rome*.
Free, as old *Rome*, as uncorrupt, as great,
London knows how a *Vernon's* Worth to rate;
Among her worthy Sons she bids him be,
And, like the Sons of *London*, dare be *Free*.
Let *Ducal Coronets* mark others *Shame*,
These *Civic Honours* give a *Real Fame*.

The Fl----r's March. A PUFF.

OF late, a dreadful Storm of Wind
Within our sleeping *Sophi* reign'd:
Dire Cholic-Pangs his Entrails tore;
He tumbled, grunted, kick'd, and swore;
In broken Phrase was heard to growl,
March!---Houndsfoot!---Donder! D—n your Soul!
Hence Fame with Trump posterior sounded
A March on windy Orders founded;
But as from Gripes it took its Rise;
Behold how in a F—t it dies!

A BOB upon THREE BOBS.

THREE Reigns three *Bobs* produc'd of equal Fame,
In *Politicks* and *Morals* all the same:
In ANNA's Days Earl *R----t's* Peace betray'd
The *Empire*, *Holland*, and the *British* Trade:
In Reign the next, the fatal *South Sea* Scheme;
Cheated the Nation with a *Golden Dream*:
In modern Times, a worse *pacific Trance*
Half *Europe* sunk, and rais'd the Pride of *France*:
Excise, Convention, useless Troops and Fleet;
Roberto's glorious Ministry compleat:
When *Britain* recollects those wond'rous Jobs,
How much she owes to three notorious BOBS!

The FOX and HOUNDS: A Fable.

A Wily Fox, who long had been
The Plund'rer of the neighb'ring Plain,
When chac'd so hard, he could not fix
On any Stratagems or Tricks;

Could no more double as he fled,
Trusted, instead of *Heels*, his *Head*;
With desperate Courage he turn'd round,
And thus address'd each gaping Hound.

"Stop, stop, ye noisy simple Pack;
"Hear me a Word:—What do you lack:
"By killing *Me* what do you win?
"A stinking Hide and tatter'd Skin:
"Some noisy Fools *halloo* you on,
"Not for your Profit, but *their* Fun:
"Now, Sirs, consider what I offer;
"It is no mean nor foolish Proffer.
"Here you have run and stand a-gape
"For nothing:—Now let me escape,
"And to your Kennel I will bring
"Presents as great as from a *King*.
"I am not *Game*:—Let me succeed,
"And I will give you *Game* indeed."

The Hounds all listen; then their Leader,
Thus answer'd the old crafty Pleader:

'Sir *Reynard*, what you've said is true;
'You shall *escape*, but we'll *pursue*:
'The *Art*'s to make our *Masters* think
'You have 'scap'd *fair*, though on Death's Brink;
'Hark! hark the Horn!—They're coming on,
'Down, down to yonder Thicket run:
'Half dead, and panting, we'll pursue,
'But there we'll *lose* both *Scent* and *View*:
'Leap the Park-Wall, we can't get over;
'And *burrow safe* in *Royal Cover*.'

Away runs *Reynard*, leaps the Wall,
And the Chace ends in—*Nought at all*.

MORAL.

If *Men* may be with *Hounds* compar'd;
If any Knave like *Reynard* far'd;

If any *Masters* have been cheated,
And know the *Pack* their Game defeated;
What should a *true bred Huntsman* do?
Why, what? but—*hang up all the Crew.*

On the Report of NEW DIGNITIES.

'TIS said, two E--s will soon be made two D--es,
One of *North*————*d*, and one of *B—ks:*
How vast their *Merit!* that they thus receive
Titles and *Honours* great as Kings can give!
What Merit shall their high Preambles tell?
How long they serv'd their Country, and how well?
No, Herald---Study---something else compose,
For how they serv'd it, the whole Nation knows.

One Thousand Seven Hundred and Forty Two.

WITH *W――le*'s Politicks the Year began;
But soon th'indignant Patriots chang'd the Man;
With Statesmen *new* the Nation hop'd *new* Schemes,
Saw *Glorious Visions*, and dreamt *Golden Dreams:*
When from a Trance of six Months they awoke,
They found *Truth* chang'd their fancy'd *Joy* to *Joke.*
Still the same Fate on *B--t--n's* Isle attends,
And wisely, as the Year *began*, it *ends.*

Occasion'd by a late Motion.

HIGH Taxes ran! the *Britons* loud complain'd;
'Twas mov'd that *Luxury* should be restrain'd:
To *lace* our Breeches was a mortal Sin,
And wear all Gold *without*, and none *within*:
This meant the *M-n-stry*, would they confess,
" The more we have *ourselves*, the * has less."
The M-mb-rs wonder'd, tho' the Motion past;
For who could fear that *Luxury* would last?

Excises,

Excises, Taxes, Sinking Fund, are spent;
And sure SEVEN MILLIONS are a high Rack Rent!
" The *Lace* you may allow us (quoth Sir *John**)
"* We soon shall have no *Coats* to put it on."
The Knight's Remark, most questionless, was shrewd,
He that can *pay no Whore,* must not be *lewd.*
   A *Briton* once said to a *Gaul* alert,
" You found the *Ruffles,*—but we found the *Shirt.*".
Without the *last,* few would the *first* promote;
And who will buy a *Lace* that has no *Coat?*

       PHYSICK *and* CARDS.

PHysick each Morn is T——t's Care, *Ld Chesterfd*
   Each Night she plays a Pool;
One helps her to an easy Chair,
   The other to a Stool.

     The PIN. *An* EPIGRAM.

AS Nature H—y's Clay was blending,
   Uncertain what her Work would end in,
Whether in Female or in Male,
A Pin dropt in and turn'd the Scale.

   On Admiral VERNON's *taking his Seat in the*
       House of Commons.

WHAT S— would have been thought, what
   P—y seem'd,
(For Honour lov'd, for Patriotism esteem'd)
Be *Thou* in Truth inflexibly the *same;*
Retrieve the Honour of the *Patriot's* Name;
Above *Ambition's* Lure, or *Envy's* Sting,
Daring to serve your *Country,* serve your *King:*
So shalt thou thus thy Country's Hopes fulfil,
And shew in *Vernon* there's a *Briton* still.
                     Proper

   † Sir J—: H——de C——ter.

Proper Rules and Instructions, without which no Person can be an Exciseman.

Quicunque Vult.

WHosoever would be an Exciseman, before all Things it is necessary that he learns the Art of Arithmetick.

Which Art unless he wholly understand, he without doubt can be no Exciseman.

Now the Art of Arithmetick is this, to know how to multiply and how to divide. *Desunt pauca.*

The 1 is a Figure, the 2 a Figure, and the 3 a Figure.

The 1 is a Number, the 2 a Number, and the 3 a Number; and yet there are *Desunt plurima.*

For like as we are compelled by the Rules of Arithmetick, to acknowledge every Figure by itself to have Signification and Form:

So we are forbidden by the Rules of right Reason, to say, that each them have three Significations or three Powers.

The 2 is of the 1's alone, not abstracted, nor depending, but produced.

The 3 is of the 1 and 2, not abstracted, nor depending, nor produced, but derived. So there is one Figure of 1. *Desunt nonnulla.*

He therefore that will be an Exciseman, must thus understand his Figures.

Furthermore, it is necessary to the Preservation of his Place, that he also believe rightly the Authority of his Supevisor.

For his Interest is, that he believes and confesses that his Supervisor, the Servant of the Commissioners, is Master and Man: Master of the Exciseman, having Power from the Commissioners to inspect his Books; and Man to the Commissioners, being obliged to return his Accounts.

Perfect Master and perfect Man, of an unconscionable Soul and frail Flesh subsisting: equal to the Commissioners, as touching that Respect which is shewn him by the Excisemen, and inferior to the Commissioners as touching their Profit and Salary.

Who although he be Master and Man, is not two, but one Supervisor.

One, not by Confusion of Place, but by Virtue of his Authority: for his Seal and Sign Manual perfect his Commission, his Gauging the Vessels, and inspecting the Excisemen's Books, is what makes him Supervisor.

Who travels through thick and thin, and suffers most from Heat, or Cold, to save us from the Addition of Taxes, or the Deficiency in the Funds, by Corruption or Inadvertency.

Who thrice in seven Days goes his Rounds, and once in six Weeks meets the Collectors, who shall come to judge between the Exciseman and Victualler.

At whose coming all Excisemen shall bring in their Accounts, and the Victuallers their Money.

And they that have done well by prompt Payment, shall be well treated.

And those that have done ill, by being tardy in their Payments, shall be cast into Jail; and the Excisemen whose Books are blotted, or Accounts unjustifiable, shall be turned out of their Places.

These are the Rules, which except a Man follows, he cannot be an Exciseman.

Honour to the Commissioners, Fatigue to the Supervisor, and Bribery to the Exciseman.

As it was from the beginning, when Taxes were first laid upon Malt, is now, and ever will be till the Debts of the Nation are paid.

AMEN.

THE LESSONS for the DAY.

Being the First and Second Chapters of the BOOK of PREFERMENT.

The FIRST LESSON.

Here beginneth the First Chapter of the Book of PREFERMENT.

1. NOW it came to pass in the 15th Year of the Reign of *George* the King, in the 2d Month, on the 10th Day of the Month at Even, that a deep Sleep came upon me, the Visions of the Night possessed my Spirits: I dreamed, and behold *Robert* the Minister came in unto the King, and besought him, saying:

2. O King, live for ever! Let thy Throne be established from Generation to Generation! But behold now the Power which thou gavest unto thy Servant is at an End, the *Chippenham* Election is lost, and the Enemies of thy Servant triumph over him.

3. Wherefore now I pray thee, if I have found Favour in thy Sight, suffer thy Servant to depart in Peace, that my Soul may bless thee.

4. And when he had spoken these Words, he resigned unto the King his Place of First Lord of the Treasury, his Chancellorship of the Exchequer, and all his other Preferments.

5. And great Fear came upon *Robert*, and his Heart smote him, and he fled from the Assembly of the People, and went up into the Sanctuary, and was safe.

6.

6. And the Enemies of *Robert* communed among themselves, saying, What shall we do unto this Man? And they appointed a Committee to Enquire concerning him.

7. Howbeit the Man from whom they sought Information was possess'd with a dumb Spirit, and he opened not his Mouth, neither spake he unto them good or bad.

8. Then the Committee were in great Wrath, and they reported this Matter unto the House; but their Report was even as a Fart, which stinketh in the Nostrils for a Moment, and is forgotten.

9. And I saw in my Sleep, and behold all they who sought for Places, rushed into the Palace in great Numbers; insomuch that the Courts of the King's House were full.

10. And they all cryed out with one Voice, saying, *Give us Places!* and the Sound of their Voice reached to the uttermost Parts of the Land.

11. And when the People understood that these Patriots only sought themselves Places, they murmured greatly, and they said among themselves, *Verily, verily, all is Vanity and Vexation of Spirit.*

12. Why therefore have we striven in vain? and why have we disquieted ourselves in vain? For behold all Men have corrupted their Ways before the Lord, there are none that doeth good, no not One.

13. Corruption, as a Moth, hath eaten up their Principles; Poverty and Shame is their Portion, and they and their Sons shall be dependent for ever.

14. Nevertheless the Cry of the Patriots continued with great Violence, and it wounded the Ears of the King, insomuch that he was compelled to stop their Mouths by giving them Places.

15. As the Cry of the Hounds ceaseth when the Entrails of the Beast are divided amongst them, so ceased the Clamours of Patriots at the Distribution of Places.

Thus endeth the first Lesson.

The Second LESSON.

Here beginneth the Second Chapter of the Book of PREFERMENT.

1. NOW these are the Generations of those that sought Preferment.

2. Twenty Years they sought Preferment, and found it not; yea, twenty Years they wandered in the Wilderness.

3. Twenty Years they sought them Places, but they found no Resting-place for the Soal of the Foot.

4. And lo! it came to pass in the Days of *George* the King, that they said amongst themselves, Go to, let us get ourselves Places, that it may be well with us, our Wives, and our little Ones.

5. And these are the Names of the Men that have gotten themselves Places in this their Day.

6. Now the first that pushed himself forward in this Affair was the Motion-maker, who being swoln with Pride and Ambition, and thirsting in his Heart after the Mammon of Unrighteousness, he determined with himself that he would ask for the Chancellorship of the Exchequer: but his Party wist not what he designed.

7. Wherefore he went privily unto the King's Palace, and he got himself placed at the Head of the Exchequer, where he sitteth unto this Day.

8. Who

8. Who now shall bring in the Place-Bill? Who now shall make a Motion for Removal? Verily, verily, it is much to be feared, that he who expecteth these Things from S——ds will be greatly disappointed.

9. And C---t—t the Scribe took the Place of Secretary of State, and H—gt--n presideth at the Council-Board, and W--l--m--gt--n the President is made First Lord of the T—f---y.

10. In these Days Lord H--r--y held the King's Signet, and to him succeeded Lord G---r.

11. And the King had a Guard called Gentlemen Pensioners, and over them he set Lord B---ft.

12. Lord L--mr---k got the Reversion after Lord P—lm—n for himself and for his Son after him; and he shall be called the King's Remembrancer from Generation to Generation.

13. Lord Ed——me was and is not; he was the King's Treasurer in the Land of *Ireland*, but he found no Favour in their Eyes, and to him succeeded Harry V——ne.

14. Henry L——g was Scribe to the Treasury, but the Name of L——g was unseemly, so he is called Henry F————n—se unto this Day.

15. Moreover it came to pass, that for his great skill in Maritime Affairs, Lord W—n-——sea was set at the Head of the Admiralty.

16. To Lord C—bh—m was given the First Troop of tall Men, called Horse-Grenadiers, and he was made a Field-Marshal.

17. So also was Lord St——r; moreover he was sent Ambassador unto the *Dutch*, and our Credit encreaseth amongst them.

18. To Lord S--d——y B—— cl———k succeeded *William* F——ch, as Vice-Chamberlain to

the King: his Brother *Edward* alſo was made Groom of the Bed-Chamber.

19. And that his Majeſty might not want good and able Counſellors learned in the Law, lo! *M-r- r—y* the Orator, and *N--th--l G———nd———y* were appointed K——— g's Council.

20. But what ſhall be done unto *P———y?* What ſhall be done to the Man whom the King delighteth to honour? For lo! the Word is gone out of his Mouth, he hath ſaid in his Wrath that he will have no Place.

21. Behold an Expedient! He ſhall no longer be called *W—m P—lt--y*, but the E--l of *B——— th*. And what is it to *W—m P—lt—y* what the E— of *B——— th* ſhall do? What is the Privilege of P-r-ge, but to do what they pleaſe uncenſured?

22. Theſe are the Men after their Generations, and many more ſhall come in unto the Land to poſſeſs it.

23. Of the Tribe of *Jacob* twelve Thouſand, of the Tribe of *Andrew* twelve Thouſand, of the Tribe of *Patrick* twelve Thouſand.

24. And all theſe Things came to paſs, that the Saying of the Prophet *Jonathan* might be fulfilled, *Thoſe that are in ſhall be as thoſe that are out, and thoſe that are out as thoſe that are in:* But the Lord of *B——— th* is over all, and bleſſed be the Name of the Lord of *B——— th.*

Here endeth the Second Leſſon.

THE
Evening LESSONS.

Being the First and Second Chapters of the Book of ENTERTAINMENTS.

The First LESSON.

1. AND the Cry of Poverty was sore in the Land.

2. And it came to pass in those Days, that the Rich People combined together among themselves, saying,

3. "Wherefore should the Poor have any Mo-
"ney, seeing they spend it in a *Vulgar* Way?

4. "Do not they spend it in Meat, and in Drink,
"and in Raiment, for themselves, their Wives,
"their Little Ones? Neither regard they the
"*sweet Singers* which *we* have *brought over*."

5. And the Saying pleased the Rulers of the Land, so that there was not found amongst *all* the Rulers, *whom* the Saying did not please.

6. So they oppressed and harrassed the Poor, till they thought they had extorted the utmost Farthing.

7. When the Poor saw this, and that they were oppressed and harrassed, and that they were evil-entreated of their Rulers:

8. They were alarm'd, and moved with Indignation, and they said one to another, "Know not
"*we* also the Use of Money?

9. Thus they communed among themselves, every Man with his Neighbour, and their Murmurings were great among them.

10. And

10. And they said, "Come now, and let *us* "seek out Places of Pleasure, and let our Hearts "know Joy and Gladness, seeing what we do not "*spend* shall be *taken from* us.

11. As it happeneth to the Prodigal, even so "happeneth it to the Industrious; there is one "Event happeneth to all: Let us Eat and Drink, "for to-morrow we shall be Taxed.

12. Now there was present a Man of Skill, and great Cunning, and when he had heard the Saying of the Multitude, he departed and went unto his own Home.

13. Nevertheless he did not forget the Saying of the Multitude, and the Resolution which they had resolved: And as he thought *thereon*, he contrived a Place of Recreation, and it is called *Vauxhall* even to this Day.

14. And the Number of the People that resorted thither, was even as the Number of the Sands that is upon the Sea-shore.

15. When *Inigo* the Builder saw this, and that the Number of those that resorted unto *Vaux-hall*, was as the Number of the Sands that is upon the Sea-shore:

16. It came to pass, that he also contrived a Place, which he called *Ranelagh*.

17. And the Building was goodly *to the Eye*, and fair *to look upon*, so that a fairer was not found, not excepting the K——'s Palace.

18. Moreover the K—— went and survey'd the Building, and, as he survey'd the Building, he said, "Lo! thus shall it be spoken of me amongst "the Nations, the Ruler of *Israel* excelleth others "in a *Cake-house*."

19. And the Diameter of the Building was 122 Cubits, and the Height 80 and one Cubit, and 336 Cubits was the Circumference thereof.

20. And the Evening was warm, and the River smooth, and the Melody of Instruments was heard upon the Waters, and I said, Lo! *now* I will go to *Vaux-hall*.

21. So I took a Companion, and the Voyage pleased me. And it came to pass as I sailed by *La* ——— *b* the P—ce of the High-priest.

22. I asked of the Man that was with me, saying, Is this P———te *alive*, or *dead*? And he answered and said, Our Friend *sleepeth*.

23. So I came unto *Vaux-hall*, and produced a Plate of Silver, and the Doors flew open before me, and I entered thereat into the Garden.

24. And as I entered, my Mind was softened unto Pleasure; the *irregular* Disposition of the Trees delighted me, but the *regular* Disposition of the Lamps displeased me.

25. Moreover at the Sound of the Organ my Soul danced for Joy; and the Man's Finger, that played upon the Organ, was a cunning Finger.

26. And there was great Harmony betwixt the Sound of the Organ, and the Sound of the other Instruments; and it happened, that whatever the Organ on *one Side* spake, the Fiddles on the *other Side* cry'd, *So say we*." This also pleased me.

27. Albeit there was not heard the Voice of Singing-men, or of Singing-women, and the Music lacked Interpretation.

28. And I said, How wot I now what is piped or harped? Verily this is as it were sounding Brass, or a tinkling Cymbal.

29. Then walked I round the Place: I praised the Colonnades, the Paintings, and the Pavilions.

30. And I said unto mine Eye, go to now and examine every Part.

31. Then

31. Then I looked *up*, and lo! a fine Alcove was built for the Reception of one of the Princes of the People.

32. Albeit *the Prince* chose a *Pavilion*, for said He, I will be *accessible*, and *upon a Footing* with my People.

33. I praised also the Statue of the chief Musician: it had gone thro' the Hands of a Cunning workman.

34. And there was an Arch before the Statue, and thro' the Arch sawest thou the Statue.

35. Then I beheld a Drawer, and he looked wistfully upon me, and his Countenance said, Sit down.

36. So I sate down, and I said, Go now fetch me savoury Meats, such as my Soul loveth; and he straitway went to fetch them.

37. And I said unto him, asked I not for *Beef?* wherefore then didst thou bring me *Parsley?*

38. Run now quickly and bring me Wine, that I may drink, and my Heart may chear me; for as to what *Beef* thou broughtest me, I wot not what is become of it.

39. Now the Wine was an Abomination unto me; nevertheless I drank, for I said, "Lest peradventure I should faint by the Way."

40. And I said, Tell me now what is to pay: and he said, Thou shalt know what is to pay.

41. Then pulled I out three Pieces of Silver, and I gave them unto him, albeit he looked displeased at me, as who should say, Pay me that thou *owest* me.

42. Have I not been thy Slave and thine Ass these five Minutes? Have not I served thee faithfully? According to the thing thou gavest me to do, even so did I.

43. Moreover have I any Wages save what thou givest me? Wherefore then dost thou with-hold from me that which is my Due, and givest me not Six-pence? So I gave him Six-pence.

34. But after this he neither bowed, nor made any Obeisance unto me, and I repented of what I had done:

45. And I said, How many Souls would this Money have comforted! Verily it would have done away Sorrow from their Hearts, and made the Eye of the Mourner to weep with *Joy*.

46. So I departed and came unto the River:

47. And as I drew near, I called " Oars;" but there was not found that answer'd, " Here am I."

48. And it rained!

Here endeth the FIRST LESSON.

The SECOND LESSON.

1. NOW there was moreover an Evening when the Sky was cloudy, and the East-Wind blew, and Men's Hearts do sink with Trouble, and I waxed exceeding sorrowful.

2. And my Companions said unto me, " Why go " we not now to *Ranelagh*-Gardens, that we may " banish Sorrow from our Hearts?

3. So we went: and it came to pass, that the Preparations by the Way-side filled our Minds with mighty Expectations.

3. And we said one to another, What Building can this Man build, that shall answer the Expectations he gives us by the Way?

5. And we drew near unto the Theatre; and as we entered the Theatre it so fell out that our Expectations were exceeded.

6. Our Hearts leaped for Joy, and I said unto myself, See now what mighty Pleasures may be purchased for a Shilling!

K   7. Where

7. Where now is the Sorrow wherewith I sorrowed, or the Grief whereof I grieved? Surely *Pain*, and *Anguish* are banished from this *Circle*: *Trouble* also and *Sorrow* have no Shilling to introduce them.

8. And the Lamps were not disposed as thou seest them in the Street, a-row; but like unto the Stars that are in the Firmament.

9. And the Organ *played*, and the Singers *sung*, and the Lamps *blaz'd*, and the Gilding *glitter'd*, and the Ladies *looked*, and I was filled with Joy; and I said, Is there now among the Sons of Men one that is happier than I?

10. Moreover the Words which the Singers sung enticed me to be *free and gay*.

11. So my Heart was enlarged, and I wished well even to mine Enemies, saving those that were my *Nation's* Enemies; to *such* wished I not well.

12. And my Soul was opened, and I talked unto the Stranger that was next me, even as thou wouldest talk unto thine Acquaintance, or thy Brother; and I said in my Heart, Are we not all one Family?

13. And the Physician that was with me said, Verily this is meet for an *English* Climate.

14. Nevertheless the *Gardens* are not *yet* to be compared to the *Gardens* on the *other side Jordan*, neither perhaps *will they*.

15. And there was a Time when the Man that ruleth at *Ranelagh* met the Man that ruleth at *Vauxhall*, and as he drew near unto him, he cried with a loud Voice, "What dost thou?

16. And the Man of *Ranelagh* bespoke him fairly, saying, Wilt thou not I should do what I will with *mine own?* Yea, verily, and with *other People's* also, seeing they have put it into my Hands.

17. If thou wilt pray for a *warm* Evening, should not I pray also for a *cool* one, that it may be well

with me? Wherefore let there be no Difference betwixt thee and me, for we are *Brethren*.

18. When the Man of *Vaux-hall* heard this, he was smitten at Heart, and he said unto himself, What shall I do now to difgrace this Man of *Ranelagh*?

19. And he said, Lo! this will I do; I will go hence unto a Seer, and I will caufe him to lie down, and it shall be that when he waketh, he shall say, I have dreamed a Dream.

20. In Condemnation of *Ranelagh* shall he dream, and in Praife of *Vaux-hall* shall he dream, and I will print his Dreamings in the *Champion*.

21. So he did even as he had faid, and the Dreamer dreamed, and the *Champion* printed, and the Readers at the Coffee-houfe interpreted the Dream.

22. Moreover the Man of *Ranelagh* caft his Eye upon a Field, and he faid, I will purchafe that Field, for fo I shall make an Addition to my Garden.

23. And he faid unto the Owner of the Field, Lo now what shall I give thee for the Field which joineth unto my Garden? And he faid, An hundred Pieces of Gold.

24. And he faid, I will not give thee an hundred Pieces, albeit ninety and nine Pieces will I give thee.

25. And it came to pafs, that while he was yet fpeaking, the Man of *Vauxhall* entered the Threfhold, and paid down the hundred Pieces; and when he had paid down the hundred Pieces, he faid, The Field is mine——

26. Now as touching a Comparifon betwixt thefe Places, I will not fay that I greatly defire it.

27. For they have both their Beauties; albeit fundry and divers are the Beauties of thefe Places.

28. For as there is a Time to eat, and a Time to drink, and a Time for neither: and a Time to walk,

walk, and a Time to fit ftill, and a Time for neither: Even fo there is a Time for *Ranelagh*, and a Time for *Vaux-hall:* Is there not alfo a Time for *neither?* G—d forbid!

29. Moreover I did eat and drink at *Ranelagh*, as I had before eaten and drunk at *Vaux-hall*; but the Wine and the Drawers were an Abomination in both Places.

30. Now when I had walked the Circle of *Ranelagh* many Times, and had beheld the fame *Faces* many times, and the fame *Laces* many times;

31. A fudden Wearinefs came upon me, and I began to moralize, and I faid, Such alfo is the Circle of Life!——

32. And as I came forth, a Coachman faid unto me, Would your Honour have a Coach?

33. And I looked, and behold it was as it were Noon-day, and the Road was lighten'd, and the Weather was grown warm, and the Feet of Travellers was heard upon the Road, and I faid, Nay, I will walk hence, for it is falutary, fafe, and pleafant.

34. So I came unto my own Home.

35. Moreover it happened that in thofe Days lived an exceeding poor Widow, and fhe faid unto herfelf, Wherewithal fhall I get Money?

36. And fhe faid, when there appeareth a Comet in the Sky, do not the People go forth at Midnight? do they not gape and ftare, and are not they greatly alarmed?

37. And do not the old Men go forth, and the Prophets prophefy? Yea, doth not *Whif—n* the Prophet prophefy *exceedingly*, albeit it cometh not to pafs?

38. Thus are they alarmed, both fmall and great! Come now therefore, let us make unto ourfelves Comets of Gun-powder, and Comets of Salt-petre; and

and it shall be, that while they gape and stare, we will pick their Pockets.

39. And she did even as she had said: according to every Word that she had spoken, even so did she: she made unto herself Comets of Gun-powder, and Comets of Salt-petre; and while the People gaped and stared, she did pick their Pockets.

40. Moreover she contrived a Sound like unto the Sound of an Organ, and a Sound like unto the Sound of a Fiddle; and it pleased the People, and they wot not that their Children wanted Bread.

41. And thus it was that the Rulers of the Land ran away with one half of the Substance of the Poor; and that Mother C—p—r, &c. challenged the other half. And nothing flourished in those Days saving the C—t and the Cake-house.

42. And when her Fire was waxed low, she had Recourse unto *Puffs*; albeit her *Puffs* were as the *Puffings* of an old Woman that hath an *Asthma*.

43. And her Devices grew stale, and her Fireworks failed, insomuch that when her Rockets rose, they were even as the Stars which cause no Admiration:

44. And when she departeth hence, shall it not be said of her, That her Days were even as the Days of a *Salamander*? She made her Nest in the midst of the Flames: even amidst the Fire of Whores and Combustibles! But the Fire is out, and her Name is extinguished; yea, even as a Rocket is she vanished, which blazes for a while, then sinks, and is forgotten.

Thus endeth the Second Lesson.

THE EPISTLE for the DAY.

Being Part of the Second Chapter of the Acts of the PATRIOTS.

1. THEN said the Man *William*, Are these Things so?

2. And when the Day of Meeting was fully come, they were all with one Accord in one Place.

3. And suddenly there came a Sound from C——t, and it filled all the House where they were sitting.

4. And many were filled with Covetousness, and began to speak with other Tongues, as the Spirit of Lucre gave them Utterance.

5. And People were amazed and marvelled, saying one to another, Behold, are not all these which speak Pat——ts?

6. And how we hear these Patriots speak the Language of the C——t?

7. And the People were amazed and in doubt, saying one to another, What meaneth this?

8. Others mocking, said, These Men are Courtiers.

9. But the Man *William* standing up, lift up his Voice and said unto them, Hearken to my Words:

10. For these are not Courtiers, as ye suppose, seeing they have not accepted Places.

11. Now when they heard this they were pricked in their Hearts, and said unto *William*, and the rest of the Pat——ts, What shall we do?

12. Then *William* said unto them, Recant, and be persuaded, and every one of you shall receive Gifts.

13. For the Promise is unto you and to your Children, even as many as our Lord the K——g shall call.

14. And

14. And with many such Words exhorted he them, saying, Save yourselves from this untoward Generation.

15. And many gladly received his Word, and were made Place-men.

16. And the Man *William* added to the Court daily such as were converted.

17. This *William* hath G——e raised up, whereof ye are all Witnesses.

18. Therefore let all the House of C——ns know assuredly, that G——e hath made that same *William* both a P—r and C——tier.

19. And it shall come to pass, that whosoever shall call on the Name of the L—d of B—th shall be promoted.

F I N I S.

THE
Foundling Hospital
FOR
WIT.

(Price One Shilling.)

THE Foundling Hospital FOR WIT.

NUMBER II.

CONTAINING,

The Ballance of *Europe*.
Prenez le Roy, to M. *Noailles*.
The Marshal's Answer.
On the C——s of *Y*—*h* making the Campaign.
On *L*—*g*—*nier*'s passing the *Rhine*.
The Lion and Frogs.
On the March of the *D*——*h*.
Britannia's Lamentation and Petition to the D—ke.
A New Ballad on Beating the *French*.
A Letter on the Blues ———.
News from the Army on the K—g and D—ke.
To Fortune, on *S*———*ys* and *W*——*le*.
The Mistake.
The Downfal of Dancing, to the Ladies of *Blackheath*.
An Epigram on Ld G—*l*—*y* and his Cook.
A Lesson from *H*——*r*.
A New Ballad on our Riches.
On *Faction Detected*.
The Carters, *John* and *Will*.
The Gracious Refusal.
On the Promotion of the Rt. Hon. H. *Pelham*.
The Interview between *Harry* and *Will*.
To the E. of *B*———*h*, on *Faction Detected*.
Epigram on the Blues.
An Ode to the New M——s.
An Ode to the Earl of *B*———*h*.
Faction Detected, a New Ballad.
A Humorous Ballad, to Lord G———*m*.
Verses occasion'd by the many Satires on the Government.
On a late Transaction, to the D— of M———*h*.

With many other Curious Pieces, some of which were never before printed.

By TIMOTHY SILENCE, *Esq*;

LONDON:
Printed for W. WEBB, near St. *Paul's*. 1749.
Where may be had any of the other Numbers.

THE
Foundling Hospital
FOR
WIT.

***

NUMBER II.

***

The BALLANCE.

WHILE in suspense the Scales of *Europe* hung,
   Doubtful to whom the Ballance did belong,
France seem'd, at all Events, its Power to gain,
Flung in its Scale a hundred thousand Men.
GEORGE smil'd; in t'other cast his single Sword;
Poiz'd were the Scales, and *Ballance* was restor'd.

Prenez le Roy. To *Marshal* Noailles.

PRenez le Roy! cries grand Marshal *Noailles*;
   But finding hard Work on't, soon took to his Heels:
And swift as the Wind o'er the River he cross'd,
For the Bridges he gain'd, tho' the Battle he lost:
So quickly he got himself out of Harm's Way,
He lost only his *Army*, the *Field*, and the *Day*.

Marshal Noailles's Answer.

I Lost not the *Field*, tho' for it' I fought;
  For how could I lose what I never had got?
And to gain such a Day, 'twas a Folly to strive:
For I never beheld a worse Day in my Life.
So the Battle I prudently turn'd to a Chase,
And sav'd my brave *Army*, by *winning the Race*.

On the French *singing* Te Deum *at* Paris.

THE *French*, tho' beat, *Te Deum* sing,
  As if they overcame us;
Fight them again, *Great Britain*'s King,
  And make them cry —— *Oremus*.

On the C———— of Y————'s making the Campaign.

WITH G—— what Hero can compare?
  Or who like him a Sword can wield,
That dares protect his *fav'rite Fair*
  Amid'st the Thunder of the Field?
The God of War outdone we see——
  In Action, *Venus* he dismiss'd,
Till he had made his Foe to flee,
  Then *slyly*, after Battle, kiss'd.
But G——, to *Love* and *War* ally'd,
  Both Deities at once admires;
And swelling big with martial Pride,
  By *Love* allays his glowing Fires.

On the British, Austrian, *and* German *Auxiliary Forces passing the* Rhine.

AS soon as on the Banks of *Rhine*,
  To pass, the *British* Forces join,
    Led on by L—g—nier:
The River God rear'd up his Head,
And with indignant Frown he said,
  ' What Bus'ness have you here?

'Think

' Think ye, like *Danube*'s Stream of Yore,
' Mine shall flow stain'd with *Gallic* Gore?
  ' Ah! *British* Chieftain, know,
' The Troops, tho' fine as e'er were seen,
' Yet *Germany* has no EUGENE,
  ' Nor *England* MARLB'RO' now.'

' 'Tis true, old God, the Chief reply'd,
' We have no EUGENE on our Side,
  ' No MARLB'RO' leads our Bands;
' What then?—instead of *Heroes two*,
' We've *One* to come, shall—Both outdo;—
  ' Know this;—for **** commands.'

Rhine smiling said,——' I know him not;
' Yet be this Maxim ne'er forgot;
  ' Whatever his Renown,
' For planning Schemes, for Martial Deeds,
' That *Two* brave *Hearts*, and *Two* wise *Heads*,
  ' *Are better far than* ONE.'

A Poetical EPISTLE *from a Great Man in the*
    ARMY.

THE K—— (save his Grace)
  Is in very good Case,
Tho' scorch'd by the Heat of the Fire;
  For all the long Day
  He heard the Guns play,
But wou'd never—no never—retire.

  His H—gh—ss the D—,
  Whose Leg a Ball took,
But did no great Harm to the Calf,
  Is so frolick and cheary,
  So pleasant and airy,
The Youngster doth nothing but laugh.

  So many fine Cloaths
  We've got from *French* Beaus,
That I've chang'd my blue Coat for a better.

From a Cottage write I,
With *Neiperg* close by,
And *Bumper 'Squire Jones* is my Letter.
For of the late Fight
In Faith I can't write,
Because I know nought of the Matter;
But in one or two Days,
I'll find out some Ways,
To make of't a damnable Clatter.
P. S. But stay, my good Lord,
By your Leave a small Word,
Of the Guns which we brought from *H—n—r*;
Without their Assistance
(What's *English* Resistance?)
With us, before G—d, 'twas all over.

An Account of the Battle between the French *and Allies, as sent into the Country.*

THE *K—, God* be prais'd,
Though his Valour was rais'd,
And was all in the Heat of the Fire,
Has receiv'd ne'er a Wound,
But is safe and sound,
As *True Briton's Heart* can desire.
The *French* pass'd the *Maine*
With some thousands of Men,
But our Army so boldly attack'd 'em,
That in greater Haste
The *Maine* they *repass'd*,
While our Conquerors hew'd 'em and hack'd 'em.
Duke C—— brave
A Shot chanc'd to have
In his *Leg*;——which *pierced the Calf
Of his Leg:* But to's *Bone*
No Mischief has done,
And his H—— is merry and safe.

All

All *in their fine Cloaths,*
Fort bien Poudre Beaus,
Of the *French* Houſhold Troops we have taken;
And Great *Noailles,* who
No doubt's *as fine too,*
From our Fellows cou'd ſcarce ſave his Bacon.
Poor *Clayton* is kill'd,
Yet with Joy we are fill'd
At our Conqueſt, and hope nought will mar it:
P. S. *I'd wrote you a better,*
And more ſenſible Letter,
But *conſider the* fourth Flaſk of Claret.

The GALLIC HEROES.

AT *Wit perplex'd,* if you would ſmile,
Think, *Reader,* of the great *Belleiſle.*
The modern *Falſtaff* would you ſee?
Bold *Broglio* is the very *He.*
Pride humbled if you would enjoy,
Turn next your Thoughts on *Maillebois.*
But if *Compaſſion* e'er prevails
Beſtow it on the poor *Noailles.*

To the EMPEROR.

WHILE *France* her treacherous Arms employs,
Thy gaſping Empire to reſtore;
Her Friendſhip half thy Realms deſtroys,
What could her hoſtile Sword do more?
Thus *Drury* Dames to Love inclin'd,
Plunder your Fob, your Noſe efface;
And fatal always when moſt kind,
Or pox or kill while they embrace.

An Excuse for the LAUREAT.

TO *C--bb--r* cries Sir *John*, ' Ye lazy Rogue,
 ' Not write a Line now *Dettingen*'s in Vogue?
' Are you not paid to sing your Prince's Fame?
' Before, such Opportunity ne'er came.'
—Here *C-bb-r* smil'd and answer'd: '*Cæsar*'s Glory,
' Without my *Rhymes*, will be admir'd in Story,
' To latest Ages stand upon Record;
' For *he Himself* has *wrote* it with his *Sword*.

An EPIGRAM.

ON the Banks of the *Maine* as our Soldiers wer walking,
On the opposite Side they heard Noise and much Talking.
Some *Frenchmen* were there, and our People espy'd,
Then in their sad Jargon thus tauntingly cry'd;
Vou, Mounsieur Inglee, vou Heretick, vou Nave,
Prie, var be dat Hero, your Clayton *de brave?*—
Of *Briton*'s bold Sons one advanc'd from the rest,
And thus (tho' not liking) retorted the Jest.
The same glorious Work, Fool, he still does pursue,
And your Maison du Roy *he be gone to review.*

The Campaign and its Historians.

ON the Banks of the *Maine*,
 Began the Campaign,
Heureusement, quoth *John** to his Friend.
 Tell *John*, if you know,
 How far you shall go,
Ere you make on't as happy an End.
 It has often been said,
 And in Papers we've read,
That the *Rhine*, Heroe *Charles* had pass'd over;

* See Lord *C——t's* Letter, *June* 16.

That

That *Noailles* and his Hoſt,
Would ſoon feel to their Coſt,
The wrath of the Prince of *H——r*.

The *Gazetteer* feigns,
And tortures his Brains,
That we with good News may grow wiſer;
When the Longitude's known,
Politicians ſhall own,
The Credit of each Adv—rt—ſer.

On the Means of perpetuating the Fame of Great ACTIONS.

*Urgentur ignoti longa
Nocte, carent quia Vate ſacro.*

VAIN are th' Atchievements of the Sword,
  To raiſe a laſting Name;
Unleſs ſome able Pen record,
  'Tis but precarious Fame.

This, *Horace* has declar'd his Senſe;
  Vain *Louis* this diſcerning,
To Poets dol'd about his Pence,
  And cheriſh'd Men of Learning.

Thrice happy *G——e!* who to rehearſe
  Thy Vict'ries o'er thy Foes,
Haſt C——r ready with his Verſe,
  And C——t with his Proſe.

Cardinal TENCHIN's PRAYER.

GReat God of Hoſts, attending the Complaints
  From Heaven alike, of Sinners and of Saints;
We thy dear ſinful Servants hope to find
Where'er our Troops advance, thy Mercy kind;
Oh let our Victories thy Love proclaim,
And think not on our Juſtice——but our Fame.

If by forswearing we can serve Thee better,
In Treaties, why shou'd Kings regard the Letter?
Reserving still, when they invoke the Sky
To hear the Oath, a Privilege to lye.
Oh grant us, Lord! to violate thy Will;
Fight against Vows——yet be good Christians still;
Attending more our Glory, than thy Word;
Since Soldiers have no Conscience—but their Sword.
The Means, as holy *Rome* has understood,
Are always righteous, if the End is good;
Which shews the Praise and Merit more sublime,
Wipes off the Stain, and sanctifies the Crime.
Fraud is no Sin, and Murder has no Guilt,
When right or wrong, *Britannia*'s Blood is spilt;
For ah! can *Bourbon*'s Arm inflict a Blow
Not lik'd by thee, when *Brunswick* is the Foe?
Even perjur'd Troops demand their just Applause,
That stab and plunder in a righteous Cause;
Which thy kind Smile for ever shou'd approve,
And claim their Laurel here, their Wreaths above.
Suppose against our Faith we cross the *Rhine*,
Thou knowest, Lord, how upright the Design!
'Gainst *George* and Heresy, we draw the Sword,
And break our Vows——according to thy Word.
Vouchsafe to hear us, Lord, while thus we pray,
Or ne'er expect a new Thanksgiving Day!
Which thy dear Church is each Campaign repeating,
For Triumphs oft——but oft'ner for a Beating.

The Lion *and the* Frogs. *A* FABLE.

A *Frog* and *Lion* made Alliance,
Which might bid all the Plain defiance.
The King of * *Cocks* (a haughty Race)
Whome'er he wou'd, with Crowns would grace;

* Gallus *is Latin for a Cock and a Frenchman.*

The

The *Lion* with imperial Sway
Rouz'd up, and check'd him in his Way;
Call'd to his aid his neighbouring *Frog:*
Who *croak'd*—but ſtir'd juſt like a *Log!*
Frogs—*twenty Thouſand* were to fight
In Morning; not to march ere Night:
Such *Faith* and *Valour* they diſcover,
That ere they *move*, the *Conqueſt*'s over.
' Why, cry the Allies, *Meſſieurs—Mynheers*,
' Such tardy, ſlow, Reſerve appears?—
Says a ſage *Frog*,—In oozy Beds
We always like to keep our Heads:
Be Famine, War, at higheſt Pitch,
We *baſk* in *Mud*, and ſtill grow *Rich:*
You've beat the *Cocks*, their Schemes perplex'd;—
One *Vict'ry more* gain;—make them vext—
—And—*we'll* dare march out to the *Next*.

A FABLE *on the late Tranſactions in* Germany.

A Strutting Cock, ambitious grown,
   His Sons diſpatches up and down,
     The Eaglet to aſſail;
They crow'd and ſtruck ſome ſparring Blows,
Then having flown from Houſe to Houſe,
     They haſtily turn'd Tail.

The Eaglet ſtretch'd her Talons forth,
(The Royal Eaglet of the North)
     And caught them by the A—ſe;
Their Feathers flew,
She pluck'd them Blue;
     Poor puny Wights of *Mars!*

Their Sire ſends forth a ſtouter Troop,
   Their Brothers to relieve;
The beſt Game Bird in all the Coop,
   To them did Orders give

To fight, whate'er stood in their Way,
The fiercest Bird, or Beast of Prey.

A Lion in the Forest stood,
His Whelps attending, all true Blood,
   Which the rash Birds assault;
But half fell dead,
The rest they fled,
   And curse their Sire his Fault.

B———a's *Lamentation and Petition.*

IN *hostile Fields* why lives my Lord,
   Now *furrow'd his fair Front* appears?
Ah! 'tis too late to wield *that Sword*,
   That sheath'd hath been *near forty Years*.

The *Damps*, and *Colds*, and *endless Toils*,
   That ever wait on *martial Deeds*,
Are they, to *Thee*, repaid with *Spoils*,
   Or *Fame*, that fond Ambition feeds?

Return, and bless my longing Arms,
   And let the G——n *Strumpet* languish;
Oh flee from *Dangers* and *Alarms*,
   And ease my *wasting inbred Anguish!*

Thou too, my *lovely darling Lad*,
   With *plumpy Cheeks* and *Sides so round*,
Put up thy *Courage* with thy *Dad*,
   Nor longer lie on the *hard Ground*.

One Wound's enough, so well receiv'd,
   Not in the *Heel*, nor yet in *Trenches:*
By *Men* thy Bravery's believ'd;
   Thou hast the Hearts of all the *Wenches*.

My *Tears* are streaming for ye *Both*;
   Return, while *yet* my Heart is *tender:*
Oh *valiant Father*, be not loth!
   Oh *charming Son*, to Love surrender!

Let S—*tacy* go back; send A—— over;
  Or some one *skilful* in his Art:
'Tis sure too much for poor H—*anovr*;
  To *council* ALL, and *act* HER PART.

With foreign *Chiefs*, no artful Dress
  Can lead the B——*ns* on to *Fame:*
They love their Country to Excess,
  And place it *second* to *no Name.*

A New BALLAD; *or,* BRITONS *Rejoice,* &c.

  To the Tune of Handel's March in Scipio.

*B*RITONS rejoice,
    Your Honour's now retriev'd,
    The *French* are beat
    Our Joy's compleat,
    And *Germany* reliev'd.
Then never fear, brave Boys,
    But boldly still advance,
    Like *Edward,* and like *Henry,*
Great *George* will conquer *France.*

  Our *Britons* brave,
Tho' they ne'er fought before,
    Are still the same
    True Cocks of Game,
  As in the Days of Yore.
Should *Edward* and the *Black Prince*
    Now rise, with Joy they'd see,
    That *Englishmen* are still the same
As they were at *Cressy.*

  The Odds were great,
And great the Game to play:
    Says *English John,*
    But three to one,
  Huzza! brave Boys, huzza!

Then

Then soon pell-mell we drove them
    Into the River *Mayne:*
      Five thousand there were drowned,
Five thousand more were slain.

  The *British* Name
All *Europe* will revere:
    No vile Disgrace,
    Nor Insult base
We now shall need to fear.
Then curse on wicked W——le,
  And all his pilf'ring Crew,
    Who ty'd those Hands
    With shameful Bands
That c uld the World subdue.

The following Lines were occasion'd by reading a Grand, Mysterious COFFEE-HOUSE ODE *on the Battle of* Dettingen; *the second Line of which is express'd in these majestical Terms:*

" All true BRITONS, sing Hallelujah! "

WHat need of *Hallelujahs,* pray,
    When you've but just begun?
'Tis Time enough, your Readers think,
    When that your Song is done.
Beside, it would be patter there;
    For all with one accord
Would then without the least Regret,
    Cry out, *O praise the Lord!*

EPIGRAM.

HIS Foe, the *Parthian* better to amuse,
    First flies, then turns, and afterward subdues:
On a much wiser Scheme *Noailles* relies;
    For *Noailles* conquers first, and after flies!

To the Queen of HUNGARY.

WHEN *Lewis* had heard by each trembling Courier,
  That his Troops were half kill'd, and the other half flying,
To *Bohemia*'s lov'd Queen, who had nothing to fear,
  He grew every day more genteel and complying.
His Armies withdrawn, and his Wrath at an end,
  He hopes your Resentment may likewise be o'er;
And begs you would think him a trusty good Friend,
  Since his Squadrons could butcher and plunder no more.
To Friendship and Peace of a sudden inclin'd,
  Now, now is your critical Time to entreat him;
Since a Monarch of *France* will be always most kind,
  The more you correct, & the oft'ner you beat him.

The SCENE CHANG'D: An EPIGRAM.

WITH haughty Pride the *French* proclaim'd,
  That they the *Austrian* Pow'r would awe;
And when th' *Hungarian* Queen they'd tam'd,
  Give on *Vienna*'s Walls their Law.
How chang'd the Scene! *Noailles* is gone,
  And *Broglio* from *Vienna* far is:
O *Lewis*, 'tis not Ten to One
  But th' Allies give *You* Law at *Paris*.

FRENCH POLICY.

IN *Lewis* see the Fate of Kings,
  O'er-run with Fraud and Pride;
Asham'd to own the secret Springs,
  Which yet they cannot hide.

To sooth *Bavaria*'s ruin'd Lord,
   Broglio is bid to roam
In private, (so he keeps his Word)
   Caress'd and welcom'd Home.

These Paths his Grandsire better trod,
   In Fraud a constant Dealer,
The Old One Robb'd ye on the Road,
   The Young One's a Sheep-stealer.

The Substance of a certain LETTER.

DEAR Friend, of the Blues
   I'll write you some News,
To wipe off our Stain,
And make the Thing plain.

   What they say of E—— S——,
I'll assure you an't fair;
To be well understood,
You must read H——w——,
And our Fault wan't abiding,
But lay in our Riding.

   You must know, we forgot
To charge on a Trot,
But gallop'd full speed,
Like a fool-hardy Breed,
To the Enemy's Line,
And there, Sir, in fine,
(Since the Truth I am writing)
We broke without fighting,
On the Foe turn'd our B———h,
But form'd out of Reach,
And by this lucky Flight,
Beat the *French*, Sir, outright;
For their eager pursuing,
Prov'd the Cause of their Ruin,
And, so tho' we run,
Yet the Battle we won.

Therefore good now stand by us,
When People bely us.
Until my L—— S——,
(And that is but fair)
Sends over a Letter,
To clear it up better:
So here ends my News,
With a thousand Adieus!

Postscript.

Once more let me beg you, speak up for the Blues,
And make, if you can, Sir, a better Excuse.

A Thought on our Army Intelligence.

IN our *Accounts*, 'tis something *rare*,
   To hear a Word of good Lord S——.
But whether *he* from hence may claim,
A *Right Hand*, or a *Left Hand* Fame,
Is what I am not *clear* in *quite*,
Since none know, yet, what's *wrong or right*.

News from the Army.

THE *News* I send in alter'd Stile,
   I leave your Friends to reconcile.
  The Duke is *cur'd:* yet not so much,
But, when he rides, 'tis in a *Coach:*
Brave D'Aremberg *some time* was well;
Tho' when he will, we now can't tell:
And Col'nel Peers, with many more,
From *Wounded*, go to the *Dead* Score.
  Prince Charles (a mighty Hero He,
Black, rough, and *all* that Man should be)
Had *cross'd* the Rhine a Week ago;
But now the Papers tell us, No.
Yet this is true; The *King* he saw,
And eke the *Army* near Hanau.

The King has nothing else to do,
But *cross* the River and *fall to*:
And somewhere he will do't 'twixt Mentz,
And Bingen, Rhinefield, or Coblentz.

Noailles, that rank *Tergiversator*,
Shoots like a *Duck* across the Water;
Entrenches, fortifies, extends;
But few believe he'll gain his *Ends*;
Spite of his Isles, and all his Works,
* He'll drive him off, who drove the Turks.

Would you have more *discordant Stuff?*
We've beat the *French*—and *that's enough.*

Hor. Book I. Ode XXXV.

Translated, Imitated, and Paraphras'd.

To FORTUNE.

OH! Goddess! thou, who rul'st at Court,
And mak'st th' ambitious Great thy Sport!
That can'st the lowest Mortal raise
And put a S——s in W——'s Place!
Yet turn to Triumphs his Disgrace.

Thee, that his Land may be thy Care,
The lowly Hind pursues with Pray'r:
The Merchant too, in dread of *Spain*,
Hopes, that thro' thee, his far-fetch'd Gain
Safe in the Channel may remain!

Thee *Hussars*, and the barb'rous Race,
That † *bang* the *French* from Place to Place:
Pandours and *Croats*, and the Host
That swarm along *Bavaria*'s Coast,
Still dread, lest the rich Spoil be lost!

Thee,

---

* *Prince Charles.*

† The Author hopes he may be pardon'd so low an Expression; but he could find none so happily adapted to the Behaviour of the *French.*

Thee, Purple Kings, o'er-stepping Law,
Lewis, or *Charles*, behold with Awe;
Lest thou their Subjects should excite
To arm in the Defence of Right,
And with their lawful Sov'reigns fight!

Necessity precedes thee still,
Arm'd with each Sort of Good and Ill!
Cannons and Swords, and Racks and Wheels,
Ribbands, and Wands, and Staffs, and Seals,
That follow close thy treach'rous Heels!

Before thy Shrine, see *Hope* attend!
And white-rob'd, scarce-found Friendship bend!
Nor when thou leav'st the fallen Great,
To all the Changes of their Fate,
Will she forsake them, with their State!

Whilst the false Croud, and perjur'd Whore,
Fly from their Friend's diminish'd Store,
And the moist Guest, when the last Flask
Proclaims the hollow empty Cask;
Alike unfit for either Task!

But Goddess! now on GEORGE attend!
On GEORGE, distracted *Europe*'s Friend!
Guide thou his Arms! protect his Cause!
Nor let him sheath the Sword he draws,
'Till tam'd *Bavaria* own his Laws!

And when the gen'rous Toil is o'er,
And haughty *France dictates* no more;
Conduct him safely o'er the Main,
And when return'd to us again,
New-point the War, and humble *Spain*.

Verses written by a HIGHLANDER *the Day before he was taken.*

YE think our *Highlands*, bleak and bare,
O' *Phœbus*' Bounty ha' na Share;
And that, becaufe far North we come,
We're glad to leave our native Home.

But much mifta'en, ye little ken
Each bonny Strath, and verdant Glen,
Where Violets blow, and Hawthorns bloom,
Of Gardens fine fupply the Room:
And *Cowdenknows* and *Yarrow* Side,
As much the blithfome *Scotfman*'s Pride,
Who near thefe pleafant Places dwells,
As *Windfor Caftle*, or *Verfailles*.

'Tis true, that we are unco' poor,
Our Lords and Lairds live on your Store,
But fare each earns whate'er he gets,
They'r ye're ane Tykes, and turn ye're Spits:
While we at hame, wi' mikle Care,
Rub thro' our Lives wi' little Gear:
Yet now and then the Piper plays,
And *Scottifh* Slaves forget their Waes,
Sing they'r ald Sangs, and are as canty
As *Englifh* Clowns wi' aw their Plenty.
Then winder not we're fcarce inclin'd
To be in martial Bands confin'd,
Sent o'er the Sea, and far away,
To make a Shew without ——.
But if this Humour's fae refented,
Banifh us hame,—— and we're contented.

Take ye a ROBIN i' th' Yard,
(And be his Cafe wi' ours compar'd)
As lang as ye your Crumbs impart
He pecks and fings wi' aw his Heart,

And

And trusting to ye're kind Protection,
Makes ay your Window his Election;
There wi' his Plaid athwart his Breast,
He seeks his Meat, or takes his Rest:
But if wi' him ye break ye're Wird,
And seize, and cage the little Bird,
Sullen at first he bears his Chain,
'Till starving quits the greater Pain.
And *Highlanders* like *Robins* be,
Alive or dead they mun be *free*.

A SUMMARY of INTELLIGENCE,
Domestic and Foreign.

TO sum up all the *current News*:
—The *Lott'ry*'s half engros'd by *Jews*:
'Tis ask'd, who governs after Spring,
Whether a *Regency* or ——
A *Lord* translated to *his Grace*;
But—not the Lord of *noble Race*.
The *Weekly Bills* increasing much:
No great Dependence on the *Dutch*:
Perhaps still less on *Prussia*'s Monarch,
Who seems to *navigate his own Ark*:
Some slight *Complainings* from the *Rhine*,
Where People know not *how* to *dine*:
We want *more News* from *Lobkowitz*,
And *something certain* from the *Switz*:
Count *Traun*, 'tis said, has beat *de Gages*;
But yet the *last* has *rais'd his Wages*:
Th' Auxil'ries marching, and the *French*,
One Side, no doubt, must soon *entrench*:
We of *West-India* hear no *more*,
Than ne'er *Columbus* made the *Shore*;
And *Matthews*, tho' Lord Paramount,
Sends from the *Streights* no *grand Account*.——

On all these Points the *grave ones lecture*:
On all—their Ground is—*mere Conjecture.*

The MISTAKE.

WHEN lately G—— and *Gallia*'s Sons
   In dreadful Combat strove,
Wide spread the Tumult round the Sky,
   And reach'd almighty *Jove.*

The Monarch whom the Heav'ns obey,
   Anxious for *Britain*'s State,
id War's intrepid God descend
   And guard the Hero's Fate.

With Joy the Martial God replies,
   I'll aid the doubtful War;
Then t'wards *Hispania*'s golden Climes
   Directs his bounding Car.

Jove saw the God's mistaken Course;
   Return, Return, he cries;
G——*shews what* British *Courage dares*
   Beneath Germanian *Skies.*

Confounded at a Truth so strange,
   The Warriour check'd his Rein,
And swore by Heaven he thought that G——
   Had been at War with *Spain*.

And Oh! might once the Muse advise,
   Return ere 'tis too late;
Humble the Pow'r *Hispania* boasts,
   And render *Britain* great.

For should you baulk the God once more,
   You'll after call in vain,
He'll rack his Wits to find you out,
   Before he thinks of *Spain*.   C. B.

A Lesson

A Leſſon from H——N——R.

THE Week ſpent in Labour, in Trouble, in Care,
The *Trader* on *Saturday* breathes the freſh Air;
From Courts and from Clients, the *Lawyer* once free,
In every *Vacation* his *Villa* muſt ſee.
And from *Sunday* to *Sunday* the briſk brawny *Prieſt*,
Leaves Scriptures and Prayers for a *Cup o' the beſt*.
If then *Peace*, and the *Place* that you love, is the Thing
For which we all ſtrive,—— Why d'ye grudge it your——?
Why rave at his *Abſence*, and make ſuch a *Fuſs*?
He's *buſy* with *You*,— and at *Eaſe* when with *Us*.

A New Ballad upon the Riches of GREAT BRITAIN.
Occaſion'd by a late Calculation.

WHY raileſt thou, *Thomas*, as if we were *poor*?
Thy *Journal* ſhall never be credited more;
It tends honeſt Minds to corrupt and bewitch;
Other Journals can prove, *We are damnable rich*.
                Derry down, down, &c.

In them may'ſt thou ſee all the *Millions* we raiſe,
And the *Uſes* for what, and the *Means* and the *Ways*.
Man, Woman, and *Child*, from the Throne to the Shed,
We come in at leaſt with our *Guinea* per Head*.
                Derry down, down, &c.

Tho' ſome never ſaw ſuch a Piece of their *own*,
What then? They ſhall raiſe it, let *S—s* but alone.
To aſk it at once, 'twou'd with Hardſhip be found:
They now never miſs it—*but all the Year round*.
                Derry down, down, &c.

* *The People of* England *are computed at between ſeven and eight Millions.*

Salt, Candles, Beer, Soap, daily Quotas bring in;
Much comes from *Tobacco,* & more comes from *Gin*:
The *laſt* was forbidden; but S—ys would *relax,*
And grant the *free Uſage* and double the *Tax.*
      Derry down, down, &c.

Thus far the Revenue affects *Common Livers*:
But let all the Merit remain with the *Givers*:
They take from the *People,* and grant to the *Crown,*
And grant, we muſt own, like to *Men of Renown.*
      Derry down, down, &c.

Five hundred and odd: Now ſuppoſe them all meet,
And each Man as heavy as *Or——d the Great*:
They at one, this Year's Gold at the other *Extream*,*
And the *Men* and their *Chapel* would ſoon *kick the
 Beam.*   *Derry down, down, &c.*

Oh! *Thomas,* then ceaſe thy *ſarcaſtical Lectures,*
And bleſs *happy Britain,* and laud her *Protectors,*
Who each, to a Man, *Pros* and *Cons* being told,
Can give *more* each Year, than his *own Weight in Gold.*
      Derry down, down, &c.

Now that we are *wealthy,* what *Churl* will diſpute?
Let thoſe who deny it henceforward be *mute*—
Effect muſt have *Cauſe* in good Logic, you know;
And what he *has not,* who the Deuce can *beſtow?*
      Derry down, down, &c.

---

* *A Pound Weight of Gold is worth, ſuppoſe, about* 50 *l.
Sterling. Allow each Man to weigh* 15 *Stone, or* 210 *Pounds,
Horſeman's Weight, and the following Calculation may give ſome
Idea of this Matter.*

  210
   50
 ―――――
 10500 £ *the Weight of each Individual in Gold.*
  558
―――――
5,859,000 *Weight of the Whole. Which is a great deal with-
 in Compaſs.*

              Then

[23]

Then why should we grumble at *Troops* sent *on far*,
To finish *an old*, or commence *a new War?*
What *Want* could ensue, should they journey to *Greece*,
While *so many Men* are worth *so much a-piece*.
                    Derry down, down, &c.

On *the* CONDUCT *of a* certain GREAT PRINCE.

' TO whom is FRED'RICK an *Ally?*
    To those who Friendship best can *buy*.
' Wherefore and when is he a *Foe?*
As *Interest* prompts him to be *so*.
Refining, varying ev'ry Day,
He keeps the *Parties* all at *Bay*,
And, without Claim of *proper Right*,
The *Ballance* holds—for which they *fight*.
This mystic *Antimachiavel**,
Does not his *Conduct* plainly tell,
That, while *against* it he disputed,
He *learn'd* the Doctrine he *refuted?*

The CATASTROPHE.

WHEN *V—rn—n* is willing to shake Hands
        with *Spain,*
And our Ladies all boast of the chaste Lady ——
When *S—nd—s* joins with *P———* in friendly Debate,
And *St J———* again holds the Rudder of State;
When *P—t* is bought off, or *No—l* brought in,
And *O·nf—*'s convinc'd that Pride is a Sin;
When Sir *W—ns* haunts Courts or *H—C—* complies,
And *C—J—W———* cries up *Y———k* to the Skies;
When *B———df—* for Power shall barter his Grace,
And *G—w—r* forfeit Honour to keep in his Place;
When *H—n—w—d* speaks of the BLUES what is
        fair,
And all *H—n—r* shews us a Man like Lord *St—;*

* *A Treatise publish'd by* M. De Voltaire, *and said to be wrote by his P———n M———y.*

Lorrain

Lorrain, and *Alsace*, and *Burgundy* likewise,
Shall submit all at once to the potent Allies:
Corruption shall yield unto Freedom and Trade,
All our Taxes shall cease, and our Debts shall be paid.

On FACTION DETECTED.

O Libel, born to endless Shame,
   Big with the foulest Lyes!
Thy Patrons, Authors, thee disclaim,
   Thy Enemies despise.

All treat thee at the self same Rate,
   The Many and the Few;
And Parties who each other hate,
   Agree in Hating you.

The CARTERS.

THINGS may well go slowly on,
   When by aukward Engines mov'd,
No Man e'er cou'd trust in *John*;
   Will by no Man is belov'd.

Well may then the Team stand still,
   Or rumble on thro' Ruts and Stones;
All Men smile at what frets *Will*;
   All wish *John* may break his Bones.

Careless, tho' they own the Cart,
   Laughing they its Dangers see;
Thoughtless that themselves must smart,
   If it once o'erturn'd shou'd be.

The GRACIOUS REFUSAL.

WHEN the Great Earl of *B*——, with most
   Dog-like Submission,
To the Army wrote over, thus ran his *Petition*;
" Tho' once, in ill Humour, I cry'd out, *No Place*,
" May it *now* please my *Lord*, and your *M*——*y*'s
   Grace,   " To

" To grant me that *Trifle* the *Tr—y's Head.*"—
C——t ſmil'd with Diſdain when the Letter he read ;
Then carry'd it up to the K—— with a Sneer :
" See P——y the *Patriot*, the *Courtier*, the *P—r* !
" Shall I draw his *Commiſſion* ?"—The Anſwer was,
  No :
Which C—t return'd, with, " Your ſervant, and ſo ;
" The K—, in mere Tenderneſs to your *good Name*,
" (Which already is blown at the *wrong End* of Fame)
" In your preſent *bad State* would protect you from
  worſe ;
" And, leſt *gen'ral Contempt* grow t'a *gen'ral Curſe*,
" Is *graciouſly pleas'd* to deny your Requeſt,
" That your L——p, at laſt, in *Oblivion* may reſt,
" And enjoy that *ſtill Life*, which you always
  call'd *beſt*."

On the PROMOTION *of the Right Honourable* Henry
Pelham, *Eſq*;

WHEN to the King the Tidings *Carteret* bore,
  That *Wilmington*, good Earl, was now no more,
And a long Liſt of Nobles, old and new,
Of Knights and 'Squires preſented to his View,
Demanding low—to whom it pleas'd his Grace,
Of all the Train, to give the late Earl's Place ?
To the moſt Worthy, the juſt Monarch ſaid ;
And ſtrait to PELHAM were the Honours paid.

The INTERVIEW.

THE Story goes,—as Fame will tattle ſtill,
  Once on a Time — 'Squire *Harry* met—Lord
  Will.
Says This to That,—If you'll the Story hear,
I'll tell you, *Hal*, a Secret—worth your Ear.

The Old Man's gone, where G—— knows what's
  his Case,
But I've declar'd—that I'll *accept* his Place.
And is it so?—Why, let me tell you, Brother,
Since one good Turn, they say, deserves another,
I too, for once, a Secret will reveal,
Which long, indeed, I cannot well conceal.
Our Master—who, y'know, ne'er breaks his Word,
Promis'd I shou'd *succeed* him at the B——,
Full low bow'd I—as Love and Duty taught,
Nor fear I much that you this Place have caught.
Will star'd and cock'd, and cock'd and star'd again;
Pleas'd, *Harry* smil'd, to see his Rival's Pain.

On a NOBLEMAN's *Arrival* at H——n-Hall.

WHILE *Europe* is divided all with Care,
  With Dawn of Peace, or Universal War;
While foreign Realms dire Desolation feel,
And *gen'rous Britons* ample Tributes al;
While *Fleury* dead can tell no Tale that's past;
And Or——d happ'ly clos'd his Scene the last,
From *Mortal Care* retires: At H————n-Hall
He *sees*, he *hears*, he *talks*, he *laughs* at All.
Ye Gods! can't be? when such his impious Toils!
No Conscience on his harden'd Breast recoils?
He boasts his *Triumphs*, and enjoys his *Spoils*.
'Tis true, he has escap'd a Mortal Jury:
But *what's to come!*—Let him enquire of Fleury.

The METAMORPHOSIS.

NO League with our *Wishes* since *Fortune* will hold,
  Our *Hope* grows as thin as a *Lath*.
The *Gazette* has *brush'd-off* our B—nn—ts bold,
  And *left* us meer K———— of the B————.

To

To the E. of B——,

Occasion'd by a late Pamphlet, entitled,
Faction detected.

YOUR Sheets I've perus'd,
    Where the Whigs you've abus'd,
And on Tories have falsely reflected;
    But, my Lord, I'm afraid,
    From all that's there said,
'Tis you, and not they, that's detected.

    Both Parties, I hear,
    Most freely declare,
That 'tis not approv'd of by either:
    If it's damn'd then by both,
    It must be the Growth
Of *somebody* who is of neither.

    'Tis easy to name
    From what Quarter it came,
And the Thing of itself stands confess'd;
    'Tis that pitiful Crew,
    Of your Creatures and you,
That both Parties scorn and detest.

    But stay———let me see———
    Which Tool could it be
That such a huge Book cou'd indite?
    For of all those you made,
    If there is one that can read,
I'm sure there's not one that can write.

    'Tis above poor Sir *John*,
    Nor by S——s could be done,
And B——e's too stupid and dark:
    O——d hardly reads well,
    Jeff. never cou'd spell,
And you know H—— V——? sets his Mark.

[28]

  Then since all your Tools
   Are such ignorant F——ls,
It must be your L———p's own doing:
   You have taken your *Plie*,
   But you'll soon own with me,
That you've settled yourself in your Ruin.

   As diff'rent Winds blew,
   Like the Weather-Cock you
Long waver'd both Parties betwixt;
   But did not you know,
   That Weather-Cocks grow
Quite useless the Moment they're fix'd?

The PARALLEL.

A Patriot of old, 'tis said,
  Full twenty Years the Zany play'd,
The *Roman* Commonwealth to save;
  For at one glorious Burst, he broke
  His own Disguise, and Country's Yoke,
And dug for Tyranny a Grave.

—— rivals the Patrician's Fame,
  In Zeal and Steadiness the same,
As many Years the Mask he wore;
  Whole Speeches seem'd to shake the Throne,
  Amidst the Faithful Few he shone,
As *Marcus Cato* did of yore.

  Then all at once shook off the Veil,
  To Truth and Freedom turn'd his Tail,
And for a Title fawn'd a Tool:
  In different Lights the Pair we view,
  The First as wise in Folly's Shew;
The last in Wisdom's Garb a Fool.

A M<small>OTTO</small>

A Motto for a Sword.

'Never dare draw me without Reason shewn;
' When drawn, ne'er put me up without Re-
" nown*."
An Exil'd Prelate's Sword this Motto bore;
The Motto just, the Sword tho' never wore.——
From This, ye fighting Heroes of the Age,
Learn what is Valour, and know what is Sage.
Learn, that a *Prelate*'s Sword can teach just Things;
Teach Heroes *Courage*, and give *Law* to Kings.

POTATOES and HEMP:
Or, Tories and Robertsmen.

When *Tory Oxford* rul'd the roast,
  To *Wharton* thus he made his boast:
' You've been in *Ireland* we know,
' And seen how there Potatoes grow:
' Let them but once get in the Ground,
' No way to root them out is found.
' We *Tories* like Potatoes are,
' (My Lord the Simile will bear)
' In vain, you aim at Conquest o'er us,
' We carry every Point before us.

But *Wharton*, witty, and a *Whig*,
Thus check'd the Minister so big:
' I've been in *Ireland*, an't please,
' And know Potatoes will *increase*:
' But give me leave, my Lord, to tell,
' We know to root them out as well:
' A little *Hemp-seed*, timely sown,
' Will clear the Ground most over-grown.

---

* *The Motto of a Sword, presented to the late Dr.* Atterbury *when he went out of the* Tower, *was*, Draw me not without Reason, nor put me up without Honour.

To *Tories* liken *Robertsmen*,
This Simile will serve again,
And shoot from *W—l—gt—n* to *P——*.
But why thus cumber they the Field?
'Tis 'cause the *Hemp* has been with-held.
Had that been *timely* sown among 'em,
And *Justice* in the Produce strung 'em,
The late Defeat had sav'd the *Realm*,
And *Englishmen* now been at *Helm*.

Britons, let *Wharton*'s Hint be taken,
'Tis ne'er too late to *watch your Bacon*.
They have not yet so full Possession,
But Hemp may grow *another S-ss—n*.
At *Or——d* how the Folks would stare,
With *H-rry* here, and *H-r—ce* there!
If *second Crops* infest your Lands,
Let *C——t* take his turn, and *S——*,
String such a goodly *Rope of Onions*,
We all shall *smile* and join *Opinions*.

Occasioned by a Paragraph in the Gazetteer.

WHEN on the Treas'ry liv'd the *Gazetteer*,
  ' *Britons*, he cry'd, What have ye now to fear?
' Ye write, ye speak, ye do just what you please;
' The Fun's your own,—the Minister's at Ease.'
But when discarded from the Publick Pelf,
The *Gazetteer* was forc'd to keep himself,
Loud he exclaimed, " Liberty's at Stake;
" Without a Risque ye neither write nor speak."
To prove which Truth ('twas all that he could bring)
A mighty innocent insipid Thing,
Sends Author, Printer, Publisher to Jail,
(As possibly they wish) and gives no Bail.——
C—rt—t, wouldst thou thy Lenity display?
E'en take the *Gazetteer* again in Pay.

The

The CARDINALS.

FRANCE lately was at *Europe*'s Head,
　Now *Europe* seems on *France* to tread;
　　Is not this mighty strange?
Young *Conti* thus the Reason gives,
Fleury is dead, and *Tenchin* lives,
　　And hence this wond'rous Change.

EPIGRAM.

IF thro' fear of Disgrace into Danger we run,
　And boldly attack those we rather would shun;
Then Cowards are brave, if the Maxim be true,
And no braver Men in the World than the *Blue*.

IMITATION of

*Audivere, Lyce, Dii mea vota, Dii
Audivere, Lyce: fis Anus, & tamen
　Vis formosa videri:
　　Ludisque, & bibis impudens.*　　Hor.

HE is grown old, he is abhorr'd,
　Whom falsely once all Men ador'd.
I thank you, Gods! for so you ought
To stamp the *Man* who merits nought.
And yet to bribe the Goddess *Fame*
　No Art by him is left untry'd;
So great is *Bubo*'s Want of Shame,
　His Drunkenness and Pride.

But know 'tis P——T that Goddess seeks,
　His shining Virtue claims her Choice;
For him alone her Trumpet speaks,
　For him alone is heard her Voice.

For Streams more crystal than her Skies
　The Goddess flies a dirty *Bath*.
O *Bubo!* thou art fill'd with Lies,
　O Virtue! he hath left thy Path.　　Nor

Nor Title can, nor Strings of Blue,
  Nor Wealth immense thy Fame restore,
Nor heav'nly Peace of Mind renew :
  What Time has bury'd, is no more.

Where is the Man who next to *W—d—m* shone,
  The Nation's Column, and the Senate's Pride :
Where is the Patriot, the *Camillus* gone,
  Of true Applause where now the swelling Tide ?

But *W—d—m* dy'd while Credit bloom'd,
  Cursed, O *Bubo !* is thy Fate,
An aged Raven thou art doom'd,
  The World's Contempt, not worth its Hate !

PLAIN THOUGHTS, &c.

A New Ballad.

ATTEND, ye brave *Britons* of ev'ry Degree,
  All you who deserve, and resolve to be free;
Plain-Thoughts will suffice, and *Plain-Language* will do
When all we assert is well known to be true.
                    Derry down, &c.

To save our old Laws a new M——h we took,
And well for those Laws an old Tyrant forsook :
And shou'd our old *England* again be at Stake,
A Curse on the Slaves who the N--w won't forsake.
                    Derry down, &c.

This M——h, unskill'd in the Nation's Affairs,
A Lover of Wealth, and a Foe to all Cares,
Resign'd to his Statesmen his Kingdom itself,
And wink'd at their Plunder to share in the Pelf.
                    Derry down, &c.

He purchas'd abroad while his Ministers jobb'd ;
And *H————r* flourish'd, while *B———n* was robb'd,
                                And

And when he chang'd hands with a fresh Set of Men,
Where those took a Shilling, these Villains took ten.
    Derry down, &c.

This M———h deceas'd, his Son did succeed;
A P———more august never came out of his Breed;
For tho' at his Birth lying Wags had a Fling,
He soon prov'd himself the true Son of a K———,
    Derry down, &c.

Like Measures he follow'd, like Servants he had;
And all Things grew worse that before were too bad:
For *W—l—e* still rul'd with Corruption and Gold;
The M———h he bought, and the Na——n he sold.
    Derry down, &c.

With Armies at Home, and with foreign Troops paid:
With Laws that cramp'd Freedom, as Taxes cramp'd
  Trade:
With Maxims quite new, he pursu'd his base Ends,
And help'd our old Foes to oppress our old Friends.
    Derry down, &c.

At length when Corruption drain'd Treasuries dry,
And none would be bought—for none offer'd to buy,
And Courtiers quit Leaders, they follow'd for Pay,
And Leaders turn Courtiers, worse R-ls than they.
    Derry down, &c.

My Tale, O ye *Britons!* this Moral does bring,
However descended, a K——— is a K———;
Whenever they're taken, most Statesmen are Knaves,
And Patriots at C—t are the lowest of Slaves.
    Derry down, &c.

ODE. *To the new M————rs.*

WITS, point your Arrows keen and quick,
  Sport Odes, Jokes, Ballads ne'er so thick
    At *S————*'s solid Head;
With safe impenetrable Weight
He stands great Leader of the State,
    Arm'd Cap-a-pie in Lead.

Let Facts convince, let Rhet'rick move,
Let *P————tt* persuade, let *W——ll——r* prove
    Wild Schemes, and *Levy-Stealing*;
Dumb, as their Bench, these Statesmen sit,
Cyphers without Reply, or Wit,
    Lost to all Shame and Feeling.

Not so Lord *B————*, less wise than they,
He contradicts himself each Day,
    Still is a great Debater,
He threatens Vengeance on the Press,
He makes our little Freedom less,
    And our great Army greater.

Thou, Genius of this Isle! arise,
See with Disdain, Grief, and Surprize
    Such Knaves, such Ideots join'd,
Join'd to destroy that happy Frame,
Which made *Old England*'s Strength and Name
    The Terror of Mankind.

A SIMILE.

To JEFFREY BROADBOTTOM, *Esq*;

DEAR *Jeffrey*, didst thou never meet
 A Beggar walking in the Street,
Who, conscious of his Want of Sight,
Trusts others to direct him right?
Out of his Doors he'll never stir
Without his knowing, faithful Cur,

         Well

Well skill'd each diff'rent Way in finding,
Who knows all Crossings, every Winding:
By him thro' all the Town he's led,
And guided safely home to Bed.

So fares it with our T———y Board,
Where, dark and blind sits ev'ry L—d,
From that grave *Thing* that wears a Ribbon,
Quite down to that grave *Nothing*, G———: *Gibbon*
Exactly fitted to each other,
Each justly calls his Neighbour, Brother;
Their Tongues can't speak, nor Heads discern,
Too dull their own dull Forms to learn:
They therefore wisely have provided
A Cur, by whom they all are guided;
No Warrant sign till he inspects it,
And take no Step till he directs it:
But conscious to his Judgment, stoop,
And all their Strings are ty'd to Sc——— *Scrope*

A NEW BALLAD.
To the Tune of Ye COMMONS *and* PEERS.

Attend to my Call,
  Ye *Jacobites* all,
Who so long have wept over this Nation,
  And with me you'll own,
  That *England* is grown
To be in a blest Situation.

  Since *W———e*, that Fool,
  No longer does rule,
But to *N———k* is gone in Disgrace;
  What mayn't ye expect
  When once ye reflect
What wise Men have come in his Place?

The Objection was good,
That no *one Man* cou'd
Alone bear the Weight of this Realm;
So, that you might be pleas'd,
And the Nation be eas'd,
There's a Dozen at least at the Helm.

They with you were once join'd,
And closely combin'd,
As Liberty's chiefest Upholders;
And if they got higher
Than you might desire,
It was by the Help of your Shoulders.

It's well known to you,
That they've nothing in View,
But the best Patriotical Ends;
For with them you agreed
In all that they did,
And for twenty long Years were their Friends.

They are still the same Men
As you knew them then,
In Action and Honour as clear;
S—— ready and bright,
B—— steady and tight,
And W—— calm and sincere.

Their Gratitude now
Resolving to shew,
To you who have got 'em their Places:
They've done such a Thing
As may ruin the K——,
And of Course must regain your good Graces.

The H————r Line
Is not Right Divine,
And therefore they know you can't bear it;
And our Army so great
You must thoroughly hate,
Since more than the D——l you fear it.

So your good old Allies,
  To stop all your Cries,
And of ev'ry Complaint to disarm ye,
  Now they're at the Helm,
  Quite out of the Realm
Have sent both the K———and the Army.

A SONG *sung in the* B———h *Camp.*
To the Tune of Cuckoo.

WHEN *British* Horse, but chiefly B———
  And whisker'd Heroes, dreadful Sight!
And many a Scarf of yellow Hue,
  Did quit the fearful bloody Fight.
    Then *I———n* brave, behind a Tree,
      Stood very close,
      Stood very close,
      Stood very close,
    And what heard he?
      But ———Cannon!
        Cannon!
        Cannon!
  O Sound of Fear,
  O Sound of Fear,
Unpleasing to *H—n—n* Ear,
To *H—n—ns*, tho' not near.

Occasioned by the sight of a Print of Lord GOWER.

BEhold the Image of a fav'rite Peer,
  Whom, for his Worth, *Britannia*'s Sons revere,
His Country's steady Friend, her boasted Pride,
By Virtue more than Titles dignify'd.
  Fir'd with the gen'rous Thirst of honest Praise,
He nobly dares, in these degen'rate Days,
To vindicate his much-lov'd Country's Cause,
Assert her Commerce, Liberty and Laws;

Stem

Stem the ſtrong Torrent of oppreſſive Might,
And plead a free-born People's ſacred Right;
In ev'ry Shape Corruption to oppoſe,
And be the Foe avow'd of *Britain*'s Foes.

Proof againſt all that lures the vulgar Mind,
To Honour fix'd, *Gow'r* ſtill unchang'd we find,
Treading the ſame bright Path to deathleſs Fame,
As did the Patriots of the *Roman* Name.

A——s.

On the Arrival of G—— O——.

ARRIVE in Safety, all ye Heroes brave,
That from *America* ſurvive the Grave.
Let Fame cry Fraud, ill Conduct or Neglect,
No INQUISITION *Britons* now expect.
Since O——d loaded with an Age of Crimes,
Eſcapes, inſulting the degen'rate Times.
Since B——h our great Palladium 'till of late,
Defends each Vice in M——s of St——e,
Well may thoſe M————rs remit the Scores
Of G——ls, A——ls, and Com——s.

A Synonymous Song *on a Shitten Subject*.
To its own proper Tune.

THE H—— of C———— we may call
   A Common-Houſe, indeed!
An Houſe that Common is to all,
   May be an Houſe of Need.

To Houſe of Need all Folks reſort,
   Each for the like Occaſion;
In H—— of C———— ſome concert
   To drain away the Nation.

C————s H——, Folks raiſe a Fund,
   Which annually they ſink;
In Houſe of Need, from ſinking Ground,
   Folks raiſe a Fund of Stink.

This Stinking Common-House of Need,
　　Some also call a Bog-house;
A Kennel for the worst of Breed
　　Must be a very Dog-house.

The H—— of C—— is decreed
　　For Members all to sit in;
And some Folks use the House of Need
　　To shew their shallow Wit in.

There, what sad Stuff the Members void,
　　A Fool sets forth in Writing;
Here, sitting Members are employ'd,
　　That Shores we shall not shite in.

In C————s-H——, 'tis thought, proceeds
　　Business from every One;
In t'other, all Men do those Needs,
　　Which can't be left undone.

Each, when the Members have a Call,
　　Must instantly go hence;
Those that defer, e'en one and all
　　Stink at the Consequence.

The H—— of C————, House of Need,
　　The same as Cut, and Caper;
Since 'tis on either Side agreed
　　They both deal in Waste-paper.

To sum the Whole, and set them right,
　　To know their Use 'tis fitting:
This is,— to sit, to write, and shite;
　　That—to shite, write, and sit in.

　　　　　　　　　　　　　Hor.

HOR. LIB. II. Ode XVI. *Otium Divos, &c.*
IMITATED.
Inscrib'd to the E. of B.

IN each ambitious Measure crost!
Each Friend, that should *support* you, lost!
By Faction's Tempest *rudely tost*!
    At length you ask the Gods for *Ease*.
But what avails your pious Care!
Your Heart pour'd out in endless Pray'r!
Ease is not *Venal*, tho' you are,
    As Wealth may *tempt*, or Titles *please*.

For not the *Tr—s—r*'s *Staff*, nor all
That *O—f—d* grasp'd before his Fall,
Or his *Successor P—lh—m* shall,
    Can *ease* the self-devoted Mind!
Care flys into the Rooms of State,
Nor can the Slaves that on him wait,
Drive the curst Phantom from the Gate,
    Care stays, when none else dare, behind!

How happier at his frugal Board,
Lives the Plebeian, tho' *no Lord*;
(His Father's Wealth his *only* Hoard!)
    Who acts within his proper Sphere!
Whilst honest *Morpheus* o'er his Brows
His choicest, mildest Poppies strows,
And Sleep (the God's best Gift!) bestows,
    Unbroke by Avarice or Fear!

Why flies our Arrow to such Heights?
Our feeble Thread spun by the Fates,
Each Hour the fatal Scissars waits,
    Nor will one Moment's Pause afford.
We bustle to be rais'd on high!
New Lands explore; new Suns descry!
Alas! 'twere well, could *Self* too fly,
    And lose the *'Squire* in the *Lord*!

Beyond the prefent Hour forbear,
The foll'wing is not worth your Care;
In Life's contracted Span how rare
    To fee one Man compleatly bleft!
Sly O—f—d wifely could lay down,
Nor give his Foes one parting Frown,
Whilft Peace his lateft hours fhall crown!
    And good old W—lm—n's at reft!

With twice ten thoufand Pounds a Year
You *yet* may live and *tafte* good Cheer,
Tho' you ne'er be Lord Tr—f—r,
    So you repent you of that Sin:
Whilft I, as others will no doubt,
(When ——— returns) with many a Shout
Shall laugh to fee your Friends *troop out*,
    As fhamefully as they *came in*.

The ART *of making* HASTY-PUDDING.
By the late W. KING, L. L. D.

I Sing of *food*, by *Britifh* Nurfe defign'd
  To make the Stripling brave, and Maiden kind.
Delay not, Mufe, in Numbers to rehearfe
The Pleafures of our Life, and Sinews of our Verfe:
Let *Pudding*, Difh moft wholefome, be my Theme,
And dip thy fwelling Plumes in fragrant Cream.
Sing then that Difh fo fitting to improve
A tender Modefty, and trembling Love;
Swimming in Butter of a golden Hue,
Garnifh'd with Drops of Rofes fpicy Dew.
    Sometimes the frugal Matron feems in hafte,
Nor cares to beat her *Pudding* into *Pafte*:
Yet Milk in proper Skillet fhe will place,
And gently fpice it with a Blade of Mace;
Then fet fome careful Damfel to look to't,
And ftill to ftir away the *Bifhop*'s *Foot*:

For if *Burnt Milk* should to the Bottom stick,
Like *over-heated Zeal*, 'twou'd make folks sick.
Into the Milk her Flour she gently throws,
As Valets now wou'd powder tender Beaus:
The liquid Forms in *hasty Mass* unite,
Both equally delicious as they're white.
In shining Dish the *hasty Mess* is thrown,
And seems to want no Graces but its own.
Yet still the Housewife brings in fresh Supplies,
To gratify the Taste, and please the Eyes.
She on the Surface Lumps of *Butter* lays,
Which, melting with the Heat, its Beams displays;
From whence it causes Wonder to behold
A *Silver* Soil bedeck'd with Streams of *Gold*.

A Midsummer Pasquinade, *found in the Streets of* London.

YE close-fisted Rogues, whom the City be-shrieves,
To make you deliver your Money, like Thieves,
What Fraud has obtain'd you may justly disown;
And swear it belongs to Persons unknown.
Or if you want Spirit to use what you've got;
You want what you have; and so have it not.
Grave *Casuists* say, Oaths solemnly made
To those who would rob you, you ought to evade.
Holy *David* advises, do well for thyself:
Take *David*'s Advice, and be true to thy Pelf.
O the wise men of *London!* Don't give 'em a Souse:
They who ruin a City, to finish a House.

The present State of Great Britain.

WHEN we review our *Britain*'s present State,
At Home, how happy we! Abroad, how great!
In *Germany*, how dreadful are our Arms
Which fill the Continent with new Alarms!

Much

Much fear the *French*; the gull'd *Bavarian* more;
Some hope that *Britain*'s King will Peace reſtore.
—All this, perhaps, without a Battle too.
Now let us take a ſhort domeſtic View——
As half the People know not what to do.
Here *Ranelagh* the Grand, *Vauxhall* the Gay,
With City *Ruckholt* various Joys diſplay:
A Thouſand other mimick Gardens glow
With Lamps or Fireworks, a ſurpriſing Show!
Here *Britons* never do a Care reveal,
No *Trade* then think of, and no *Tax* they feel,
In ſuch bleſt State what Nation round us lies,
At Home ſo *Merry*, and Abroad ſo *Wiſe*.

FACTION DETECTED.

A New BALLAD.
To the Tune of Derry down.

QUOTH S——s to P——y, ſince Words may cauſe Fighting,
I have left off Debating and taken to Writing.
Your Project, quo' P——y, may do very well,
But ere you do write, you ſhould learn how to ſpell.
      Derry down, &c.

My Spelling, ſays S——s, by O——d's corrected,
And the Preſs ſhall by him be with Caution inſpected.
M——y too has ſupply'd ſome fine Words that come pat in,
And chequer'd the Work here and there with old Latin.
      Derry, &c.

But, tho' to theſe Scholars I owe all my Learning,
The Reaſ'ning is all from my own keen Diſcerning;
And that it is mine has this clear Demonſtration,
It proves thee a *ſteady* good Friend to this Nation.
      Derry, &c.

Our Friends the *W—lp—l-ns*, but gently I lash them,
But as for the *Tories*, I damnably thrash 'em:
From *St-nh-pe* and *C-bh-m*, to *W-ll-r* and *P-tt*,
I prove each Opposer a rank *Jacobite*.
         Derry, &c.

That we who came *in* had no View to our Profit,
The Argument's plain, tho' the *Faction* may scoff it:
And thence it doth follow by Inference true,
That they who staid *out* had their Profit in View.
         Derry, &c.

I next do demonstrate how false those Asserters,
Ah! Country ungratefull who calls us *Deserters*;
For when we insisted that things should be mended,
We writ, talk'd, and swore—what we never intended.
         Derry, &c.

The P——r, much delighted, straight seiz'd on the Page,
And dash'd in some Strokes of rhetorical Rage.
So thus was produc'd, supervis'd, and corrected,
That doughty Performance call'd *Faction detected*.
         Derry, &c.

On the Death of the Duke of ARGYLL.

SOLDIER, compleat in *Bravery* and *Art*;
 Statesman, that scorn'd *Duplicity* of Heart;
Patriot, that stemm'd the *ministerial* Tide;
Noble, that ne'er his *Dignities* bely'd:
' *Argyll*, the State's whole Thunder born to wield,
' And shake alike the *Senate* and the *Field*,'
Descends to *Dust*.—Oh *Britain!* lift thine Eyes,
And in *this Loss* conceive what *Judgment* lies.
Corruption's dire Effects what *Hand* shall stay,
When thy *few guardian Sons* are snatch'd away?

On hearing that the Duke of ARGYLL *had recover'd the free Use of his Reason before his Death.*

IN vain *Argyll*, with god-like Virtue stood,
   To stem the Torrent of Corruption's Flood;
Britannia's sickly State with Grief he sees,
And *weeps* to find her fond of her Disease.
Nor matchless Worth, nor Eloquence can move,
Nay (more than all) not ev'n her Country's Love.
What could he do, since no Success he had,
But, like the World, be knavish, or be mad?
No narrow, selfish Soul, no C—rt—r he,
Knavish alas! he knew not how to be:
But, as no useless Faculty he'd have,
Reason he dropt, when Reason could not save:
Lethargick Visions o'er his weary'd Mind
Steal unperceiv'd; but no long Welcome find.
(Short is the Nap of Judgment, with the Wise)
He wakes, sees *England* sleep, and strait he dies.

On the Death of JOHN, *Duke of* ARGYLL.

WHat dreadful Judgments threaten this our Isle!
   W——le still lives; and *thou* art dead, *Argyll*.

An EPITAPH *on a poor honest Man; intended to be plac'd on a Stone in the Chancel of the Church of* Bromham *in the County of* Wilts.

'TIS not the Tomb in Marble polish'd high,
   The venal Verse, or flattering Titles nigh,
The classick Learning o'er an impious Stone,
Where *Latin* tells what *English* blush'd to own,
Shall shroud the Guilty from the Eye of God,
Incline his Ballance, or avert his Rod.

His Hand can raise the Crippled and the Poor,
Spread on the Way, or fainting at the Door;
And blast the Villain, tho' to Altars fled,
Who robb'd us, living; and insults us, dead.

The DOWNFALL *of* DANCING; *or a bright Thought of the Squire's. An original* SONG, *most humbly addrest to the young Ladies that frequent the* Green-man *Assembly on* Blackheath.

By RICHARD WRONGHEAD, *of* Blunder-hall *in the Island of* Sheepy, *Esq*;

Tempora mutantur, & nos mutamur in illis.
    Anglice,
Your own dear Dicky *the Self-same still is.*

TO you gay Girls of *Greenwich* Town,
 I *Wretch unworthy* write;
And sighing do with Sorrow own
 I've lost my *Dancing* quite.
Ah! what avails it now to *me*,
Soft Sinks and Rises———one-two-three?
    With fal-lal, la-tha-ra, la.

La Belle Assemblée's now no more,
 Blackheath is not the same;
The *Green-man* guards the guestless Door,
 And startles at the *Name*.
Say, *Fair-ones!* was it always so?
F——zg——ld answers, no—no—no.
    Fal, lal-lal, la-tha-ra, la.

How strange th' Effects of subtle *Art* !
 Pow'r once did bear the Sway;
But now *we* find, with aching Heart,
 That *Power* must obey.
The * *Solebay* beat the *Frigate* far:
But † *Grace* now beats th *Man* of *War*.
    Fal-lal, &c.

* *Name of the Mistress of the* Green-man *Assembly*.
† *The celebrated* Grace Tosier *on* Black-heath.

Adieu, soft *Song*, and merry *Tale*,
    That once my *Soul* inspir'd!
Mirth, *Wit*, and *Jests*, no more prevail,
    The charming *Nymphs* retir'd.
Adieu, sweet *Smile* and am'rous *Glance*,
The dear Delights of sprightly *Dance*.
                   Fal, lal, &c.

My gold-lac'd *Vest*, of green *Velour*.
    So wond'rous gay and nice;
My silver *Snuff-box* figur'd o'er,
    And *Lid* of smart Device,
My Chevron'd Clocks and silk-bound *Shoes*
Are thrown aside, no more for Use.
                     Fal, lal, &c.

My *Feet* almost forget to walk,
    For want of *Patty*'s-*Mill*;
My *Tongue* (sometimes) forgets to *talk*,
    That *never* could lie *still*;
And I a very *Cypher* grown,
That was too full of — *all my own*.
                     Fal, lal, &c.

The *Scene* is chang'd, and 'stead of *you*,
    At *Cards* I nightly play;
I deal with *Kings* and *Queens*, 'tis true,
    And cast the *Knaves* away:
And I'd discard the *Courtly Train*,
Might I enjoy my *Girls* again.
                     Fal, lal, &c.

Hang *Sorrow*——cast old *Care* behind,
    Nor think of what is past;
But let's some new *Expedient* find——
    I've thought on *One* at last;
Let's all agree and *act a Play*.
We'll fix the *Name* another Day,   Z. Z.
                     Fal, lal, &c.

An EPITAPH *on his Wife* BESS.

By TIMOTHY STONECUTTER.

Beneath this rugged Stone doth lie
  The rankeſt Corps that e'er did die;
Whoſe ſofteſt Word to deareſt Friend,
Would make your Hair to ſtand an End.

  You'd think Storms riſing when ſhe ſung;
Thunder was Muſick to her Tongue;
When in her real Storms did riſe,
Light'ning was Twilight to her Eyes.

  Her mildeſt Look ſo fierce a Sight,
Great Chance you'd catch an Ague by't;
And when her Perſon mov'd——huge Rock
No Earthquake gave ſo great a Shock.

  Where ſhe abides ſeek not to know;
If they want Sulphur, ſhe's below:
If ſhe's above——Gods, hear my Pray'r,
And ſend me—any where but there.
Amen.

The Cave of POPE. *A Prophecy.*

When dark Oblivion in her ſable Cloak
  Shall wrap the Names of Heroes and of
    Kings;
And their high Deeds, ſubmitting to the Stroke
  Of Time, ſhall fall amongſt forgotten Things;

Then (for the Muſe that diſtant Day can ſee)
  On *Thames*'s Bank the Stranger ſhall arrive,
With curious Wiſh thy ſacred Grott to ſee,
  Thy ſacred Grott ſhall with thy Name ſurvive.
Grateful

Grateful Posterity, from Age to Age,
  With pious Hand the Ruin shall repair:
Some good old Man, to each enquiring Sage
  Pointing the Place, shall cry, The Bard liv'd there,

Whose Song was Music to the listening Ear,
  Yet taught audacious Vice and Folly, Shame;
Easy his Manners, but his Life severe;
  His Word alone gave Infamy or Fame.

Sequester'd from the Fool and Coxcomb-Wit,
  Beneath this silent Roof the Muse he found;
'Twas here he slept inspir'd, or sate and writ;
  Here with his Friends the social Glass went round.

With aweful Veneration shall they trace
  The Steps which thou so long before hast trod;
With reverend Wonder view the solemn Place,
  From whence thy Genius soar'd to Nature's God.

Then, some small Gem, or Moss, or shining Ore,
  Departing, each shall pilfer, in fond hope
To please their Friends, on ev'ry distant Shore,
  Boasting a Relick from the Cave of POPE.

This BALLAD, *tho' wrote some time ago, was never in Print, and is too good to be lost.*

COme listen awhile, and I'll tell you some News,
  Just piping hot from Court;
'Tis not of a Peace, nor yet of a Truce,
  But yet 'twill make you Sport:
Six Dozen of Smocks the Maids had lost,
  My good Lord *G—t—m* said;
There's never a Maid, but rather had lost
  By far her Maidenhead.
The Nation all its Money has lost,
  The Merchants all their Trade;
Gibraltar and *Portmahon*, to our Cost,
  Are lost too I'm afraid.

N° II.   H   But

But what are all thefe Loffes now?
　　We value e'm not a Pin,
For the Maids fo poor, have ftill loft more,
　　They're ftrip'd quite to their Skin.
A Maid of Honour with nothing upon her,
　　Her M—— y then cry'd,
Without Fig-leaf, like Grandame *Eve*,
　　Her Nakednefs to hide,
Shall never with me abide, forfooth,
　　Nor in my Court appear;
For nothing fo like the naked Truth,
　　Shall ever inhabit there.

But if by Chance, to take a Dance,
　　Like Goddeffes on *Ida*,
Thefe Maids fhould come to the Drawing-room,
　　Good lack! what would they hide-a?
The P——e to one an Apple might give,
　　As *Paris* did of old;
But alas! poor P——e, I fear thy Dad
　　Won't allow thee an Apple of Gold.

The K—g, God blefs him, next let's addrefs him,
　　For he's a gallant Lover;
So frank and free, gives Money with Glee,
　　His Maidens for to cover:
For he, good Man, five Pounds a Piece
　　To each Maiden fair has fent,
Of the Hundred and fifteeen thoufand Pounds
　　He got from his P——t.

STANZAS *written to obviate an Objection to an* Englifh *Lady.*

LOVE, thy Vot'ry let me live,
　　I'll to thee devote my Lay;
In the Joys you only give
　　Let me laugh my Time away.

Fairer

Fairer than the Queen of Love,
  Ever faithful, ever new,
Polly can to Rapture move,
  Can compel me to be true.

Let the Rich have Gold and Care,
  Pomp, and Fear the Proud obtain;
Let the Heroe madly dare,
  And the Learn'd be gravely vain,
Let *them* take the varied Woe,
  Pomp, or Wealth, or Fame, impart,
All beneath my *Feet* I throw,
  Holding *Polly* to my *Heart*.

VERSES *occasion'd by seeing such innumerable* SATIRES *writ against the Government; address'd to all true Lovers of their Country.*

BElieve me, Friends, whate'er ye do,
  You'll find this Maxim ever true,
    In Spite of all your Arts:
Write what you will, say backward Prayers
There's no one Ruler knows, or cares,
    Its coming from your Hearts.

Some write for Profit, some for Praise,
And some,—for want of better Ways
    To vent their Spite aloud:
And would you, who your Country love,
And truly would its Glory prove,
    Now mix with such a Crowd?

Many there are, (believe this too,
For much I fear, it is too true)
    Fierce Anger will display,
Who bearing in the common Cry,
The easier lets——his Brother by,
    So slyly steal away.

Tho'

Tho' all your Anger now is just,
To this, my Friends, I'd have you trust,
   And not to idle Noises;
Bear bravely in your Mind and Heart
The truly just and honest Part,
   In hopes of casting Voices.

Many there are, would gladly come,
At Sound of Trumpet, and of Drum;
   To give their Country Glory:
But ne'er will join the simple Strife,
And throw away both Peace and Life
   For meerly Whig or Tory.

This let your better Judgment guide,
And this be too your honest Pride,
   That all you did was free:
Then you shall say, with Joy of Heart,
Rejoicing in your noble Part,
   How few have done like me!

But now, as Vice is at its Height,
So hard it is to manage right,
   All are glad they have not kept it:*
And while this Cry of Knaves and Fools,
Declare 'tis only Mob that rules,
   No wise Man will accept it †.

EPIGRAM

On his Excellency the late Lord Galway *and his* Cook.

SAYS my Lord to his Cook, you Son of a Punk,
  Hows comes it I see you, thus, ev'ry Day drunk?
Physicians, they say, once a Month do allow
A Man for his Health to get drunk —— as a Sow.
That is right, quoth the Cook; but the Day they
   don't say;
So for fear I should miss it I'm drunk ev'ry Day.

HYMEN's

* *The right Way.*   † *Power.*

HYMEN's TRIUMPH.

On the Marriage of the Rev. Mr. RICHARD BEAUCHAMP, *to Miss* JULIANA KEATING, *on Thursday May* 5*th*, 1743.

By the Rev. WILLIAM DUNKIN, M. A. *of Trin. Col. Dublin.*

ONCE *Hymen,* abus'd for the Matches he made,
   (Since Beauty was barter'd, and Wedlock a
      Trade)
By *Pallas* instructed to pitch on a Pair,
Join'd DICK the Facetious to JULIA the Fair.

So true was *his* Passion, so decent *her* Carriage,
Not even *Diana* cou'd censure the Marriage.
Apollo was charm'd with her Mind, and his Parts,
And tun'd the soft Notes of his Lute by their Hearts:
The Muses in Chorus obey'd his Command,
And hymn'd to the Graces, who danc'd Hand in
      Hand;
The Birds of the Grove, from the Branches above,
Sang Sponsals, and chatter'd the Tydings of Love.

To gather a Garland, the Nymphs and the Fawns
Dismantled the Meadows, the Vallies and Lawns:
The gay, living Colours by *Flora* were wreath'd,
And *Zephyr* cool-sigh'd to the Odour she breath'd.

Vertumnus was present in Garment of Green,
And thus gaily spoke to the Bloom-bearing Queen.
' Now the Nymphs and the Fawns may lavishly bring
' The Paintings of Nature, and Pride of the Spring,
' Faint Emblems of Beauty, *Vertumnus* employs
' The Season, to ripen more delicate Joys,
' Rich Omens of Issue! with Blossoms you suit
' The Virgin; but I shall adorn her with Fruit.
                        Then

Then *Mercury* said as he look'd on the Bride,
With an envious Eye, calling *Venus* aside,
' Alas, idle Maid! what a Part hath she acted,
' To wed with a Parson?—it makes me distracted:
' My Measures are broken, my Purposes crost:
' I meant her a Lord—but her Market is lost.
' Her Sisters are like her: She gives us a Sample,
' And copies exactly her Mother's Example:
' It flows from the Fountain; her Blood must inherit
' This Oddness of choosing out Men for their Merit.
' Well, since she rejected the Baits of my Store,
' Adieu to the Pleasures of sweet *Nara-more*.

Quoth *Venus*, ' You have little Cause to repine,
' The chief Disappointment and Anguish are mine;
' You meant her a Title of *Honour* and *Pence*,
' I meant her a Beau—but she truckled to *Sense*.
' I long since might know she would baffle my Sport,
' For, Brother, I never could bring her to Court:
' Yet *Cupid*, to whom I committed her Beauty,
' Was blindly defective in doing his Duty.

' Arraign not thy *Cupid*, glad *Hymen* replies,
' For once he hath shewn that his Godship has Eyes.

A SKETCH *of* PARIS. *In* 1741.

By GALLO-ANGLUS.

LADIES, whose Dress, Wit, Sprightliness, and Air,
Charm, till their plaster'd Cheeks, like Spectres scare.
Men learn'd, polite; and yet so much the Prig,
Their Genius seems quite center'd in their Wig.
Ferries, and Ferrymen*, begrim, like *Charon*:
Plump, chuckling Priests, drest gorgeously as *Aaron*.
Pulpit Enthusiasts, foaming like mad *Tom*:
Coarse Vixens, ogling lewd in *Nôtre Dame* †.

* On the River *Seine*.   † The Cathedral.

Pert,

Pert, fallow, flip-fhod Damfels loofely drefs'd;
As ris'n from Bed, and panting to be prefs'd.
Shades §, which the Gazer for *Elyſium* takes,
Till his ftung Nofe fufpects the neighbouring Jakes.
Nuns joking now; now fighing " *Fleſh is Grafs:*"
Friars who Catches roar, and toaft a Lafs.
An Opera-Houfe large as our City Halls;
Fine Action, Words, Cloaths, Dreffes :—difmal
    Squalls.
Round from *Pont-Neuf*, the View fuperb and rich;
Grand Keys;— the River a genteel *Fleet Ditch*.
Lame, Hackney Horfes; as their Drivers lean,
Figures unnumber'd, *Anti's* to the Spleen.
Old wither'd Crones, in gaudy Silks difplay'd:
Monks ‖ with Toupees, and Tonfors in Brocade.
Taudry, patch'd Sempftreffes, begrim'd with Snuff:
Long-rapier'd Pygmies, hid behind a Muff.
Shoe-Boys with Ruffles; Lacqueys drefs'd like
    Qual.—
Such Oddities! the Town feems all a Droll.
Turn where we will, our Eyes new Splendors greet,
Whilft half the City glares a *Monmouth Street*.
Still motlier (VANITY) wou'd be thy Fair,
Had the fam'd Painter, *Bunyan* † fweet, been here.

   § The *Tuilleries*, very fine, and very foul.
   ‖ One of the Princes of the Blood is an Abbot.
   † The Celebrated Author of the *Pilgrim's Progrefs. See his elegant Defcription of* Vanity-Fair.

ECHO

ECHO de MARLI.

JE suis dans ces lieux personne ne m'écoute,   *Ecoute.*
J'entend qu'on me repond, qui est donc avec moy; *Moy.*
C'est toi, charmant Echo, repond à mes demandes. *Demandes.*
Ne pourroit-on sçavoir si *Prague* sera prise ?   *Prise.*
Cette Reine en couroux, me'n voudroit elle encore ? *Encore.*
Mais les Princes *Lorrains*, ne s'en iront ils point ? *Point.*
L'Empereur, que fait-il, est-il mal à *Franckfort* ? *Fort.*
A prendre la loy d'eux, sera-t'il donc contraint ? *Contraint.*
La *France*, cette fois sera-t'elle domptée ? *Domptée.*
Après tant de lauriers, me voila donc perdu ? *Perdu.*
Que peut-on ajoûter à mes douleurs ? *Douleurs.*
Ah Dieu ! dois-je attendre apres tant de malheurs ? *Malheurs.*
A demander la paix, seray je donc reduit ? *Reduit.*
Mes enemis sont fiers, comment faut-il s'y prendre ? *Rendre.*
Quoy ! rendre ce que j'ay conquis par mes faits inouis ? *Oui.*
Qu'auray je donc gagné par ma gloire & mes peines ? *Peines.*
Que veux-tu que je fasse apres tant d'injustice ? *Justice.*
Mais qu'auront mes sujets reduits à la besace ? *Besace.*
Que deviendront ces gens conquis & malheureux ? *Malheureux.*
Tant de peuples vaincus ne me craindront-ils plus ? *Plus.*
Autrefois mon seul nom imprimoit la terreur ? *Erreur.*
Laisse-moy, je te prie, et souffre que je pleure. *Pleure.*

On a late TRANSACTION.

BY various Paths the great ascend
   Those rugged Heights that lead to Praise;
While Crowds who on their Steps attend,
   Affrighted at their Labours, gaze,

What Courage, *Marlb'rough*, swell'd thy Breast,
   Of well-fought Fields the Glory thine !
Like Fire thy Offspring has exprest,
   Restrain'd from Fight—he durst *Resign*.

Upon a very late Piece of HAGUE INTELLIGENCE.

THE *puffing Art*, how vaſtly it improves!
  Ale-men their *Drink* and *Ladies puff* their
    Loves.
In *Weekly Puffs* Clare-market CHAMPION *hectors*;
Quacks puff their *Drugs,* and *Pr——ſts* their *gratis*
    Lectures;
Books, Brandies, Wigs, the *Opera* and *Play,*
Welch Fair, and *Tott'nam Court,* are *puff'd away*:
Each *married Man,* and ev'ry *widow'd Fair,*
Now *Paragraphs it* with a *puffing Air*;
Long *Lott'ry Puffs* ſupply the Place of *News,*
Conſtables puff their Zeal againſt the *Stews.*
So when we hear *affronted S —— r* maintain
The mighty great Effects of this *Campaign*;
And *Fenelon, ſubmiſſive* and *perplext,*
Make early Overtures to ſhun the *next,*
What can we think of ſuch *October Stuff,*
Or call it, but a *M——n——ſt——l Puff?*
Say, means it aught in *H——v——n Love,*
But, eaſy Britons GIVE us, GIVE us more?
Scorn, *Britiſh Sen——rs,* the *Emp'rick Bill,*
And never SWALLOW ſuch another PILL.

SISYPHUS.

HE's *Siſyphus,* that ſtrives with mighty Pain
  To get ſome Offices, but ſtrives in vain;
Who poorly, meanly begs the Royal Grace,
But ſtill refus'd, he ne'er obtains the Place:
For ſtill to ſeek, and ſtill in Hopes devour,
And never to enjoy deſired Pow'r;
What is it, but with Torture of the Soul
Againſt the Hill a mighty Weight to roll?
Thus, while *Will Wabble* waddles up the Hill,
The Stone recoils, and backward *waddles Will.*

CONTENTS.

THE Ballance of Europe — — Page	1
Prenez le Roy, to Marſhal Noailles —	ibid.
Marſhal Noailles's Anſwer —	2
On the French Singing Te Deum at Paris	ibid.
On the C———s of Y———h's making the Campaign	ibid.
On the Auxiliary Forces paſſing the Rhine commanded by General L—g—nier — —	ibid.
A Poetical Epiſtle from a great Man in the Army, on the K———g and D———e — —	3
An Account of the Battle, as ſent into the Country	4
The Gallick Heroes, Belleiſle, Broglio, Maillebois, and Noailles — — —	5
The Emperor on his gaſping Empire —	ibid.
An Excuſe for the Laureat's not writing on the Battle of Dettingen — — —	6
An Epigram on an Engliſh and French Soldier on the Mayne — —	ibid.
The Campaign and its Hiſtorians — —	ibid.
On perpetuating the Fame of great Actions —	7
Cardinal Tenchin's Prayer —	ibid.
The Lion and Frogs, a Fable addreſs'd to the D—h — — —	8
A Fable on the Affairs in Germany, between the Cock and Eaglet — — —	9
Britain's Lamentation, and Petition to the D—ke	10
A new Ballad, or Britons Rejoice, on beating the French — —	11
On ——— All true Britons Rejoice —	12
An Epigram on Marſhal Noailles — —	ibid.
On the Queen of Hungary —	13
The Scene chang'd, an Epigram —	ibid.
French Policy — —	ibid.

The

The Substance of a certain Letter on the Blues	
A Thought on our Army Intelligence	15
News from the Army on the K—g *and the* D—ke	ibid.
To Fortune, on S———s *and* W———le	16
Verses by a Highlander *the Day before he was taken*	18
A Summary of Intelligence, Domestick and Foreign	19
The Mistake, on G———s *making War in* Germany *and not in* Spain	20
A Lesson from Hanover	21
A new Ballad on the Riches of Great Britain	ibid.
On the Conduct of a certain great Prince	23
The Catastrophe	ibid.
On Faction Detected	24
John *and* Will *the Carters*	ibid.
The gracious Refusal	ibid.
On the Promotion of the Right Hon. H. Pelham	25
The Interview between 'Squire Harry *and* Lord Will	ibid.
On a Nobleman's arrival at H———n-Hall	26
The Metamorphosis	ibid.
To the E—— *of* B———, *on Faction Detected*	27
The Parallel	28
A Motto for a Sword	29
Potatoes *and* Hemp, *or* Tories *and* Robertsmen	ibid.
Verses on a Paragraph in the Gazetteer	30
The Cardinals	31
Epigram on the Blues	ibid.
Imitation of Horace *to* P——t	ibid.
Plain Thoughts, a new Ballad	32
An Ode to the new M——rs	34
A Simile to Jeffry Broadbottom	ibid.
A new Ballad on the new M———rs	35
A Song in the B——h *Camp*	37
Verses on the Sight of a Print of Lord Gower	ibid.
On the Arrival of G———O———	38
A synonymous Song on a S———n *Subject*	39

I

An Ode inscrib'd to the E—— *of* B——h	40
Art of making Hasty-Pudding	41
A Midsummer Pasquinade *found in the Streets of* London	42
The present State of Great Britain	ibid.
Faction Detected, a new Ballad, to S——s *and* P——y	43
Poems on the Death of the Duke of Argyll	44
An Epitaph on a poor honest Man	45
The Downfal of Dancing, to the Ladies on Blackheath	46
Timothy Stonecutter's *Epitaph on his Wife* Bess	48
The Cave of Pope, *a Prophecy*	ibid.
A humorous Ballad, to Lord G———m	49
Stanzas on an English *Lady*	50
Verses occasion'd by the many Satires on the Government	51
An Epigram on Lord G—l—y *and his Cook*	52
Hymen's *Triumph on the Marriage of the Rev.* Richard Beauchamp	53
A Sketch of Paris	54
Echo de Marli	55
On a late Transaction of the D—— *of* M———h	60

FINIS.

THE
Foundling Hospital
FOR
WIT.

Intended for the Reception and Preservation of such Brats of WIT and HUMOUR whose Parents chuse to Drop them.

NUMBER III. to be Continued Occasionally.

CONTAINING,

1. Ode to the E—— of B——.
2. The Heroes: To the Commanders of the 15 New Regiments.
3. Arms and the Man: To the D——.
4. Important Question resolved: To Sir J—n B——.
5. Honesty the best Policy.
6. An Epigram on W—x—n W—— W—— and C—n—n.
7. An Epigram by the E—— of C——d.
8. The Ball at W'——.
9. P——s executed.
10. Battle of Falkirk: To G—— H——.
11. On the Stocks in W—— Chapel.
12. On Cha. S————pe, Esq; drinking Tar-Water.
13. The Monkies: To our Modern Beaus.
14. A Song on Miss Mol'y Carr.
15. An Epilogue intended to be spoke by Mrs. W*ffington*.
16. An Ode from P——lF—y to N—t T—y.
17. Orpheus and Hecate: To Lady B——.
18. Sir J. Suckling, a Ballad, adapted to a Modern General.
19. A Ballad on Lord D—n—l's altering his Chapel into a Kitchen.
20. A D————'s Ghost to P————.
21. The Unembarrassed Countenance.
22. Long and Short Verses: To P——
23. Verses on the D——s of M————b.
24. Advice to Clara, by Mr. P————.
25. Universal Business, 1st and 2d Part.
26. Modern Fine Gentlemen and Lady.
27. An Epilogue on the Duke's Birth-Day: Spoke by Mr. *Garrick*.
28. The Surprising History of a late long Administration.

With many Curious Pieces never before printed, and a General Table of Contents to the Whole.

By TIMOTHY SILENCE, Esq;

LONDON: Printed for W. WEBB, near St. *Paul's*. 1746.

Where may be had Number I and II. Containing all the Satires, Odes, Ballads, and Epigrams, by the Prime Wits of this Age since the Change of the late Earl of O————d's Administration.

The INDEX.

AN Ode from the E——l of B——h to Ambition. p. 1
The Heroes: A new Ballad. 3
Arms and the Man: A new Ballad. 5
The important Question resolved. 7
Honesty the best Policy. ibid.
To Mr. P——— on the Hanover Troops. ibid:
An Epigram. 8
——— on Miss *Eleanor Ambrose* of *Dublin*, by the E—— of C———d. ibid.
An Answer to the foregoing. ibid.
The Ball.
On *Larissa*. 12
P——tt excused. ibid.
Nature and Fortune: To the E-- of C———ld. 13
On Love and Wine, in Imitation of *Anacreon*. 14
The Gazette of Jan. 23, 1745-6, versified. ibid.
A Song, to the Tune of the Cut-Purse. 16
An Epigram on *Will* and *John*. 17
Upon seeing a Pair of Stocks in W———for Chapel. 18
On *Ch*———. *St*———pe, Esq; drinking Tar-Water. ibid.
The Monkies: To our Modern Beaus. ibid.
Anacreontic. 20
Epigram. ibid.
A Song on Miss *Molly Carr*. Brussels 1744. 21
A Song. 23
An Epilogue intended to be spoken by Mrs. *Woffington* in the Habit of a Volunteer, &c. 24
An Ode from P———l F———y to N———s F--- y, Esq; in Imitation of Ode IX. Book 2. of *Horace*. 26
Orpheus and *Hecate*, an Ode. 28
Sir *John Suckling*, an old Ballad adapted to a Modern General. 30

A New Ballad, on Lord *D-n--l*'s altering his Chapel at *Gr——e* into a Kitchen. 33
A D———ss's Ghost to Orator *H--P--tt*. ibid.
The Unembarrassed Countenance, a New Ballad. To the Tune of a Cobler there was, &c. 30
An Epistle to *William Pitt*, Esq; 37
Short Verses, in Imitation of long Verses, in an Epistle to *William Pitt*, Esq; 40
Verses on, the late D———ss of M———. By Mr. *Pit*. 42
To *Clara*. 43
Universal Business, Message the First. 45
Message the Second. ibid.
The Modern Fine Gentleman. 46
The Modern Fine Lady: Or a Counterpart to a Poem lately published, called, The Modern Fine Gentleman. 49
Martial, Lib. X. Ep. 67. 53
An Epitaph for Lady ———. ibid.
Epigram on the K-- of *Pr*——— 54
Extempore, left on Mad. *De Pompadour*'s Toilet, by *Voltaire*, while she was Drawing. ibid.
A Poem on his Excellency the Earl of *Chesterfield*'s being about to leave *Ireland*. 55
An Epilogue on the Birth-Day of his Royal Highness the Duke of *Cumberland*. Written by the Farmer, and spoken by Mr. *Garrick*. 56
The Surprising History of a late long Administration; shewing the wonderful Transactions, the wise Negotiations, the prudent Measures, and the great Events of that most astonishing Period. By *Titus Livius*, Jun. 58
A Letter of Recommendation from Cardinal *Richlieu*. 62

THE
Foundling Hospital
FOR
W I T.

NUMBER III.

An ODE *from the* E—— *of* B—— *to* Ambition.

Peccat ad extremum ridendus.

AWAY, Ambition, let me rest;
   All Party-Rage forsake my Breast,
  And Opposition cease.
Arm me no more for future Strife,
Pity my poor Remains of Life,
  And give my Age its Peace.

I'm not the Man you knew before,
For I am P————y now no more,
  My Titles hide my Name.
(Oh how I blush to own my Case!)
My Dignity was my Disgrace,
  And I was rais'd to Shame.

To Thee I facrific'd my Youth,
Gave up my Honour, Friendſhip, Truth
   My K—— and C——nt—y's Weal.
For Thee I finn'd againſt my Reaſon,
The Daily Lie, the Weekly Treaſon,
   Proclaim'd my blinded Zeal.

For Thee I ruin'd O————d's Pow'r.
O had I well employ'd that Hour,
   My Reign had known no End:
But then (Oh Fool) like *Brutus*, I
Left able, pow'rful *Antony*,
   T' avenge his fallen Friend.

He drives me to this abject State,
And ſtill he urges on my Fate,
   And heaps my Meaſure full:
All O————d's Wrongs are now repaid,
I'm fall'n into the Pit I made,
   And roar in my own Bull.

Leave me, and to great *Varus* go,
On him reſiſtleſs Smiles beſtow,
   Inflame his kindled Heat:
Diſplay thy Pow'r, thy Temptings ſhew,
The glorious Height, the ſunny Brow,
   With all that charm and cheat.

Varus, on whom, while yet a Child,
You, Goddeſs, favourably ſmil'd,
   And form'd him for your Tool;
Bid him the Path of Greatneſs try,
Teach him to conquer or to die,
   To ruin, or to rule.

Here

Here all my Views of Greatneſs ceaſe,
I only aſk Content and Peace,
  Which I will never barter
For all the Gifts that you can ſhow'r;
The Pride of Wealth, the Pomp of Pow'r,
  Employments, and a Garter.

But at that Word what Thoughts return!
Again I feel Ambition burn,
  My Dreams, my Hopes obey;
There all my Wiſhes crown'd I feel,
Enjoy the Ribband, Treas'ry, Seal,
  Which vaniſh with the Day.

The HEROES: A new BALLAD.

To the Tune of —— Sally in our Alley.

OF all the Jobbs that e'er have paſt
    Our Houſe, ſince times of Jobbing;
Sure none was ever like the laſt,
    Ev'n in the Days of *Robin*:
For he himſelf had bluſh'd for Shame
    At this polluted Cluſter,
Of fifteen N—bles of great Fame,
    All brib'd by one falſe Muſter.

Two D—kes on Horſeback firſt appear,
    Both tall and of great Prowefs;
Two little B-r-ns in the Rear
    (For they're, you know the loweſt:)
But High and Low they all agree
    To do whatever Man dar'd;
Thoſe ne'er ſo tall, and thoſe that fall
    A Foot below the Standard.

B 2   Three

Three Regiments one D–ke contents,
　　With two more Places, you know;
Since his B—*th* Kn—ghts, his Grace delights
　　In Tri-a junct' in U-no.
Now *B–lt–n* comes with Beat of Drums,
　　Tho' Fighting be his Loathing;
He much diflikes both Guns and Pikes,
　　But relifhes the Cloathing.

Next doth advance, defying *France*,
　　A Peer in wond'rous Buftle;
With Sword in Hand he ftout doth ftand,
　　And brags his Name is *R-ſſ-l:*
He'll beat the *French* from ev'ry Trench,
　　And blow them off the Water;
By Sea and Land he doth command,
　　And looks an errant Otter.

But of this Clan, there's not a Man
　　For Bravery that can be,
(Tho' *An*———*r* fhould make a Stir)
　　Compar'd with M———s *Gr*———*by:*
His Sword and Drefs both well exprefs
　　His Courage moft exceeding;
And by his Hair, you'd almoft fwear
　　He's valiant *Charles* of *Sweden.*

The next are *H*———*t, Ha*———*x,*
　　And *F*———*h,* choice Commanders!
For thefe the Nation we muft Tax,
　　But ne'er fend them to *Flanders.*
Two Corps of Men do ftill remain,
　　Earl *Ch*———*ly*'s and Earl *B*———*ley*'s;
The laft, I hold, not quite fo bold
　　As formerly was *Herc'les.*

And

And now, dear G——r, thou Man of Pow'r,
    And comprehensive Noddle;
Tho' you've the Gout, yet as you're stout,
    Why wa'n't you plac'd in Saddle?
Then you might ride to either Side,
    Chuse which K—— you'ld serve under;
But, dear Dragoon, change not too soon,
    For fear of th' other Blunder.

This faithful Band shall ever stand,
    Defend our Faith's Defender;
Shall keep us free from Popery,
    The *French* and the PRETENDER.
Now God bless all our M-n-try,
    May they the Crown environ,
To hold in Chain whate'er P——e reign,
    And rule with Links of Iron.

ARMS and the MAN. *A new Ballad.*

GOD prosper the King and the King's noble Sons,
    May their Praises resound from the Mouth of their
Till Rebellion and all Civil Discord may cease,   [Guns:
And these Realms be restor'd to a flourishing Peace.

How this War first began, and the Progress it made,
Has never been Sung, tho' 't has often been Said;
Yet great Deeds to record, to great Poets belongs,
As *Homer* and *Virgil* set forth in their Songs.

The *Scots*, as the *Swiss*, who make Fighting a Trade,
Betraying for ever, for ever betray'd;
Like the Frogs, sick of Log, chose a K—— of their own,
'Twill ne'er out of the Flesh, what is bred in the Bone.

                                      From

From *Rome* a young Heroe well known they invite,
To accept of a Crown which he claims as his Right;
In City and Town they their Monarch proclaim,
And their old K— and new K— are one and the same.

When these Tidings reach'd *England*, three Chieftai[ns]
Rebellion to rout, and his Progress oppose: [they cho[se]
But first, second and third, were all struck with Disma[y]
Thrice happy the Man, who could first run away.

Now great Preparations proclaim their great Fears;
The Militia, the *Dutch*, the Troops rais'd by the Dea[n]
They associate, subscribe, fast, vote and address,
For your true loyal Subjects can do nothing less.

Horse, Foot, and Dragoons from lost *Flanders* they ca[me]
With *Hessians* and *Danes*, and the Devil and all;
Your Hunters and Rangers, led by O———pe,
And the Church at the Arse of the B———p of *Y—k*.

And pray who so fit to lead forth this Parade,
As the Babe of *Tangier*, my old Grandmother *Wade*?
Whose Cunning so quick, and whose Motion so slow,
That the Rebels march'd on, while He stuck in the Sno[w]

Poor *London*, alas! is fear'd out of its Wits
With Arms and Alarms, as sad Soldiers as Cits;
Sure of dying by Inches, whatever Cause thrives,
Since in parting with Money they part with their Live[s]

But the Genius of *Britain* appears in the D———,
Their Courage to raise, and their Fears to rebuke;
He march'd Day and Night till he got to the Rear,
And then sent us Word, he had nothing to fear.

A

All Night under Arms, the brave D— kept his Ground,
But the Devil a Rebel was there to be found;
The Foot got on Horseback, the News gives account,
But that wou'd not do, so the Horsemen dismount.

Here a fierce Fight ensu'd by a sort of Owl-Light,
Where none got the Day, because it was Night;
And so dark, that we ne'er to the Truth on't shall get,
Unless 'tis clear'd up by another Gazette.

The IMPORTANT QUESTION Resolv'd.

TO what does *France* her present Greatness owe?
    Some say to * *Charles*'s Death; I answer, No.
Whence the fell Discord that o'erspreads our Land,
And *England* ravag'd by a Highland Band?
From the same fatal Source each Plague began:
B-rn-rd's loud Clamour for a War with *Spain*.

* The late Emperor *Charles* VI.

HONESTY the best POLICY.

THAT Patriotism's a Joke, we must allow,
    For *P—t*, the last Professor, owns it now;
But rigid *V——n* keeps his steady Plan,
And claims no Title —— but of Honest Man.

To Mr. P—— on the Hanover Troops.

THAT Rock which gave thee Glory prov'd thy Doom,
And was at once thy Trophy and thy Tomb.

An

An EPIGRAM.

SAYS *W-k-n* to *C-tt-n*, "I thought my Lord *G—r*,
"(You told me) intended to leave us no more."
Says *C-tt-n*, 'He has not'.—— Says *W-k-n*, "You lie.
"And you too, Sir *J—n*, have a Place * by the Bye.
"I thought all your Boastings wou'd end in a Farce,
"Pray where's the *Broad Bottom?*" Says *C-tt-n*, 'My
  Arse.'

* Which happen'd to prove true.—

An EPIGRAM on Miss ELEANOR AMBROSE, a celebrated Beauty in Dublin. By the E— of C———d.

IN *Flavia*'s Eyes is every Grace,
  She's handsome as she cou'd be;
With *Jacob*'s Beauty in her Face,
  And *Esau*'s where it shou'd be.

An ANSWER.

FLAVIA's a Name a deal too free
  With holy Writ to blend her;
Henceforth let *Nell Susanna* be,
  And *C———d* the Elder.

The BALL.

AS late at *W———* it fell out,
  To have a kind of Dancing-bout;
When Innocence divinely sprung,
Dwelt on *Belinda*'s heavenly Tongue:

Where

Where Mirth and Gayety appear'd,
And nothing thought and nothing fear'd;
They strike the Ground in circling Dance,
The pleasing Rounds of mimic *France*.

See N————y clouded in a Fool,
And M————y at the Dancing School.
The custom'd Officer wants Sense,
But that supplies with Impudence:
The ruffled Publican looks great,
Bigger than Minister of State;
Pleas'd to behold the lovely Fair,
He apes the Mimick to a Hair.
Next comes the Beau, the powder'd L————ds,
Who'd rather dance than tell his Beads;
And talks of lonely Groves and Meads:
How blooming Nature doth excell,
In Her that's more than Parallel!
Fee Simple next leads up the Van,
And is saluted by the Fan:
Alas! he sighs, he now is ty'd
To one less fair, a brawling Bride.

Young *Orpheus* sweeps the sounding Lyre,
The willing Notes do all conspire
To charm the Groves, and move the Floods;
Try the Experiment, O Woods!
See *Cælia, Sylvia,* all conspire,
To raise the Flame, and fan the Fire;
View all the Pageantry of Love,
The Bow, the Quiver, and the Dove:
But, Muse, forbear to fly too high,
The Bird unfeather'd cannot fly;
Tho' Instinct tells him that's the Sky.

View *Bacchus* ornamented here,
Drest like a grape-leav'd Ribbon Peer;

See Glasses now and Claret brought,
As quick as Light'ning, or as Thought:
They quaff nectar'ous Draughts of Wine,
And all agree that 'tis divine;
Divine, crys *Bacchus* with a Nod,
And plumes himself that He's the God;
Contention now and Strife appear'd,
And all the Bacchanalian Herd;
Now Noise and Nonsense interfere,
Enough to rend the Hemisphere.

    See gentle Innocence oppreſt,
And lab'ring in the fair one's Breaſt;
N———y with Hick-ups,—ſcarce—can—ſpeak,
Yet makes the faireſt Lady ſqueak;
Immodeſty now proves him drunk,
He uſes all like W——re, or Punk;
Forgets his Company for Shame,
And offers Things I dare not name.
Now M———y, N———y, C———t, all
Reel as they ſtand, and ſtagg'ring fall;
They with them pull the fair Ones down,
And grapple with them on the Ground:
See Hoops and Petticoats fly up,
As high as *Cupid* us'd to ſup;
Who can expreſs the amorous Sight,
Or tell the Revels of the Night?
Nigrelia's now ſtark-ſtaring mad,
Concludes the Ladies all were bad,
As bad as ſhe herſelf has been,
Tho' M———d —e'en with m———d Men:
For they who always are the worſt,
Are ſure to cry out W———re the firſt.
Next Morn perplext, ſhe tells the Tale,
Falſe Facts to add, ſhe does not fail;
Her H———d and her Lover there,
Jealous ſhe Friend nor Foe does ſpare;

                             And

And, say *Belinda* sure was d——k,
Such is the Frenzy of the P——k;
And how extravagantly rude
Is the Distraction of the Prude!

" Now Aggravation tells the Story,
" Which don't redound to female Glory;
" Which like a Snow-ball gathers more
" By rolling, than it did before;
" From House to House the Tale is carry'd,
" How such a one of late miscarry'd,
" And that which makes it worst of all,
" It happen'd at a Publick Ball;
" Had Privacy been usher'd in,
" 'Twould not have signify'd a Pin;
" Its being publick makes the Sin:
" But all know the very Case,
" It may be so, indeed, alas!

What Care can Innocence e'er help,
The Rudeness of each Booby Whelp?
Insulted Beauty merits Aid,
For who wou'd wrong the injur'd Maid?
Much less misuse a second Time,
Without the Shew of Wit or Rhime:
Already 'tis too much to bear
Reflections on the gentle Fair:
How often is the tender Maid
To Wrongs and Insults here betray'd?
How oft unguarded Innocence
Is left alone without Defence?
Defence they want not, when 'tis said,
That each went home a thorough Maid.

Let Envy then not shew her Head,
And Calumny be ever dead;
As Virtue is its own Reward,
If to the Right you shew Regard.

Fair

Fair Ones, from henceforth all beware.
Who loves a *Fool*, or trusts a *Bear*.

On LARISSA.

AS *Larissa* on the Billows
    Of a purling River swims,
Cupid hies him from the Willows,
    Lighting on her tender Limbs:
She affrighted at the Matter,
    Scream'd and squeal'd, and cry'd alack!
And to drown the Wag in Water,
    Turn'd, and swam upon her Back.

P——TT Excus'd.

PIQU'D at the C——t, she knew not why,
    And ostentatious of her Plenty,
Old S——H, when she came to die,
    Bequeath'd her *Thousands, Ten* and *Twenty*:
Not that or CH————D, or P—TT,
    She valu'd, farther than their *Name*;
But hop'd the *Orator* and *Wit*
    Would leave her *twice as much in Fame*.
No * *future Ties* on them she cast,
    But gave, *unlimited*, the Sum:
'Twas the *Reward* of Virtue past,
    Nor Wages for the Time to come.
' Who then, says P—TT, dare censure *Me*,
    ' Or call my *new Opinions*——strange?
' 'Tis plain the D————fs left me *free* ;
    ' And where lies *Freedom*——but in *Change?*

---

* See her Will with regard to the H———le Mr. S———r.

Nature

Nature and Fortune, to the E— of CH———LD.

NAture and *Fortune* blithe and gay,
    To pass an Hour or two,
In frolick Mood agreed to play
    At *What shall this Man do?*
Come, I'll be judge then, *Fortune* cries,
    And therefore must be blind;
Then whipt a Napkin round her Eyes,
    And ty'd it fast behind.
This done, she stump'd upon her own,
    And loll'd on *Nature*'s Knees:
So Courtiers cringe; but make the Throne
    A Pillar for their Ease.
Nature had now prepar'd her List
    Of Names on Scraps of Leather,
Which roll'd, she gave them each a Twist,
    And husled them together.
Thus mixt, which ever came to hand,
    She very surely drew:
Then bade her Sister give Command,
    For what that Man should do.
'Twould almost burst one's Sides to hear,
    What strange Commands she gave;
That C——r should the Laurel wear,
    And C———e an Army have.
At length when * STANHOPE's Name was come,
    Dame *Nature* smil'd, and cry'd,
Now tell me, Sister, this Man's Doom,
    And what shall him betide?
That Man, said *Fortune*, shall be One
    Blest both by You and Me:—
Nay, then, quoth *Nature*, let's have done;
    Sister, I'm sure you *see*.

    * Lord C—fi———d.

On LOVE and WINE.

In Imitation of ANACREON.

GIVE me generous Love and Wine,
  Give me *Champaign* ere I dine;
Let me Nectar freely quaff,
Which will make me love and laugh.
Happy *Bacchus* with his Vine,
Shall intangle thee in Twine;
He shall call my Limbs to move,
Pliant in the Joys of Love:
Venus too shall lend her Aid,
Who was ne'er of Love afraid;
She shall Joys delightful prove,
Fit alone for Wine and Love:
Joys that make us all divine;
For what are Joys, but Love and Wine?
Blessings which the Gods enjoy,
Blessings which can never cloy;
Love dispells all gloomy Care,
And Wine does banish all Despair.

   Since these conspire to make me great,
   Let Love and Drinking be my Fate.

The G—z—e *of* January 23, 1745-6: *Versified.*

I'LL tell you a Tale for a Groat,
   That highly advances our Glory,
Of a Battle so gallantly fought,
   As not to be equall'd in Story.

To *Scotland* repairs Chieftain *H⸺y*,
   The fierceſt of *Britiſh* Commanders,
He promis'd the K⸺g he would maul ye,
   The cowardly Rebel Highlanders.

And now all ſo brave on the Green
   This Hero his Army aſſembled:
Were ever ſuch Myrmidons ſeen?
   O how the blue Bonnet Men trembled!

But ſcarce had your Fears drove you back,
   When Aid from the Welkin was ſent ye,
And all of a ſudden alack!
   Et veniunt en claſſica Venti.

Reſiſtance and Courage were vain,
   The South-Wind blew louder and louder,
Then down fell a Deluge of Rain,
   Which ſpoil'd in a trice all our Powder.

'Twas time to give over the Fight,
   And prudently make a Retreat,
So to *Lithgow* we came in wet Plight,
   Where we found not a Morſel to eat.

From thence by mere Hunger drove out,
   To *Edinburgh* ſtrait we ran on,
The G⸺l look'd ſharply about,
   And ſwore that he miſs'd all his Cannon.

Some think in a Trap they were caught,
   The Highland Men ſtole them away;
But others more juſtly have thought,
   By the Wind they were all blown away.

                                And

And now he that rightly can ken
  My Tale, tho' the Truth may be doubted,
Muſt own, by a Handful of Men.
  The whole Highland Army was routed.

A SONG.

To the Tune of, The Cut-purſe.

THE old *Engliſh* Cauſe knocks at ev'ry Man's Door,
  And bids him ſtand up for Religion and Right;
It addreſſes the Rich as well as the Poor,
  And for Liberty bids them like *Engliſhmen* fight,
    And ſuffer no Wrong
    From a Popiſh Throng,
Who if they're not quell'd will enſlave us ere long;
  Moſt bravely then let us our Liberty prize,
  Nor ſuffer Deluſion to blind all our Eyes.
    CHORUS.
  Or each Highlander Cut-purſe will ſoon give us Law;
  Each Rebel's as daring as Tyler *or* Straw.

From *Paris Cartouche* to *Scotland* is come,
  And Banditti's of *Scots* will rob your Eſtates:
Theſe Robbers are all protected by *Rome*;
  Conſult but their Annals, record but their Dates.
    It's their Politicks
    To burn Hereticks,
Or poiſon by Water that's fetch'd from the *Styx*.
  Let *Frenchify'd* Bigots in vain then attempt
  To bring or our Church or our King to contempt.
    CHORUS.
  Or each Highlander, &c.

The

The Farces of *Rome*, with her Host,
  Are laugh'd at and jeer'd by the Learned and Wise,
And all her thin Tinsel's apparently lost,
  Her Stories of Reliques and sanctify'd Lies.
    Each ignorant Joke
    Believe, or you smoke,
If ever you're conquer'd, or receive the Pope's Yoke.
Let no Popish Invader lay claim to your Choice,
But boldly exclude him with Arms and with Voice.
      C H O R U S.
    Or each *Highlander*, &c.

Let Curses most vile and Anathemas roar;
  Let half-ruin'd *France* and the *Pope* Tribute pay,
Our thund'ring Cannon shall guard *Britain*'s Shore,
  Great *George* shall defend us, and him we'll obey.
    Then *France* and proud *Spain*
    Have labour'd in vain;
For the Mountain has brought forth a huge Mouse again.
The Pretender must scamper and quit every Clan,
And drive for old *Rome*, and get home if he can.
      C H O R U S.
No Highlander Cut-purse shall then give us Law,
Tho' the Devil should help him, or Tyler *and* Straw.

E P I G R A M.

*W*ILL and *John* at a Plumber's once happen'd to stop,
    Where a *Tully*'s Head stood in the Front of the Shop:
Will crys out, " O that I had such a Head !"
' You have, replies *John*; for — behold it is lead.'

D   *Upon*

Upon seeing a Pair of Stocks in W——for *Chapel.*

'TIS plain, ye holy Sinners!
　　Within thefe facred Walls
The *Stocks* are plac'd —— for Simony
　　Is common to you all.

On CH—— S——PE, *Efq; drinking* Tar-Water.

WHEN *Charles* by Rule Epifcopal
　　Tar-Water firft began;
Methinks, he cry'd, I feel myfelf
　　Become a double Man.

Its Prowefs then refolv'd to try,
　　But Oh! with Shame and Trouble,
He found of all his boafted Parts,
　　One Thing alone was double.

Enrag'd, he curft the filly Book,
　　The Bifhop and the Tar;
And fwore the Beggar's Blefling was
　　A better Boon by far.

The MONKIES.

To our Modern BEAUS.

WHOE'ER with curious Eye has rang'd
　　Through *Ovid*'s Tales, has feen,
How *Jove*, incens'd, to Monkies chang'd
　　A Tribe of worthlefs Men.

Repentant,

Repentant, soon th' offending Race
    Intreat the injur'd Pow'r,
To give them back the Human Face,
    And Reason's Aid restore.

Jove, sooth'd at length, his Ear inclin'd,
    And granted half their Pray'r;
But th' other half he bade the Wind
    Disperse in empty Air.

Scarce had the Thunderer giv'n the Nod,
    That shook the vaulted Skies,
With haughtier Air the Creatures strode,
    And stretch'd their dwindled Size.

The Hair in Curls luxuriant now
    Around their Temples spread;
The Tail, that whilom hung below,
    Now dangled from the Head.

The Head remains unchang'd within,
    Nor alter'd much the Face;
It still retain its native Grin,
    And all its old Grimace.

The hollow Cheeks began to fill,
    Yet meagre look'd and wan;
The Mouth incessant chatter'd still,
    But mock'd the Voice of Man.

Thus half transform'd, and half the same,
    Jove bade them take their Place,
(Restoring them their ancient Claim)
    Among the Human Race.

Man with Contempt the Brute survey'd,
    Nor would a Name bestow:
But Woman lik'd the motly Breed,
    And call'd the Thing a BEAU.

ANACREONTIC.

BEauty's gay Queen, fair *Aphrodite*,
    Parent eternal of Delight,
Forsake awhile thy *Paphian* Groves,
To *Avon*'s Banks direct thy Doves,
Instruct the am'rous Boy, thy Son,
To wound those Hearts that ne'er were won:
Then shall a thousand Altars rise,
And Vows be wafted to the Skies.
Here, gentle Goddess, shalt thou find
Attendants meet of ev'ry Kind;
To wait thy Steps the Graces three,
Shall *Franklin*, *Beckford*, *Shadwell* be,
Fair *Child* shall weave thy golden Zone,
And add new Graces of her own;
A thousand Nymphs shall crowd thy Train,
A thousand Youths shall bear thy Chain.
O *Venus*, hear my humble Prayer;
Form these Nymphs gentle as they're fair;
Bring with thee Mirth and Converse free,
And Youth, which owes its Charms to thee;
Bring Self-persuasion to beguile,
The speaking Glance, the dimpled Smile;
Sighs, that can melt the stony Mind,
Thou can'st make them fair, and kind.

I Have lost my Mistress, Horse, and Wife,
  And when I think on human Life,
    Cry Mercy 'twas no worse.
My Mistress sickly, poor and old,
My Wife damn'd ugly, and a Scold
    I am sorry for my Horse.

A SONG

On Miss MOLLY CARR. —— Brussels, 1744.

WHEN I from my Window am gazing,
    'Tis not at a Comet or Star,
But an Object more bright and more pleasing,
    The Eyes of my sweet MOLLY C—R.

No *Phœbe*, no *Daphne*, no *Phillis*,
    Tho' Poets put them on a Par,
With the Beauties of Roses and Lillies,
    Can vie with my sweet MOLLY C—R.

You Soldiers, so stout in your Prattle,
    Yet always hope Danger is far,
You're more safe from the Cannon in Battle,
    Than a Glance from my sweet MOLLY C—R.

The Prelate so famous for Teaching
    The excellent Virtues of Tar,
Had he seen her, would leave off his Preaching,
    And write on my sweet MOLLY C—R.

His *Τὸ E-ge-mo-ni-con* * Fire,
    His Æther, affirm it I dare,
Can be found in Perfection much higher
    Existing in sweet MOLLY C—R.

The

---

* Τὸ Ἡγεμονικὸν. An Epithet, or rather an Attribute given by Dr. Berkley, Bishop of Cloyne, to Fire or Æther of the most exalted Nature, and which, he thinks, exists in Tar-Water. (See his Treatise on the Subject.) But with great Deference to that learned Prelate, I think it more applicable to a fine Girl. I would explain the Meaning of the Word; but it is *Greek*, and would therefore seem Presumption in a Soldier to attempt it; tho' was I capable I should chuse to give to all fine Gentlemen an Opportunity of shewing their Learning to the Ladies.

The Lawyers, who make themselves Drudges
  To much dirty Work at the Bar,
Would quit both their Fees and the Judges,
  To plead to my sweet MOLLY C—R.

The Doctors, so knowing in Physick,
  Who Nature's just Crisises mar,
May search, but they'll find no Specific
  So certain as sweet MOLLY C—R.

The *Pandours* and *Croats* most savage,
  Whose greatest Delight is in War,
Would stop from their Plunder and Ravage,
  At the Name of my sweet MOLLY C—R.

If, as rich as a *Crœsus* in Treasure,
  In Kingdoms as great as a *Czar*,
All, all I would lay down with Pleasure
  At the Feet of my sweet MOLLY C—R.

Let those out of Play of the Nation,
  With the Great Ones eternally jar;
I'm humbly content with my Station,
  So smiles but my sweet MOLLY C—R.

Tho' a glorious Campaign now is ended,
  Without wooden Leg or a Scar;
How, ye † *Dutch!* shall our Troops be defended
  From th' Charms of my sweet MOLLY C—R ?

A Mon—h breaks Faith with his Allies,
  And ‖ others, like Cocks do but § spar.
                                    Sad

---

† It may seem odd and whimsical to invoke the *Dutch*; but it is impossible to avoid joking with our best Friends sometimes; —— no Reasons must be given; there are Secrets in all Families, Brother, &c.

‖ I don't mean any of the Allies of the Queen of *Hungary*.

§ A Word us'd by Cockers, when their Cocks do not strike home, but rather seem to play with one another.

Sad Doings! I never shall tell Lies,
  Or trifle with sweet MOLLY C—R.

If St——r had commanded in *Flanders*,
  The *French* had been ruin'd by gar;
Hold, — Muse, not a Word of Commanders,
  Sing always of sweet MOLLY C—R.

A SONG.

AWAY, let nought to Love displeasing,
    My *Winifreda*, move your Care;
Let nought delay the heavenly Blessing,
    Nor squeamish Pride, nor gloomy Fear.

What tho' no Grants of Royal Donors
    With pompous Titles grace our Blood,
We'll shine in more substantial Honors,
    And to be noble, we'll be good.

Our Name, while Virtue thus we tender,
    Will sweetly sound where-e'er 'tis spoke,
And all the Great Ones, they shall wonder
    How they respect such little Folk.

What tho' from Fortune's lavish Bounty
    No mighty Treasures we possess,
We'll find within our Pittance Plenty,
    And be content without Excess.

Still shall each kind returning Season
    Sufficient for our Wishes give:
For we will live a Life of Reason;
    And that's the only Life to live.

Thro'

Thro' Youth and Age in Love excelling,
  We'll Hand in Hand together tread;
Sweet smiling Peace shall crown our Dwelling,
  And Babes, sweet smiling Babes, our Bed.

How should I love the pretty Creatures,
  While round my Knees they fondly clung;
To see them look their Mother's Features,
  To hear them lisp their Mother's Tongue!

And when with Envy Time transported,
  Shall think to rob us of our Joys,
You'll, in your Girls, again be courted;
  And I'll go wooing in my Boys.

An EPILOGUE *intended to be spoken by Mrs.* Woffington, *in the Habit of a Volunteer, upon reading the* Gazette, *containing an Account of the late Action at* Falkirk.

PLague of all Cowards, say I—why bless my Eyes—
  No, no, it can't be true——the Gazette lies.
Our Men retreat! before a Scrub Banditti!
Who scarce could fright the Buff-Coats of the City!—
Well, if 'tis so, and that our *Men* can't *stand*,
'Tis Time we Women take the *Thing* in *Hand*.
Thus in my Country's Cause I now appear,
A bold, smart *Kevenhuller'd* Volunteer;
And really, mark some Heroes in the Nation,
You'll think this no unnat'ral Transformation:
For if in Valour real *Manhood lies*,
All Cowards are but Women in Disguise.

They

They cry, thefe Rebels are fo ftout and tall!—
Ah lud! *I'd lower the proudeft of them all.*
Try but my *Mettle*, place me in the Van,
And poft me, if I don't—*bring down my Man.*
Had we an Army of fuch valorous Wenches,
What Man, d'ye think, would dare attack our *Trenches?*
Oh, how th' Artillery of our *Eyes* would maul 'em!
But, our *mask'd Batteries,* lud! how they would *gall 'em!*
No Rebels 'gainft fuch Force dare take the Field;
For, d—mme, but we'd *die* before we'd yield.
Jefting apart—We Women have ftrong Reafon
To ftop the Progrefs of this Popifh Treafon:
For fure when Female Liberty's at Stake,
All Women ought to *buftle* for its Sake:
Should thofe audacious Sons of *Rome* prevail,
Vows,--CONVENTS,--and that Heathen Thing--the VEIL
Muft come in Fafhion. O! fuch Inftitutions
Would fuit but oddly with our—CONSTITUTIONS.
What gay Coquet would brook a Nun's Profeffion?
And I've fome *private* REASONS 'gainft Confeffion.
Befides, our good Men of the Church, they fay,
(Who now, thank Heav'n, may *love* as well as pray)
Muft then be only wed to cloifter'd Houfes,
Slap then we're nick'd of Twenty thoufand Spoufes;
Faith, and no bad ones, as I'm told: then judge ye,
Is't fit we lofe our BENEFIT of CLERGY?

In Freedom's Caufe, ye Patriot-Fair, arife,
Exert the facred Influence of your Eyes;
On valiant Merit deign alone to fmile,
And vindicate the Glory of our Ifle;
To no bafe Coward proftitute your Charms,
Difband the Lover who deferts his Arms:
So fhall you fire each Hero to his Duty,
And *Britifh* Rights be fav'd by *Britifh* Beauty.

An ODE. *Imitated from* ODE XI. Book II. *of* Horace.
From P—l F—y *to* N—s F—y, *Esq*;

By a PERSON of HONOUR.

Studiis florentem ignobilis oti.   VIRG.

NEVER, dear *Faz*, torment thy Brain
  With idle Fears of *France* or *Spain*,
 Or any thing that's foreign:
What can *Bavaria* do to Us?
What *Prussia*'s Monarch, or the *Russ*?
 Or ev'n Prince *Charles* of *Lorrain*?

Let us be chearful whilst we can,
And lengthen out the short-liv'd Span,
 Enjoying ev'ry Hour.
The Moon itself we see decay;
Beauty's the worse for ev'ry Day,
 And so's the sweetest Flow'r.

How oft, dear *Faz*, have we been told,
That *Paul* and *Faz* are both grown old,
 By young and wanton Lasses!
Then since our Time is now so short,
Let us enjoy the only Sport
 Of tossing off our Glasses.

From *White*'s we'll move th' expensive Scene,
And steal away to *Richmond Green*;
 There free from Noise and Riot,
Polly each Morn shall fill our Tea,
Spread Bread and Butter, and then we
 Each Night get drunk in Quiet.

Unless

Unless perchance Earl L———r comes,
As noisy as a dozen Drums,
   And makes a horrid Pother:
Else might we quiet sit and quaff,
And gently chat and gayly laugh
   At this, and that, and t'other.

Br————*w* shall settle what's to pay,
Adjust Accounts by Algebra;
   I'll always order Dinner:
Pr————*w*, tho' solemn, yet is sly,
And leers at *Poll* with roguish Eye,
   To make the Girl a Sinner.

Powell, (d'ye hear?) let's have the Ham,
Some Chickens and a Chine of Lamb;
   And what else—let's see—look ye,
Br—*w* must have his damn'd Bouilli;
B—*b* fattens on his Fricaffée;
   I'll have my Water-Suchy.

When Dinner comes, we'll drink about,
(No Matter who is in or out)
   Till Wine or Sleep o'ertake us;
Each Man may nod, or nap, or wink;
And when it is our turn to drink,
   Our Neighbour then shall wake us.

Thus let us live in soft Retreat,
Nor envy nor despise the Great;
   Submit to pay our Taxes;
With Peace or War we'll be content,
Till eas'd by a good Parliament,
   Till *S*—*pe* his Hand relaxes.

Never enquire about the *Rhine*,
But fill your Glass and drink your Wine,
   Hope Things may mend in *Flanders*.
The *Dutch*, we know, are good Allies;
So are they all with Subsidies;
   And we have choice Commanders.

Then here's the K—g; God bless his Grace!
Tho' neither you nor I have Place,
   He has many a sage Adviser;
And yet no Treason sure's in this,
Let who will take the Pray'r amiss,
   God send them all much Wiser!

ORPHEUS and HECATE.

An ODE. *Inscribed to the Patroness of the* Italian *Opera*.
To Lady B————.

Tantum Odiis, Iræque dabat————
————————illa Sorores
Nocte vocat genitas————   Met. lib. 4.

When *Orpheus*, as old Poets tell,
   Carry'd his Music down to Hell,
He fill'd the Shades with Joys;
Alecto, and *Tisiphone*,
Megæra, with *Brown* HECATE,
   Transported heard his Voice.

And whilst He led the Song divine,
The Spectres all in Chorus join;
   Such was grim PLUTO's Will!
Tantalus quaff'd a flowing Bowl,
Sisyphus ceas'd his Stone to roll,
   Ixion's Wheel stood still.

His Perſon, Melody, and Lyre
Set the infernal Queen on Fire,
  Who courted him to ſtay;
But PLUTO, to prevent all Strife,
Order'd the Poet, with his Wife,
  Back to the Realms of Day.

Joyful they ſpeed for upper Air;
When, to divide the happy Pair,
  HECAT' contrived a Spell:
Now, now, ſhe cry'd, in rapt'rous Tone,
His Harmony is all my own!
  I'll make a Heav'n in Hell!

For me, and my *Tartarean* Crew,
Endleſs the wanton Song renew!
  O ever touch the Lyre!
But ſtill the Bard, in heav'nly Lays,
Would ſing his King's and Maker's Praiſe,
  And kindle martial Fire.

Enrag'd, the * triple-headed Dame
Howl'd; in a Trice the *Furies* came,
  Threat'ning a dreadful Fate;
'Till PHOEBUS, with the tuneful *Nine*,
And lovely *Graces*, all combine
  To ſhield him from their Hate.

Thus ſav'd from Death, He ſhares the Love
Of Men below, and Bleſt above,
  The Virtuous, Brave, and Wiſe;
While every chaſte, and pious Mind,
To Vice averſe, to Good inclin'd,
  Muſt HECAT's Name deſpiſe.

---

* Tuque *triceps* HECATE.———   Met. lib. 7.
The Antients repreſented *Hecate* with three Heads, that of a Horſe,
a Bitch, and a Savage; the ſecond is ſuppoſed to be the Head uſed on
this Occaſion.

Sir

Sir JOHN SUCKLING, an old BALLAD,

Adapted to a Modern General.

SIR *John* he bought him an ambling Nag,
 To *Scotland* for to ride, *a*,
An hundred Horse besides his own,
 Did guard him on each side, *a*.

The Ladies all ran to their Windows, to see
 So noble and gallant a Sight, *a*;
And as he rode by, they all did cry,
 Sir *John*, why will you go fight, *a*?

But still the cruel Knight rode on,
 His Heart would not relent, *a*;
For till he came there, he felt no fear,
 Why then should he repent, *a*?

None lik'd him so well, as his own Colonel,
 He took him for *John de Wort*, *a*,
But when they made Shews of Gunning and Blows,
 Sir *John* he was nothing so pert, *a*.

For when the *Scots Army* came in Sight,
 And all prepar'd to fight, *a*,
He ran to his Tent, and they ask'd, what he meant?
 He said he must needs go and sh——, *a*.

His Colonel sent for him back again,
 To place him in the Van, *a:*
But Sir *John* he did swear, he came not there,
 To be kill'd the very first man, *a*.

To cure him of Fear, he was sent to the Rear,
 Some five or six Miles or more, *a*.

Sir

Sir *John* he did play, try trip and away,
And ne'r saw the Enemy more, *a.*

A New Ballad.
On Lord D—n——l's altering his Chapel at Gr——e into a Kitchen.

BY *Ovid*, 'mongst many more Wonders, we're told
What chanc'd to PHILEMON and BAUCIS of old,
How their Cott to a Temple was conjur'd by JOVE;
So a Chapel was chang'd to a Kitchen at *Gr—e.*
                                    Derry down, &c.

The Lord of the Mansion most rightly conceiting,
That his Guests lov'd good Prayers much less than good
                Eating;
And possess'd by the D-v-l (as some Folks will tell ye)
What was meant for the Soul, he assign'd to the Belly.
                                    Derry down, &c.

The Word was scarce given, but down dropt the Clock,
And strait was seen fixed in the Form of a Jack;
'Tis shameful to say, Pulpit, Benches and Pews,
Form'd Cupboards and Shelves for Plates, Saucepans,
                and Stews.
                                    Derry down, &c.

Pray'r-books turn'd into Platters, nor think it a Fable,
And Dressers sprung out of the C--mm--n Table;
Which instead of the usual Repast, B—d and W—e,
Is stor'd with rich Soup and good *English* Sirloin.
                                    Derry down, &c.

No

No Fires, but what pure Devotion could raise,
Till now had been known in this Temple to blaze:
But, good Lord, how the Neighbours around did admire,
When the Chimney rose up in the room of a Spire!
Derry down, &c.

For a *Jew* many People the Master mistook,
Whose *Levites* were Scullions, whose High-Priest a Cook;
And thought that he meant our Religion to alter,
When they saw the Burnt-Offerings smoak at the Altar.
Derry down, &c.

The Bell's solemn Sound, which was heard far and near,
And oft rous'd the Chaplain unwilling to Pray'r,
No more to good Sermons now summons the Sinner,
But blasphemous rings in the Country to Dinner.
Derry down, &c.

When my good Lord the B—p had heard the strange Story,
How the Place was profan'd, that was built to G--d's Glory;
With Zeal he cry'd out, Oh, how impious the Deed,
To cram Christians with Pudding instead of the Cr--d!
Derry down, &c.

Then away to the *Gr—e* hy'd the Church's Protector,
Resolving to read his Lay-brother a Lecture;
But he scarce had begun, when he saw plac'd before 'em
An Haunch piping hot from the *Sanctum Sanctorum*.
Derry down, &c.

Troth, quoth he, I find no great Sin in the Plan,
What's useless to God, to make useful to Man;
Besides, 'tis a true Christian Duty we read,
The Poor and the Hungry with good Things to feed.
Derry down, &c.

Then

Then again on the Walls he bestow'd Consecration,
But reserv'd the full Rights of a free Visitation;
Thus 'tis the Lord's House, only varied the Treat,
Now there's Meat without Grace, where was Grace
without Meat.
Derry down, &c.

A D——ss's Ghost to Orator H————r P————tt.

AS musing on his Bed the *Speecher* lay,
 Conning Harangues for some important Day;
Labouring to make the Turns harmonious fall,
And to the Taste attune 'em of *Whitehall*:
A sudden Noise, Career of Fancy stops,
And a pale Phiz within the Curtains pops.
The Phiz his opening Eye no sooner meets,
Than quick he dives between th' unsavory Sheets:
Not Proof against the Visage of her *Grace*,
Down sinks;—— till now, that *unembarrass'd* Face.

 The Spectre thus: " No sooner laid my Head,
" But all thy Patriot Sentiments are fled:
" And I in my atoning Project chous'd,
" The latest and the best I e'er espous'd.

 " To my Trustees (since Fate forbids to me,)
" Return, base V-l-n! my retaining Fee;
" Bequeath'd to save that Country thou wou'dst sell.
" Refund———— not such a *Judas* roars in Hell.

 " That soften'd Thief, by Sense of Guilt dismay'd,
" Threw back the Price of him he had betray'd;
" But, Wretch! my Purse in thy polluted Paws
" Meant to support, thou turn'st to crush the Cause.

F " Tho'

"Tho' loft on thee, yet hear thefe Rules I teach:
"Ufage like this wou'd make the Devil preach.
"No Weight to Words can Eloquence impart,
"Tho' ne'er fo clear the Head, if foul the Heart:
"Men's Words, the World will by their Actions fcan:
"The *Orator* muft be the *Honeft* Man.
"No Proftitute the generous Bofom warms,
"The *Whore* peeps thro' the Bloom, and blafts her Charms.

"Once with Applaufe was heard thy flowing Tongue,
"And on its Motions fweet Perfuafion hung: [ney)
"But now thofe Lips (and Thanks to *Sarah's* Mo-
"That in thy Country's Struggles dropt down Honey,
"Shall pleafe no more! (take my prophetick Word,)
"Nor all their Flourifhes be worth a T—d.

"But fee! the Morning ftreaks the Eaftern Sky:
"Now crows the fcaring Cock: from hence I hye,
"And leave thee to the lafh of loft Integrity.

The UNEMBARRASS'D COUNTENANCE,
A New Ballad. To the Tune of, a Cobler there was, &c. &c.

———*Sume fuperbiam*
Quæfitum meritis. Hor.

Behold young *Balaam*, now a Man of Spirit,
Afcribes his Getting to his Parts and Merit. Pope.

To a certain old Chapel well known in the Town,
 The Infide quite rotten, the Outfide near down,
A Fellow got in who cou'd talk and cou'd prate,
I'll tell you his Story, and fing you his Fate.
     Derry down, &c.

At

At firſt he ſeem'd modeſt and wonderous wiſe,
He flatter'd all others in order to riſe:
Till out of Compaſſion he got a ſmall Place,
Then full on his Maſter he turned his A—ſe.
　　　　　　　　　　Derry down, &c.

He bellow'd and roar'd at the Troops of *Hanover*,
And ſwore they were Raſcals who ever went over:
That no Man was honeſt who gave them a Vote,
And all that were for 'em ſhould hang by the Throat.
　　　　　　　　　　Derry down, &c.

He always affected to make the Houſe ring
'Gainſt *Hanover* Troops and a *Hanover* K—g:
He applauded the Way to keep *Engliſhmen* free,
By *digging* Hanover *quite into the Sea.*
　　　　　　　　　　Derry down, &c.

By flaming ſo loudly he got him a Name,
Tho' many believ'd it wou'd coſt him a Shame:
But Nature had given him, ne'er to be harraſs'd,
An unfeeling Heart, and a Front unembarraſs'd.
　　　　　　　　　　Derry down, &c.

When from an old Woman, by ſtanding his Ground,
He had got the Poſſeſſion of ten thouſand Pound,
He ſaid that he car'd not what others might call him,
He wou'd ſhew himſelf now the true Son of Sir
　Balaam *.　　　　　　*Derry down*, &c.

* See Pope, Vol. 2. Epiſtle 3. ver. 361, &c.

Poor *Harry*, whom erſt he had dirtily ſpatter'd,
He now crouch'd and cring'd to, commended and flatter'd;
Since honeſt Men here were aſham'd of his Face,
That in *Ireland* at leaſt he might get him a Place.
        Derry down, &c.

But *Harry* reſentful firſt bid him be huſh,
Then proclaim it aloud that he never cou'd bluſh;
Recant his Invectives, and then in a trice
He would ſhew the beſt Title to an *Iriſh* VICE.
        Derry down, &c.

Young *Balaam* ne'er boggled, but turned his Coat,
Determin'd to ſhare in whate'er cou'd be got,
Said, I ſcorn all thoſe who cry impudent Fellow,
As my Front is of Braſs, I'll be painted in Yellow.*
        Derry down, &c.

Since Yellow's the Colour that beſt ſuits his Face,
And *Balaam* aſpires at an eminent Place,
May he ſoon at *Cheapſide* ſtand fix'd by the Legs,
His Front well adorn'd, all daub'd o'er with Eggs.
        Derry down, &c.

Whilſt *Balaam* was poor, he was full of Renown;
But now that he's rich, he's the Jeſt of the Town;
Then let all Men learn by his foul Diſgrace.
That Honeſty's better by far than a Place.
        Derry down, &c.

---

* A Liſt of the Names of thoſe who voted for the *Hanover* Troops two Years ago was printed in yellow Characters.

An EPISTLE to WILLIAM PITT, Esq;

SInce * One there is, who with uncommon Art
   Boasts the fond Friend, but acts the Censor's Part,
Who blames your Conduct, yet so nicely blames,
All have allow'd he innocently aims:
Bear yet another Friend, whose feeble Lays
Much more may injure, while they strive to praise.

  Blest Genius! with each shining Talent born,
Whom Letters polish, and whom Arts adorn;
Fit, as thy Country calls, with equal Skill
To watch her Dangers, or her Triumphs fill;
Erst, *Tully*-like, ordain'd to loud Applause,
You pleaded Liberty's, and *Britain*'s Cause;
Foremost in ardent Patriot Bands you stood,
A firm Opposer for the Publick Good:
Whilst Pow'r's rude Hand, tho' by Yourself disdain'd,
You felt indignant for an injur'd Land;
This Danger past, becalm'd you now declare
A gen'rous Truce, nor wage a needless War.
By sharing Pow'r be now your Candour seen;
A private Station wou'd be errant Spleen.
To prove your Justice, you must Greatness bear;
And suffer Honours you are doom'd to wear.

  When some bright Comet first in Heav'n appears,
He moves our Wonder, but alarms our Fears.
Yet as he comes, diffusive Virtues flow,
And Health and Vigour spread on all below:
Nations and Worlds the gracious Boon declare,
And the fierce Meteor shines a Ruling Star.

    * Vide *H--r--y*'s Letter to *P—t*.

Thus does thy Soul, to one great Purpose true,
Bent to one End, its radiant Course pursue;
On ev'ry partial Aim with Scorn look down;
Virtue like yours no Party knows but one:
The gen'ral Weal you urge by various Ways;
Nor yield to less than universal Praise:
To guard, to save, the Work's but half compleat;
'Tis yours to strengthen, and to wield the State.

Strange Rule! to nicer Moderns only known,
That Parts and Worth must needs avoid the Throne.
Who with unsully'd Honour stands confest,
For Pow'r's high Trust, the ablest and the best,
To touch her Shrine fit Saint allow'd before,
But touches only, and is fit no more.
As the bright Maid who sought celestial Fires,
And in the Instant that she meets, expires.

Is then superior Lustre but design'd
To dazzle only, not to guide Mankind?
Must Patriots for a Nation's Weal contend,
But drop the Means, when nearest to the End?
When most approv'd, be most expos'd to Blame;
Lost to the Publick, or be lost to Fame?

But boldly Thou thy Sov'reign's Call obey;
To Courts, to Kings new Ornaments display.
Let fainter Worth the Light discreetly shun;
Yours shall, like Diamonds, brighten in the Sun.
Go soar, and shine in yon resplended Sphere;
'Tis such as You alone, that triumph there.
Exalted Merit shall for once be own'd,
A Patriot still, tho' in a Palace found.
Yes; 'tis reserv'd for Your peculiar Fame
To change your Station, and be still the same;
'Tis You shall dignify a Courtier's Name.

See where glad Armies wide their Wings extend,
Fond to embrace the Brother and the Friend.
Rouz'd at Thy Name, the Vet'ran rais'd his Head,
New Hopes reviving, to new Conquests led.
To win Thy Praise, again Ambition fires;⸺
And Thy own Spirit ev'ry Breast inspires.
Oh! might the Soldier be your destin'd Care;
Might You assist while WILLIAM leads the War:
No more, foul Triumph to the Rebel-Foe!
Would *English* Valour sleep in *Scotia*'s Snow;
Nor unreveng'd so long had GARDNER's Shade⸺
Mourn'd *Preston*'s Debt, at *Falkirk* ill repaid.
Britain once more her laurell'd Sons should see,
Sons fit to be enroll'd by Fame and Thee.

But now awhile *Hibernia*'s happy Land
Shall feel, shall bless Thy uncorrupted Hand.
Long has our Sister-Isle dejected sate,
And suffer'd more than suits a Sister's Fate:
To ease her Pains; to swell her scanty Store,
STANHOPE and Thee at once to grace her Shore!
What can she ask, or GEORGE indulge her more?

Yet fear we not; tho' now in western Skies
You seem to sink, 'tis but again to rise.⸺
When in those Strains, which wond'ring Senates hear,
You win with sacred Truth the Royal Ear;
And stand ere long a Fav'rite near the Throne
(For to be favour'd, is but to be known.)
Then *British* Annals shall new Wonders trace,
Wide Power unenvy'd, and Domestic Peace;
Charm'd into Rest, loud Factions shall agree;
Nor fear a Minister, when PITT is He.

Short

Short Verses, in Imitation of Long Verses: in an Epistle to W——M P——TT, *Esq*;

Naughty, paughty, Jack-a-dandy.   Namby Pamby.
Sic parvis componere magna solebam.   Virgil.

SINCE one hath writ,
To thee, O *P-tt!*
Whom none can know,
If Friend or Foe;
Deign to smile on,
Lank *Ly-tl-on:*
For tho' his Lays
May squint two Ways;
They're meant for Praise.

 Sir *Bob* to hang
Thou didst harangue,
While he in Joke
The Cornet broke.
But *Hal* now flatter'd,
Then whipp'd, then spatter'd,
With Fear full fraught,
Thy Favour bought:
The *Patriot* ends,
And ye are Friends,
Like *Cæsar* He,
As *Tully* was, to Thee.

 As when much tir'd,
In Roads bemir'd,
Men see by Night
A Fairy-Light,
Which they pursue
With eager View,
In hope to win
A Friendly Inn;
But by Mistake,
In some foul Lake

Surpriz'd they're flung,
Of Mud or Dung,
From whence the *Meteor* sprung.
So far'd the *Crew,*
Who follow'd *You:*

 Or as a Maid,
On Back first laid,
By dire Mishap
She gains a C—p:

 Such was your Case,
Scarce warm in Place,
Defil'd all o'er,
An errant Whore,
You chang'd your Stile,
Thou Turn-Coat vile.

 What, still refrain
From long-sought Gain?
Still to entice
A higher Price?
No, no, my *P-tt!*
Once near being bit,
Did not the Band
Their K—g withstand;
And bring him low,
As K—g cou'd go?
Tho' *France* did threat
The Royal Seat;
Tho' Rebels dire
Spread Sword and Fire;

Careless

Careless of all
That could befall
The Crown or Realm,
They quit the Helm;
Cabal, combine,
Revile, resign;
One, One and All,
From *London-Wall*,
To *P--m* * Cock-Crower
   of *Whitehall*.

  Then go my Boy!
No more be coy,
Go force your Way
To C---rt for Pay!
Nor Fear nor Shame
Should now reclaim;
Courtier or Patriot, thou
   art still the same.

  Our Colonels all
For thee loud call,
By *All* I mean,
The great *Fourteen*:
Like thee large-soul'd,
Despising Gold.
These never ran
From *Preston*'s-*Pan*,
Nor did they yield
Base *Falkirk*'s Field;
Far, far from both,
To fight, full loth,
They will not go
To lie in Snow,
Till *William*'s Blade [Aid.
Hath got thy Tongue for

  Hibernia, smile!
Thrice happy Isle!

* An Officer of great Antiquity.

On thy bless'd Ground,
Twelve thousand Pound,
For *Stan—pe*'s found;
Three thousand clear,
For *P-tt*, a Year;
So shalt thou thrive,
Industrious Hive;
While these and more
Increase thy Store.
Thrice envy'd Land!
Reserv'd to pay *Britannia*'s
   Patriot Band.

  Sunk in the *West*,
As in the *East*;
For all allow
Thou art sunk now;
Yet soon, when near
The Royal Ear,
Thou with such Things
Shall sooth our K---gs,
As gain'd Huzzas,
Of loud Applause,
From *Syd---am* glad,
And *Ca--- w* mad;
Then shall for War
The *Dutch* declare.
Then we the *Russ*
Shall meet and buss.
Then, then shall *France*
Fall in a Trance.
Then, then shall *Spain*
Yield to thy Strain.
None, from that Hour,
Shall envy Power,
In high Degree
Of Majesty, [be
When *P-tt* Minist r shall
  G   *VER-*

VERSES upon the late D———ſs *of* M———

By Mr. P———

BUT what are theſe to great *Atoſſa*'s Mind,
Scarce once herſelf, by Turns all Womankind?
Who with herſelf, and others from her Birth,
Finds all her Life one Warfare upon Earth;
Shines in expoſing Knaves and painting Fools,
Yet is whate'er ſhe hates or ridicules.
No Thought advances, but her eddy Brain
Whirls it about, and down it goes again.
Full Sixty Years the World has been her Trade,
The wiſeſt Fool much Time has ever made:
From loveleſs Youth to unreſpected Age,
No Paſſion gratify'd, except her Rage;
So much the Fury ſtill out-ran the Wit,
The Pleaſure miſs'd her, and the Scandal hit:
Who breaks with her, provokes Revenge from Hell,
But he's a bolder Man who dares be well;
Her ev'ry Turn with Violence purſu'd,
Nor more a Storm her Hate, than Gratitude:
To that each Paſſion turns or ſoon or late,
Love if it make her yield, muſt make her hate.
Superior's Death! an Equal, what a Curſe!
But an Inferior, not Dependent, worſe.
Offend her, and ſhe knows not to forgive;
Oblige her, and ſhe'll hate you while you live.
But die, and ſhe'll adore you † —Then the Buſt
And Temple riſe,—then fall again to Duſt.
Laſt Night her Lord was all that's good and great;
A Knave this Morning, and his Will a Cheat.
                                                      Strange!

† Alludes to a Temple ſhe erected with a Buſt of Queen *Anne* in
it, which mouldered away in a few Years.

Strange! by the Means defeated of the Ends,
By Spirit robb'd of Power; by Warmth, of Friends;
By Wealth, of Followers; without one Distress,
Sick of herself through very Selfishness.

Atossa's curs'd with ev'ry granted Prayer,
Childless with all her Children, wants an Heir:
To Heirs unknown, descends th' unnumber'd Store,
Or wanders, Heaven directed, to the Poor.

N. B. These Verses are Part of a Poem, entitled, *Characters of Women*. It is generally said, the D⸺ss gave Mr. *P* 1000 *l*. to suppress them: He took the Money, yet the World sees the Verses; but this is not the first Instance where Mr. *P*'s practical Virtue has fallen very short of those pompous Professions of it he makes in his Writings.

To CLARA.

Dear thoughtless *Clara*, to my Verse attend,
Believe for once thy Lover and thy Friend.
Heav'n to each Sex has various Gifts assign'd,
And shewn an equal Care of human Kind;
Strength does to Man's Imperial Race belong,
To yours that Beauty which subdues the Strong.
But as our Strength, when misapply'd, is lost;
And what should save, urges our Ruin most:
Just so, when Beauty prostituted lies,
Of Bawds the Prey, of Rakes th' abandon'd Prize;
Women no more their Empire can maintain,
Nor hope, vile Slaves of Lust, by Love to reign.

Superior Charms but make their Case the worse;
When what was meant their Blessing, proves their Curse.
O Nymph! that might, reclin'd on *Cupid*'s Breast,
Like *Psyche* sooth the God of Love rest:
Or, if Ambition mov'd thee, *Jove* enthral,
Brandish his Thunder, and direct its Fall;
Survey thyself, contemplate ev'ry Grace
Of that sweet Form, of that angelick Face.
Then *Clara* say, were those delicious Charms
Meant for lewd Brothels, and rude Ruffians Arms?
No, *Clara*, no; that Person, and that Mind,
Were form'd by Nature, and by Heav'n design'd
For nobler Ends; to these return, tho' late,
Return to these, and so redress thy Fate.
Think, *Clara*, think, (nor will that Thought be vain)
Thy Slave, thy *Harry*, doom'd to drag his Chain
Of Love, ill-treated and abus'd, that he
From more inglorious Chains might rescue thee;
Thy drooping Health restor'd by his fond Cares,
Once more thy Beauty its full Lustre wears.
Mov'd by his Love, by his Example taught,
Soon shall thy Soul, once more with Virtue fraught,
With kind and generous Truth thy Bosom warm,
And thy fair Mind, like thy fair Person, charm.

To Virtue thus, and to thy self restor'd,
By all admir'd, by one alone ador'd,
Be to thy *Harry* ever kind and true,
And live for him, who more than dy'd for you.

UNI-

UNIVERSAL BUSINESS.

Message the First.

LADY *Dorothy Drum* sends her Compliments
To Sir *Francis*, my Lady, and both the Miss *D—nts*;
Hopes they're all well, and that they have been told,
She's been ill of a violent Fever and Cold,
Or else she would have waited upon them to-day.
Lets 'em know her Assembly is put off till *May*;
But her Fever abating, to-morrow intends
To see them, and about five hundred more Friends.
Let's 'em know, that last *Monday* she heard at three
Lady *C--p--n* last *Sunday* at Six was found out   [Routs,
With a Lord and a Merchant, a Jew, and a Trooper,
A Council, a Player, and poor Mr. *C—p—r*.
Desires my Lady'd remember to send
Those things and the Books which she promis'd to lend,
The Puns and Conundrums—the Shuttle to knot,
My Lord (she knows whose Works) and the Shells for
      the Grott.

Message the Second.

SIR *Francis*, my Lady, and both the Miss *D—nts*,
Sincerely return Lady *Dorothy*'s Compliments;
Are sorry to hear she has been so ill,
And are mightily pleas'd she is not so still.
Will attend her to-morrow and bring her some News,
Of Prudes who accept what they seem to refuse.
Believe there's some Spite in Lady *C—p—n*'s Affair,
And that list'ning and peeping won't make it appear;
Can tell them new Tricks by Lady *I'——* play'd,
And that half ripe Miss *Ed——* is no longer a Maid,

Will remember the Books and the things she desires,
And Wit of the Lord for whom she enquires,
With the Tale of a Man unembarrass'd in Face,
Who swapp'd t'other Day his good Name for a Place.

The Modern FINE GENTLEMAN.

*Quale portentum neque militaris
Daunia latis alit esculetis,
Nec Jubæ tellus generat leonum
Arida nutrix.*

JUST broke from School, pert, impudent, and raw,
Expert in Latin, more expert in Taw,
His Honour posts o'er ITALY and FRANCE,
Measures St. PETER's Dome, and learns to dance.
Thence, having quick thro' various Countries flown,
Glean'd all their Follies, and expos'd his own,
He back returns, a Thing so strange all o'er,
As never Ages past produc'd before,
A Monster of such complicated Worth,
As no one single Clime could e'er bring forth:
Half Atheist, Papist, Gamester, Bubble, Rook,
Half Fiddler, Coachman, Dancer, Groom, and Cook.

Next, because Bus'ness now is all the Vogue,
And who'd be quite polite must be a Rogue,
In Parliament he purchases a Seat,
To make th' accomplish'd Gentleman compleat.
There safe in self-sufficient Impudence,
Without Experience, Honesty, or Sense,
Unknowing in her Int'rest, Trade, or Laws,
He vainly undertakes his Country's Cause:

Forth

Forth from his Lips, prepar'd at all to rail,
Torrents of Nonsense burst like bottled Ale,
Tho' shallow muddy, brisk, tho' mighty dull,
Fierce without Strength, o'erflowing, tho' not full.

Now quite a *Frenchman* in his Garb and Air,
His Neck yok'd down with Bag and Solitaire,
The Liberties of BRITAIN he supports,
And storms at Place-men, Ministers, and Courts;
Now in cropt greasy Hair, and Leather Breeches,
He loudly bellows out his Patriot Speeches:
King, Lords, and Commons ventures to abuse,
Yet dares to shew these Ears, he ought to lose.

From hence to WHITE's our virtuous CATO flies,
There sits with Countenance erect, and wise,
And talks of Games and Whist, and Pig-tail-Pies.
Plays all the Night, nor doubts each Law to break,
Himself unknowingly has help'd to make;
Trembling, and anxious stakes his utmost Groat,
Peeps o'er his Cards, and looks as if he thought;
Next Morn disowns the Losses of the Night,
Because the Fool would fain be thought a Bite.

Devoted thus to Politicks and Cards,
Nor Mirth, nor Wine, nor Women he regards;
So far is ev'ry Virtue from his Heart,
That not a gen'rous Vice can claim a Part;
Nay, lest one human Passion e'er should move
His Soul to Friendship, Tenderness, or Love,
To *Figg* and *Broughton* he commits his Breast,
To steel it to the fashionable Test.

Thus poor in Wealth, he labours to no End,
Wretched alone, in Crowds without a Friend;

Insensible

Infenfible to all that's good, or kind;
Deaf to all Merit, to all Beauty blind;
For Love too bufy, and for Wit too grave,
A harden'd, fober, proud, luxurious Knave,
By little Actions ftriving to be great,
And proud to be, and to be thought a Cheat.

And yet in this fo bad is his Succefs,
That as his Fame improves, his Rents grow lefs;
On Parchment Wings his Acres take their Flight,
And his unpeopled Groves admit the Light;
With his Eftate his Intereft too is done,
His honeft Borough feeks a warmer Sun,
For him, now Cafh and Liquor flow no more,
His independent Voters ceafe to roar:
And *Britain* foon muft want the great Defence
Of all his Honefty and Eloquence.
But that the generous Youth, more anxious grown
For publick Liberty than for his own,
Marries fome jointur'd antiquated Crone:
And boldly, when his Country is at Stake,
Braves the deep-yawning Gulf, like *Curtius*, for its Sake.

Quickly again diftrefs'd for want of Coin,
He digs no longer in th' exhaufted Mine,
But feeks Preferment, as the laft Refort,
Cringes each Morn at Levees, bows at Court,
And, from the Hand he hates, implores Support:
The Minifter, well pleas'd at fmall Expence
To filence fo much rude Impertinence,
With Squeeze and Whifper yields to his Demands,
And on the venal Lift enroll'd he ftands;
A Ribband and a Penfion buy the Slave,
This bribes the Fool about him, that the Knave.

And

And now arriv'd at his meridian Glory,
He sinks apace, despis'd by Whig and Tory;
Of Independence now he talks no more,
Nor shakes the Senate with his Patriot Roar,
But silent votes, and with Court-Trappings hung,
Eyes his own glitt'ring Star, and holds his Tongue.
In Craft political a Bankrupt made,
He sticks to Gaming, as the surer Trade;
Turns downright Sharper, lives by sucking Blood,
And grows, in short, the very Thing he wou'd:
Hunts out young Heirs, who have their Fortunes
   spent,
And lends them ready Cash at *Cent per Cent*;
Lays Wagers on his own, and others Lives,
Fights Uncles, Fathers, Grandmothers, and Wives;
'Till Death at length, indignant to be made
The daily Subject of his Sport and Trade,
Veils with his sable Hand the Wretch's Eyes,
And groaning for the Betts, he loses by't, he dies.

The MODERN FINE LADY. *Or, A Counterpart to a Poem lately published, called,* The Modern fine Gentleman.

Beauties in vain their pretty Eyes may roll,
Charms strike the Sight, but Merit wins the Soul.
                                  POPE.

AT *Hackney*, or at *Chelsea* bred,
   To dance, lisp *French*, and toss the Head,
To romp, coquet, Untruths to tell,
And scribble, tho' she cannot spell,
The Fair, (for that's their gen'ral Name,)
Burns with the Thirst of publick Fame,

With Love of Empire fondly glows;
And aims at captivating Beaus;
On Beauty builds her sole Pretence,
For Beaus are seldom Men of Sense.
For this survey her in the Morning,
With Care and Cost herself adorning,
Learn in the Glass how to behave her,
And spoil the Face that Nature gave her:
Improve in patching, practise Airs,
And in the Hurry miss her Pray'rs;
Then stuft in Chariot roll away,
To hear the Whisper of the Day,
Spread Scandal, or a Lie proclaim,
To blast and wound another's Fame;
Or else perhaps the City haunt,
And cheapen what she does not want:
Refuse to pay her Mercer's Bill,
To save her Honour at Quadrille.

On, Fancy, stretch the fruitful Scene,
And view the Lady in the Spleen,
The Lap-dog sick, or *Betty* lazy,
Or Tea-Cup broke, or Weather hazy;
No Billet from the Count To-day,
Nor Assignation at the Play;
O Time! what Method shall we use
To kill thee, and ourselves amuse?
To compass this, our modern Dame
Will hazard Fortune, Ease, and Fame,
Will stake her Cash, deny Repose,
And dare the Malice of her Foes,
Who fond of Scandal, are prepar'd
To double ev'ry Word they've heard.

Thus sir it with ev'ry Vice in Fashion,
And careless of her Reputation,

Despis'd

Despis'd by Men of Sense, who hate
Alliance with her Self-Conceit;
Enamour'd with the Thirst of Rule,
She weds a fashionable Fool:
Secur'd by Jointure from the Cares
That wait on Family Affairs,
Nor Home, nor Husband, she regards,
But slights 'em both, and sticks to Cards;
As Fortune smiles, or frowns upon her,
She's rich, or forc'd to pawn her Honour,
Ne'er quiet if she is a Gainer,
'Till some more knowing Sharper drain her.

O Woman! born to sooth Mankind,
And ease the Anguish of our Mind,
By Heav'n design'd the Balm of Life,
Who mixt all Comforts in a Wife,
How by thy Folly art thou made
Slave to the Devil, and a Spade!

But Years quick rolling hold their Pace,
And spoil the Beauties of her Face;
Her Beauty flown, what Charm can hide
Her Scorn, her Malice, and her Pride?
'Tis Storm and Tempest, nought can charm her,
Tho' ev'ry Trifle can alarm her;
Her Spouse, who hitherto had been
Slave to her Shape, and Eyes, and Skin,
And with the Glare of Beauty smit,
Had thought that all she said was Wit:
The Fair unmask'd, he chang'd his Song,
And swore that ev'ry Word was wrong:
Hence distant Carriage, sep'rate Coaches,
Cold Complaisance, and warm Reproaches,
Ill-nature, Fretfulness, Debate,
And Silence testify their Hate,

While

While Jealousy improves the Smart,
And aids the Quarrel, till they part.
State most accurs'd! where our Relief
Springs from the Subject of our Grief;
Where Hate and Interest are combin'd,
To break the Union of the Mind.

Now left at large, and void of Shame,
She fearless owns her guilty Flame,
To some young Spendthrift falls a Prey;
Who flatter less for Love, than Pay:
Proud of her Conquest, she repairs,
With Art, the Ruins of her Years;
Intent on Mischief, helps the Want
Of Beauty, with the Use of Paint,
Till old, neglected, and forlorn,
She finds herself the gen'ral Scorn:
Too full of Pride and Spleen for thinking,
As her last Comfort, takes to drinking:
Thus lulls the Vapous as they rise,
And keeps her stupid till she dies.

Unwilling thus the Muse has sung
The Follies of the Fair, and Young;
There still remains a noble Theme,
On which to build immortal Fame:
Still *Britain* boasts a lovely Throng,
To grace the Land, and Poet's Song,
Who 'midst the Conquest of their Eyes,
Attract the Virtuous, and the Wise;
Charm'd by their Conduct and their Wit,
The World applauds, the Brave submit

MARTIAL, Lib. X. Ep. 67.

PYrrhæ *filia*, Nestoris *noverca*,
   Quam vidit Niobe *puella canam*,
Laertes *aviam senex vocavit*,
Nutricem Priamus, *socrum* Thyestes,
Jam cornicibus omnibus superstes,
Hoc tandem sita prurit in sepulcro
Calvo Plotia *cum* Melanthione.

EPITAPH *for* LADY ———.

In Imitation of the above Epigram.

HEre lies, who in her Farthingale and Ruff,
   Her Gown of Taffeta, her Gloves of Buff,
Whoop'd many an Hour, and laugh'd her Belly-full,
O'er *Fletcher*'s Bawdry at the * *Hope* and * *Bull*.
Queen *Bess*'s Maids, grown old in courtly Gears,
Taught her their Quips and Cranks, and Quirks and
      Jeers.
Sister to *Harry Martin* all acknowledge,
Was she not tutor'd in a hopeful College?
Grandame to *Titus Oates*, illustrious Clerk,
Her Cousin-German *Pym*, and *Prynn* her Spark.
Claypool demure her hoyden Rompings knew,
And oft her Busk rapp'd *Falkland*'s Knuckles too.
At length she's under, Nature at a Stand,
Senior to all the Crows in *British* Land;
Yet still her Ashes itch for youthful Deeds,
And long-surviving Passion Power succeeds.

      * *Playhouses.*

EPIGRAM on the K. of Pr——.

ROY, guerrier, phliosophe, auteur, musicien,
 Poete, Franc Maçon, politique, econome;
Pour le bien de l'Europe, ah, que n'est il chretien!
Pour celui de la Reine, helas! que n'est il homme!

English'd.

KING, Hero, Philosopher, Author, Musician,
 Free mason, Oeconomist, Bard, Politician;
If a Christian, how happy would *Europe* have been!
And alas! if a Man, how transported his Queen!

EXTEMPORE left on Mad. DE POMPADOUR's Toilet, by VOLTAIRE, while she was Drawing.

POmpadour, ce crayon divin
 Devroit desiner ton visage,
Jamais une si belle main
 N'auriot fait un plus bel ouvrage.

In English.

THAT Pencil, happy to be thine,
 Should thy own Features, *Pompa*, trace.
Thy Hand, tho' blest with Skill divine,
 Can ne'er produce a fairer Face.

A POEM

A POEM *on his Excellency the Earl of* Chesterfield'*s being about to leave* Ireland.

WOU'D he were gone! what Rout is here!
No Sound but *Stanhope* strikes my Ear!
All Ranks their Gratitude proclaim,
And add their Mite to *Stanhope*'s Fame.
Again they harp, and harp agen on't,
This Novelty—a good Lieutenant!
Make Parallels, and talk of Jobbing,
And Arms, ——, and Robbing;
That *Stanhope* ne'er knew what was little,
Nor e'er came here to rob the Spittle;
Talk of his Savings to the Nation,
And what he'as still in Contemplation;
What Good he'as done, what Good intends us,
And how sincerely he befriends us;
What Schemes, what Projects he has laid,
To raise to Life our Arts, and Trade.
Are these the Feats that make this Pother?
Why, Fools! the Man can do no other;
'Tis Novelty, indeed, to you,
But what Applause to him is due?
'Tis but the Way he ever acted,
A Habit, by meer Use contracted;
He only just prefers the Bent
Of his own Mind to Precedent:
Thus all his Favour to our Nation's
A meer indulging of his Passions.

But I, to publick Good a Stranger,
Like not such Centries in our Manger,
Who'll neither Job, nor suffer Jobbers,
But thinks, and calls 'em downright Robbers;
Yet he must have the Kingdom's Praise,
For Innovations such as these.

O!

O! had the wise *Athenian* Clown
This Idol *Chesterfield* but known,
He ne'er had *Aristides* sent,
But *Stanhope* into Banishment.

An EPILOGUE

On the Birth - Day of his Royal Highness the Duke of Cumberland.

Written by the Farmer, *and spoken by Mr.* Garrick.

'TIS not a Birth to Titles, Pomp, or State,
That forms the Brave, or constitutes the Great;
To be the Son of *George*'s just Renown,
And Brother to the *Heir* of *Britain*'s Crown;
Tho' Proud these Claims, at best, they but adorn,
For Heroes, cannot be, like Princes—— Born;
Valour and Worth must confecrate their Name,
And Virtue give them to the Rolls of Fame.

Hail to the Youth, whose Actions mark this Year,
And in whose Honour you assemble here!
'Tis not to grace his natal Day we meet,
His Birth of Glory, is the Birth we greet.

How quick does his progressive Virtue run!
How swift ascend to his meridian Sun!
Before its Beam, the Northern Storms retire,
And *Britons* catch the animating Fire.

Yet rush not too precipitate, for know,
The Fate you urge, wou'd prove our greatest Foe,

Religion

Religion, Law, and Liberty's at Stake,
Repress your Ardour for your Country's sake;
The Life you prize not, *Britain* may deplore,
And Chance may take what Ages can't restore.

O, did the Gallant *Cumberland* but head
Such Troops, as here our Glorious *William* led!
Bold Names, in *Britain*'s History renown'd,
Who fix'd her Freedom on *Hibernian* Ground,
'Till Death, imbattel'd for their Country stood,
And made the *Boyne* immortal by their Blood.
Such were your Sires, who still survive in Fame;
Such are the Sons who would atchieve the same.

Young *William* then should rival Trophies raise,
And emulate our great *Deliverer*'s Days,
By equal Actions win the like Applause,
Alike their Name, their Glory, and their Cause.

May Heav'n's peculiar Angel shield the Youth,
Who draws the Sword of Liberty and Truth!
By him *Britannia*'s Injuries redress,
And crown his Toil, his Virtue, with Success;
Make him the Scourge of *France*, the Dread of *Rome*,
The Patriot's Blessing, and the Rebel's Doom.

Then seize, *Hibernia*, seize the present Joy,
This Day is sacred to the Martial Boy!—
The Morrow shall a diff'rent Strain require,
When, with thy *Stanhope*, all Delights retire,
And (a long polar Night of Grief begun)
Thy Soul shall sigh for its returning Sun.

I.

The surprising History of a late long Administration, shewing the wonderful Transactions, the wise Negotiations, the prudent Measures, and the great Events of that most astonishing Period.

By Titus Livius, *jun.*

Printed originally in the Size of Tommy Thumb's *Song Books.*

Whereas our trusty and well beloved Truffe Mushroom has at great Labour and Expence compiled the History of our Administration: We have thought proper, at his humble Request, to permit him to print it; and we order that no other Person do presume to pirate the same at their Peril.

Done as one of our greatest Acts, this last Moment of our Administration.

       Granville G——L.
       Bath B——H.

INTRODUCTION.

THere is not any Thing so eagerly read by the Publick, as those shining Periods of History, which are fill'd fill'd up with the important Negotiations and sagacious Conduct of some great Politician. But the Qualities which must conspire to form an Author capable of doing Justice to so grand a Period, are so rarely to be met with, that it will perhaps be esteemed an unpardonable Presumption in a common Writer, to attempt so arduous a Task. Yet invited by the Grandeur of the Subject, and spurr'd on by the Love of Glory, who can forbear to enter on so great a Design? The Work will immortalize the Workman. In Hopes therefore of a glorious Immortality, and inspir'd with the Dignity of the Subject, I sit down to write the ensuing History with all the Candour, Truth and Impartiality that becomes an Historian, entering on the Performance of so elaborate and magnificent a Work.

PART the First.

ON the 10th Day of *February* one thousand seven hundred and forty-five, his Grace the D—— of N——, and the Right Honourable the E—— of H——, resigned the Seals into his M——y's Hands. And

The K—— was pleased to appoint the Right Hon. *John* Earl of G—— to be Principal Secretary of S——e.

And now was to commence such a Revolution in our Political Conduct as was to astonish all *Europe*. The King of *France*, the Queen of *Spain*, the Pope, the Devil, and the Pretender were all to be demolish'd in the Twinkling of an Eye. It was prophesied by the *London Evening Post*, that several *dark Passages* in our modern Annals were to be cleared up; that *certain Trials*, which had been for some Time suspended, were to go on without a *Screen*; and many other great Things were to be accomplished.

complished. In order thereto several Changes were to be brought about; one in particular is told by a tart Historian of the present Times in the following Manner.

A certain Wag, well known by the Name of *Will Waddel*, played a comical unlucky Trick the other Day, with a Companion of his who is lately come from *Carlisle*. *Will* told this Youth, that he could procure him an *admirable* Place in the Family of a certain Great Man of his Acquaintance; and accordingly took the Youth, who had powdered and bedress'd himself in a very smart Manner, to the Gentleman's House. *Will* went in to the Gentleman, and left his Friend without to cool his Heels, as the Phrase is, in the Anti-chamber, having acquainted him that he should soon be call'd in and hired. The *Carlisle* Lad waited a long Time expecting the Return of *Will*, who had slipt down a *Pair of Back Stairs* and departed; at last the House-Maid coming to sweep the Rooms, found this young Man walking backward and forward, and instead of getting his Place, he narrowly escaped being carried before Justice *De Veil*, on suspicion of having a felonious Design on the House.

Many other Changes and Experiments were to have been attempted; but Heaven always tries the Virtues of a Hero by some Disappointments, which baulk his Hopes and baffle all his great Designs; as you will see in the second Part of our important History,

---

PART *the Second.*

ON the fourteenth Day of the same Month of *February*, in the very same Year of our Lord One thousand seven hundred and forty-five, the Right Hon. the E—— of G—— resigned the Seals into his M——'s
Hands,

Hands, which his M——— was pleafed to deliver to his Grace the D—— of N———, and to the Right Honourable the E—— of H———. And thus endeth the fecond and laft Part of this aftonifhing Adminiftration, which lafted forty-eight Hours, three Quarters, feven Minutes and eleven Seconds; which may truly be called the moft wife and moft honeft of all Adminiftrations; the Minifter having, to the Aftonifhment of all Men, never tranfacted one rafh Thing; and what is more marvellous, left as much Money in the T———ry as he found in it. This worthy Hiftory I have faithfully recorded in this Mighty Volume, that it may be read with the valuable Works of our immortal Contryman *Thomas Thumb*, by our Children, Grand Children and Great Grand Children, to the End of the World.

A Letter of Recommendation from Cardinal RICHLIEU.

Mr. *Campoa, Savoyard* and Frier of the holy Order of St. *Bennet*, is to be the Bearer to you of some News from me, by Means of this Letter: He is one of the most discreet, wise, and least vicious Persons that I ever yet knew, amongst all I have convers'd with, and hath earnestly desir'd me to write to you in his Favour, and to give him a Letter for you of Credence in his Behalf and my Recommendation, which to his Merit (I assure you) rather than his Importunity I have granted; for he deserves greatly your Esteem, & I should be sorry you should be backward to oblige him by being mistaken in not knowing him, I should be concern'd if you were as very many others have been already upon that Account, who are of my best Friends. Hence, and for no other Motive, I am desirous to advertise you that you are oblig'd for my sake to take especial Notice of him, to pay him all possible Respect, and to say nothing before him that may offend or displease him in any sort; for I may truly say, he is a worthy Man, and assure you, there can't be a more convincing Argument of an unworthy Person in the world, than to be able to injure him. I am sure that as soon as you cease being a stranger to his virtue, & have any Acquaintance with him, you will love him as well as I, and I shall receive thanks for the advice. The Assurance I have of your Civility hindereth me to write farther of him to you, or to say any more on the Subject.

FINIS.

THE
Foundling Hospital
FOR
W I T.

Intended for the
Reception and Prefervation of fuch Brats of WIT and
HUMOUR whofe Parents chufe to Drop them.

NUMBER IV. to be Continued Occafionally.

CONTAINING,

1. Ode to H—y F-x, on the Marriage of the Duchefs of M——r.
2. Ode to the Author of the Conquer'd Duchefs.
3. Rural Reflections of a *Welch* Poet.
4. W--d--m and P—tn--y; or the Vifion at *Bath*.
5. Tar-Water: A Ballad.
6. The *Highlanders* Flight.
7. The Fire-Side.
8. Ode to *Stephen Poyntz*, Efq;
9. Epilogue to *Tamerlane*.
10. Ode to Sir *C. H. IV*.
11. *Auftria*'s Deliverance.
12. The *Sweet William*.
13. The Appeal of *Morgan*'s Ghoft.
14. Monf. *D'Argenfon*'s Letter, and the Burlefque.

With many Curious Pieces never before printed, and a General Table of Contents to the Whole.

By TIMOTHY SILENCE, *Efq;*

LONDON:
Printed for W. WEBB, near St. *Paul*'s. 1763.
[Price One Shilling.]

Where may be had Number I, II, and III, containing all the Satires, Odes, Ballads, and Epigrams, by the Prime WITS of this Age, fince the Change of the late Earl of O——d's Adminiftration.

The CONTENTS.

AN Ode to H——y F—x, on the Marriage of the Duchess of M————r to H—ff—y, Esq; Page	1
An Ode addressed to the Author of the Conquered Duchess	3
The Rural Reflections of a Welch Poet	5
W—ndh—m and P——lt——y: or the Vision at Bath	8
Tar-Water, a Ballad	12
The Highlanders Flight	14
The Fire-Side: a Pastoral Soliloquy	17
An Ode to Stephen Poyntz, Esq;	19
Epilogue to Tamerlane, on the Suppression of the Rebellion	21
An Ode to Sir C——H——W——s	24
Verses written at Bath; Inscrib'd to A——H——, Esq;	25
A——H——, Esq; his Answer written by himself	26
A Dream	ibid.
Austria's Deliverance	28
Stella's Death, a Pastoral Essay	32
The Sweet William	35
The Appeal of Morgan's Ghost	37
On a certain Methodist Teacher, being caught in Bed with his Maid	46
On passing the Window Tax	47
P————m defended	ibid.
An Epigram on the Life and Character of Cicero	48
A Tarpaulin Opinion upon some new Promotions	ibid.
A Specimen of a Birth-Day Ode	49
One Thousand Seven Hundred and Forty Seven	50
An Epitaph on a Vice-Ad——l lately dead of the Gout	ibid.
Stanzas of Consolation, written in the Sternholdian, or C-bb—n Stile	51
Grace after Meat	52
Ex Martiale. Epigram. 1. Applied to G. and E. C——r	ibid.
An Epigram on the different Behaviour of the Earl of Kilmarnock, and Balmerino, &c.	ibid.
Tyburn's terrible Quarrel with Tower-Hill, about L————d L————t	53
A Copy of Lord Lovat's Letter to the Duke of Cumberland	54
The Duke of C————d's Answer to Lord Lovat's Address	56
A Modern Visit	ibid.
Monf. D'Argenson's Letter	58
The same Versified	60

THE

THE
Foundling Hospital
FOR
WIT.

NUMBER IV.

An ODE *to the Honourable* H—— y F—— x, *on the Marriage of the* Du———s *of* M——r *to* H—s—y, *Esq;*

C*LIO, behold this charming Day,*
   The Zephyrs blow, the Sun looks gay,
   The Sky one perfect Blue;
Can you refuse at such a Time,
When F-x *and I both beg for Rhyme,*
   To sing us something new?

The Goddess smil'd, and thus begun:
   've got a pleasing Theme, my Son,
      I'll sing the conquer'd D———s;
I'll sing of that disdainful Fair,
Who, scap'd from Scotch *and* English *Snare,*
      Is fast in Irish *Clutches.*

B   Sunk

Sunk is her Pow'r, her Sway is o'er,
She'll be no more ador'd, no more
    Shine forth the publick Care:
Oh! what a Falling-off is here,
From her whose Frowns made Wisdom fear,
    Whose Scorn begot Despair!

Wide was th' Extent of her Commands,
O'er fertile Fields, o'er barren Lands
    She stretch'd her haughty Reign:
The Coxcomb, Fool, and Man of Sense,
Youth, Manhood, Age, and Impotence
    With Pride receiv'd her Chain.

Here *L--c--t--r* offer'd brutal Love,
Here gentle *C--b-r-y* gently strove,
    With Sighs to fan Desire;
Here *C--h--l* snor'd his Hours away,
Here drowsy *S--n--pe* every Day
    Sat out her Gr--'s Fire.

Here constant *B--t--n* too we saw
Kneeling with reverential Awe,
    T' adore his high-flown Choice;
Where you, my *F--x*, have sigh'd whole Days,
Forgetting Kings and Peoples Praise,
    Deaf to Ambition's Voice.

What Cloaths you made! how fine you drest!
What *Dresden* China for her Feast!
    But I'll no longer teaze you;
Yet 'tis a Truth you can't deny,
Tho' Lady *C--r--l--e* is nigh,
    And does not look quite easy.

                              But

But careful Heaven defign'd her Grace
For one of the *Milefian* Race,
    On ftronger Parts depending;
Nature indeed denies them Senfe,
But gives them Legs and Impudence,
    That beats all Underftanding.

Which to accomplifh, *H--ff--y* came,
Op'ning before the noble Dame
    His honourable Trenches;
Nor of Rebukes nor Frowns afraid,
He pufh'd his Way (he knew his Trade,)
    And won the Place by Inches.

Look down, St. *Patrick*, with Succefs,
Like *H--f--y*'s all the *Irifh* blefs,
    May they all do as he does;
And ftill preferve their Breed the fame,
Caft in his Mould, made in his Frame,
    To comfort *Englifh* Widows.

An ODE *addreffed to the Author of the* Conquered Duchess. *In Anfwer to that Celebrated Performance.*

WHAT Clamour's here about a Dame,
    Who, for her Pleafure, barters Fame!
    As if 'twere ftrange or new,
That Ladies fhou'd themfelves difgrace,
Or one of the *Milefian* Race
    A Widow fhou'd purfue.

She's better, sure, than S—d—m—e,
Who, while a Duchess, play'd the Wh—re,
    As all the World has heard:
Wiser than Lady H—r—t too,
Whose foolish Match made such a Do,
    And ruin'd her and B—rd.

Yet She is gay as Lady V—ne,
Who, should she lift her am'rous Train,
    Might fairly man a Fleet;
Sprightly as Or—f—d's Countess she,
And as the wanton T—wn—s—d free,
    And more than both, discreet.

For She had Patience first to wed
Before she took the Man to Bed;
    And can you say that's bad?
Like *Diomede*'s, your Arrows rove;
Like him you wound the Queen of Love,
    And may like him run mad.

There was, Sir Knight, there was a Time,
If you invok'd your Muse for Rhyme,
    That all the World stood gazing;
You sung us then of Folks that sold
Themselves and Country too for Gold,
    Or something as amazing.

How S—ds, in Sense, in Person queer,
Jump'd from a Patriot to a Peer,
    No Mortal yet knows why;
How P—t—y truck'd the fairest Fame
For a Right Honourable Name
    To call his Vixen by.

How C——— rose, when W—l-p-le fell,
'Twas you, and only you could tell,
   And all the Scene disclos'd:
How V——ne and R--sh--t, B—th—st, G—w—r,
Were curs'd and stigmatiz'd by Power,
   And rais'd, to be expos'd.

To Heights like these your Muse shou'd fly,
To others leave the middle Sky,
   Whose Wings are weak and flaggy;
Leave these to some young *Foppington*,
Who takes your Leavings, *W—ff—g—ton*,
   And tunes his Odes to *Peggy*.

For you, who know the Sex so well,
Must own that Women most excell
   When ruling, or when rul'd.
While young, they others lead astray;
When old, they every Call obey,
   Still fooling, or befool'd.

Scheme upon Scheme must still succeed,
They every Coxcomb's Tale must heed,
   Until their Brains grow muzzy;
And then by one false Step 'tis seen,
How slight the Difference is between
   The Duchess and the *Hussey*.

The Rural Reflections of a Welch Poet.

STOP, stop, my Steed! hail *Cambria*, hail,
With craggy Clifts and darksome Vale,
   May no rude Steps defile 'em!
Your Poet with a Vengeance sent
From *London* Post, is hither bent
   To find a safe Asylum.   Bar,

Bar, bar the Doors, exclude e'en Fear,
Who prefs'd upon my Horfe's Rear,
    And made the Fleet ftill fleeter;
Here fhall my hurried Soul repofe,
And undifturb'd by IRISH Profe,
    Renew my Lyric Metre.

Thus *Flaccus* at *Philippi*'s Field
Behind him left his little Shield,
    And fculk'd in *Sabine* Cavern:
Had I not wrote that curfed Ode,
My Coward Heart I ne'er had fhew'd
    The Jeft of every Tavern.

Ye Guardians of *Mercurial* Men,
I boaft from you my fprightly Pen,
    I rhyme by your Direction:
Why did you partial Gifts impart?
You gave a Head, but gave no Heart,
    No Heart for Head's Protection.

Hence 'tis my Wit outruns my Strength,
And fcans each Inch of H--s--y's Length,
    His Length of Sword forgetting;
Hence angry Boys my Rhyme provoke
I ne'er (too ferious proves the Joke)
    Can think on't without Sweating.

What the* Lieutenant once deny'd,
My inaufpicious Wit fupply'd,
    And forc'd me into Action;
To me, as to this Scribe indite,
HIBERNIA's Sons —— I cannot write,
    To give them Satisfaction.

    * Lord Lieut. of I------d.

Fool,

Fool, cou'd I sing for others Sport,
The taking of the Duchess' FORT,
    And which the Way to win her;
I, undisturb'd, my Town enjoy'd,
Then (NERO like) with Fire destroy'd,
    By springing Mines within her.

Oh! had I sung sweet Roundelay,
Great *George*'s Birth, or New-year's Day,
    As innocent as *Colly*,
Your other *Pope*, (oh hear, ye Nine!)
He'd gladly all his Odes resign,
    And screen himself in Folly.

Ah! since my Fear has forc'd me hither,
I feel no more that sweet blue Weather
    The Muses most delight in;
Dark and more dark each Cloud impends,
And ev'ry Message from my Friends
    Conveys sad Hints of fighting.

To harmless Themes I'll tune my Reed,
Listen, ye Lambkins, whilst you feed.
    Ye Shepherds, Nymphs, and Fountains;
Ye Bees, with soporiferous Hums,
Ye pendent Goats, if H—ss—y comes,
    Convey me to your Mountains

There may I sing secure, nor Fear
Shall pull the Songster by the Ear,
    T'advise me whilst I am writing:
Or if my Satire will burst forth,
I'll lampoon Parsons in my Wrath,
    Their Cloth forbids them fighting.

Whene'er I think, can W————s brook
To sculk beneath this lonely Nook,
    And tamely bear what few will?
H--r---t like *Priam*'s Son appears,
Cries as he shakes his bloody Ears,
    Beware of *Irish* Duel.

I flutter like *Macbeth!* Arise
Strange Scenes, and swim before my Eyes;
    Swords, Pistols, bloody——shocking!
Whole Crowds of *Irish* cross my View,
I feel th 'involuntary Dew
    Run trickling down my Stocking.

Sure Sign how all's within, I trow:
C--n—l once forc'd such Streams to flow;
    So dreadful he to meet is;
Shou'd gentle C-rnb--y, Lie———r, B—h,
Or drowsy S—h—e wake in Wrath,
    'Twould cause a Diabetes.

Oh *Patrick*, Courage-giving Saint,
Reverse my Pray'r thou late did'st grant,
    Or I'm for ever undone!
Rust all their Pistols, break their Swords,
And if they'll fight it out in Words,
    I'll come again to *London*.

W—NDH—M and P—LT—Y: *or the Vision at* Bath.

An Imitation of that excellent old Song, WILLIAM *and* MARGARET.

B—— vex'd with *Courts*, the *Country* sought,
    To *ease* his *troubled* Mind,
But little *dreamt* the angry P——r
    More *Trouble* there to find.

He strove to lay aside all *Cares*,
    Ev'n those for *Wealth* and *Fame*;
Nor brought a *Spark* of *Malice* down,
    Except against the *Game*.

The live-long *Day* in *Sport* he spent,
    His *Soils* surviv'd the *Light*;
And yet tho' wearied *Home* he came,
    He *slept* not *sound* at *Night*.

O THOUGHT, thou busy, restless, Thing!
    In Peasant and in Peer;
How durst thou *plague* so great a *Man*,
    Who holds his *Peace* so dear?

A Man so great, *three* Nations once
    Did on his *Steps* attend;
Ev'n STATESMEN *trembled* at his *Frown*,
    And K— to him did *bend*.

Yet Him at times thou durst *reproach*,
    Durst *tax* Him with his Deeds;
Thus boldly should a Man presume,
    For his *Offence* he *bleeds*.

To *stir* his *Soul* yet 'scape his *Ire*,
    An Act who would not *boast*?
Knowing no *Mortal* venture might,
    THOUGHT introduc'd a GHOST.

The Night was as *Corruption* dark,
    Like *Justice* Mankind *slept*;
When in his L—d—p's *working Brain*
    This *dreadful Vision* crept.

C

His Mind revolving *paſt Events*,
  His *Conſcience*, *Fancy* caught;
And ſudden to his *aching Sight*
  Great *W——m*'s *Shadow* brought.

With aweful *Grandeur* ſtalk'd the Spright,
  With *Terror* ſhook the *P——*;
When thus the dread *Harangue* began,
  He *hear'd*, or ſeem'd to *hear*.

" O *P——y*, liſten, *W——m* ſpeaks,
  " To *Him* and *Truth* attend;
" Who *living*, ſtill your *Cauſe* eſpous'd,
  " And now in *Death* your *Friend!*

" How *bright* thy *Thought*, thy *Words* how *free*,
  " How *upright* ſeem'd thy *Soul*;
" As if no *Hope* thy *Heart* could *ſeize*,
  " Nor any *Fear* controul!

" Why didſt thou ſeem ſo *wiſe* and *good*,
  " And yet but act a *Part*;
" Why when applauded for that *Skill*,
  " Did this not *touch* thy *Heart?*

" How, once believing Virtue *fair*,
  " Be to her *Cauſe* untrue;
" Or *fancy*, after acting thus,
  " A *Title* was thy *Due?*

" Why *Juſtice* ſeek, why *Fraud* expoſe,
  " If this you did not *mean?*
" Or having both to *Light* reveal'd,
  " Why after turn a Screen?

        " How

" How could you *zealous* seem for *Right*,
　　" While meditating *Wrong*;
" Or how believe an *ill-got Pow'r*
　　" Should e'er continue *long?*

" By *Friends* admir'd, by *Nations* lov'd,
　　" Like Cato's, P——'s Name;
" How could'st Thou slight so *great a Good*,
　　" How *fool away* such *Fame?*

" How *sprightly* St——pe could you *quit*,
　　" Deceive the *great* Arg—ll,
" How cheat the *gen'rous-hearted* P—t,
　　" Sir W—— how *beguile?*

" How *slight* thy *Faith*; how *break* thy *Word*;
　　" Thy *Country* how *undo*;
" Who'd from a Briton this *expect*,
　　" Of Britons *all*, from *you?*

" Ah *foolish Man*, to barter *Fame*
　　" For *Titles* tinsel *Grace!*
" And poorly *sell* thy *own Desert*,
　　" To *dignify* thy *Race*.

" Yet know, that *this* thou *can'st not do*,
　　" 'Tis *Virtue* gives a *Name*;
" For *Titles*, if they're *basely got*,
　　" Are but *entailing Shame.*"

The *Cock* had *crow'd*, the Morning *dawn'd*,
　　And *Clowns* began to *wake*,
Before the *Chief* could from his *View*
　　This *dreadful Vision* shake.

Then up he *started* from his *Bed*,
    And *hurried* back to *Town*;
So his *Return* made as much *Noise*
    As did his *going down*.

But tho' his *Body* chang'd its *Place*,
    Yet as arch *Horace* writes,
His *Mind* was just *still* where it *was*,
    He could not *sleep* a-nights.

He *Bus'ness* hates, forgets his *Post*,
    From *Council* stays away;
And what made *People* stare at C——,
    He miss'd the ——'s *Birth-day*.

Since then He *sullen* is, or *sad*,
    Of *great Affairs* makes *flight*;
Talks much of *being* what he *was*,
    And *setting* all things *right*.

Now ——'preserve our *glorious* K——,
    And send his *Bishops* Grace,
Keeping *all Lords* for evermore
    From —— unhappy Case.

TAR-WATER, a *Ballad*. *Inscribed to the Right Honourable* PHILIP *Earl of* Chesterfield.

SINCE good Master *Prior*,
    The Tar-Water 'Squire,
Without being counted to blame,
Vulgar Patrons has scorn'd,
And his Treatise adorn'd
    With the Lustre of CHESTERFIELD's Name.

                                        Great

Great *Mecænas* of Arts!
And of all Men of Parts,
   (Tho' they're not much the Growth of this Time)
I hope 'twill be meet
To lay at your Feet
   The same lofty Subject in Rhyme.

Then come, let us sing!
Death, a Fig for thy Sting!
   I think we shall serve thee a Trick;
For the Bishop of *Cloyne*
Has at last laid a Mine,
   That will blow up both Thee and Old Nick.

Have but Faith in his Treatise,
Tho' you've Stone, Diabetes,
   Gout, or Fever, Tar-Water's specifick;
If you're costive, 'twill work;
If you purge, 'tis a Cork;
   And, if old, it will make you prolifick.

All ye fair ones, who lie sick,
Leave off Doctors and Physick,
   Tar-Water will cure all your Ails;
Have you Rheums or Defluxions,
Or Whims, or Obstructions,
   It will set right your Heads, and your Tails.

See, each tall slender Maid
Now lifts up her Head,
   Like a beautiful Fir on the Mountain!
White salubrious flow,
* From a Fissure below,
   The Streams of a Turpentine Fountain.

---

* Turpentine, the principal Ingredient in Tar, is thus extracted from the Fir Tree.

Each

Each Nymph from afar
Is so scented with Tar,
 That, unless they're permitted to feel,
All the Devils in Hell
(So alike is the Smell)
 Can't know a ——— from a Cart Wheel.

Great Physician of State!
(Tho' call'd in so late
 To a truly well-meant Consultation)
In this Fever of War,
Like the Spirit of Tar,
 Thy Skill must preserve this poor Nation.

Tho' now quite exhausted,
Her Vitals all wasted,
 She's as meagre, and weak as a Lath;
Yet we hope, that thy Art
Will recover each Part,
 Without the Assistance of *BATH*.

The HIGHLANDERS *FLIGHT*.

A new Grubstreet BALLAD.

Vicit Amor Patriæ.

WHEN an ample Relief
 For *Austria*'s fair Chief
At length was decreed by these Islands;
 We summon'd our Force,
 Dragoons, Foot, and Horse,
And a Regiment fetch'd from the Highlands.

In their own Country Plad
They were cleverly clad,
And seem'd as well furnish'd for War;
That one would have thought,
They'd as fiercely have fought
As a *Croat*, *Pandour*, or *Huſſar*.

Our Troops croſt the Water,
The K—— follow'd after,
But the *Highlanders* would not go over;
For though they all ſwear,
Yet none of them care
To fight for the H—— of H——.

They would not agree
To croſſing the Sea,
And a doubtful Campaign to go thro';
For receiving their Pay,
Their Sixpence a Day,
Was all they thought they muſt do.

They remember'd *A*————
What he did e'erwhile,
And they follow'd that Step of his Grace's;
Who ſeeing from far
That there muſt be a War,
Reſign'd his Command and his Places.

So when Danger was nigh
They determin'd to fly,
And on *England* each Man turn'd his Breech;
And with Joy they run home
To the Place whence they come,
To Beggary, Oatmeal, and Itch.

Do our Regents act right,
Who hinder their Flight,
And to *Scotland* won't let them repair?
They are surely too strict,
For can they inflict
A worse Punishment than to go there?

O yes there is one,
And I wish it was done,
In spight all S---*m*---*le* may say;
Since they won't march or fight,
Disband them outright,
And strip them of Cloaths and of Pay.

We have sometimes been told,
That the *English* of old
Have fled from their Enemies Blows;
But the *Scotch*, for their Glory,
Are the first in all Story
That run without seeing their Foes.

What then would they have done
At the Attack of a Town,
Where the Bullets and Bombs would have hit 'em,
At the first Walls or Ditches,
If they'd had any Breeches,
They certainly would have b———t 'em

G———, stand thy own Friend,
And never depend
On such *Jacobite* R——ls as these are;
They're for another K———all,
And wou'd fly to his Call,
As *Lepidus*' Troops did to *Cæsar*.

[17]

The FIRE-SIDE; *a Pastoral Soliloquy: On the* E—— *of* G———— *taking the* S—ls.

THrice happy, who free from Ambition and Pride,
   In a rural Retreat has a quiet *Fire-Side!*
I love my *Fire-Side*, there I long to repair,
And *drink* a delightful *Oblivion* of Care:
Oh! when shall I 'scape to be truly my own,
From the Noise, and the Smoke, and the Bustle of Town!
Then I live, then I triumph, whene'er I retire
From the Pomp and Parade that the Many admire:
Hail the Woods and the Lawns, shady Vales, sunny Hills,
And the Warble of Birds, and the Murmur of Rills,
Ye Flowr's of all Hues that embroider the Ground,
Flocks feeding, or frisking in Gambols around;
Scene of Joy to behold! Joy, that who would forego,
For the Wealth and the Power a Court can bestow?
I have said it at Home, I have said it Abroad,
That the Town is Man's World, but that this is of God;
Here my Trees cannot flatter, Plants nurs'd by my Care,
Pay with Fruit or with Fragrance, and incense the Air;
Here contemplative Solitude raises the Mind,
(Least alone when alone) to Ideas refin'd.
Methinks hid in Groves, which no Sound can invade,
Save when *Philomel* strikes up her sweet Serenade,
I revolve on the Changes and Changes of Things,
Pitying all who submit to be favour'd by K——s.

  Now I pass with old *Authors* an indolent Hour,
And reading at Ease, turn *Demosthenes* o'er:
Now facetious and vacant, *I nurse* the gay *Flask*
With a Sett of old Friends — *who have nothing to ask*;
Thus happy, I reck not of *France* or of *Spain*,
Nor the *Balance of Power*, what Hand shall sustain.

D   The

The *Balance of Power?* Ha! till that is restor'd,
What solid Delight can Retirement afford?
Some must be content to be Drudges of State,
That the Sage may securely enjoy his Retreat.
In Weather serene, when the Ocean is calm,
It matters not much who presides at the *Helm*;
But soon as Clouds gather and Tempests arise,
Then a *Pilot* there needs; a Man *dauntless and wise*.
If such can be found, sure HE ought to come forth,
And lend to the Publick HIS Talents and Worth.
Whate'er Inclination or Ease may suggest,
If the State wants HIS Aid, HE has no Claim to Rest.
But who is the Man, a bad Game to redeem?——
HE whom *TURIN* admires, who has *PRUSSIA*'s Esteem,
Whom the *Spaniards* have felt; and whose Iron with Dread,
Haughty *LEWIS* saw forging to fall on his Head.
HOLLAND loves HIM, nor less in the NORTH all the Pow'rs
Court, honour, revere; and the EMPRESS adores.
Hark! what was that Sound? for it seem'd more Sublime
Than befits the low Genius of Pastoral Rhyme:
Was it WISDOM I heard? or can *Fumes of the Brain*
Cheat my Ears with a Dream? Ha! repeat me the Strain.
Yes, WISDOM, I hear thee; thou deign'st to declare
ME, ME, the sole ATLAS to prop this *whole Sphere*;
Thy Voice says, or seems in sweet Accents to say,
Haste, and save sinking *Britain*——— resign'd, I obey.
And O! witness ye Powers, that *Ambition* and *Pride*
Have no Share in this Change—*for I love my Fire-Side*.
Thus the SHEPHERD; then throwing his Crook away, steals
Direct *to* St. *JAMES*'s, and *takes up the Seals*.

An ODE *to the Right Honourable* STEPHEN POYNTZ,
Esq; &c. &c. &c.

*Sensere quid Mens rete, quid Indoles
Nutrita faustis sub penetralibus
Posset ———
Doctrina sed vim promovet insitam,
Rectique cultus pectora roborant.*

      HOR. Od. IV. Lib. IV.

WHilst WILLIAM's Deeds and WILLIAM's Praise,
 Each *English* Breast with Transport raise,
  Each *English* Tongue employ;
Say, POYNTZ, if thy elated Heart
Assumes not a superior Part,
  A larger Share of Joy?

But that thy Country's high Affairs
Employ thy Time, demand thy Cares,
  You shou'd renew your Flight;
You only shou'd this Theme pursue———
Who can for WILLIAM feel like You?
  Or who like You can write?

Then to rehearse the Hero's Praise,
To paint this Sunshine of his Days,
  The pleasing Task be mine——
To think on all thy Cares o'erpaid,
To view the Hero you have made,
  That pleasing Part be thine.

Who first should watch, and who call forth
The youthful Prince's various Worth,
  You had the publick Voice;
Wisely his Royal Sire consign'd
To Thee the Culture of his Mind,
  And *England* blest the Choice.

You taught him to be early known
By Martial Deeds of Courage shewn:
  From this near *Mena*'s Flood,
By his victorious Father led,
He flesh'd his maiden Sword, He shed,
  And prov'd th' Illustrious Blood.

Of Virtue's various Charms You taught,
With Happiness and Glory fraught,
  How her unshaken Pow'r
Is independent of Success;
That no Defeat can make it less,
  No Conquest make it more.

This, after *Tournay*'s fatal Day,
'Midst Sorrow, Cares, and dire Dismay,
  Brought calm, and sure Relief;
He scrutiniz'd His noble Heart,
Found Virtue had perform'd her Part,
  And peaceful slept the Chief.

From Thee He early learnt to feel
The Patriot's Warmth for *England*'s Weal;
  (True Valour's noblest Spring)
To vindicate her Church distrest;
To fight for Liberty opprest;
  To perish for his King.

Yet say, if in the fondest Scope
Of Thought, You ever dar'd to hope
  That bounteous Heav'n so soon
Would pay thy Toils, reward thy Care,
Consenting bend to ev'ry Prayer,
  And all thy Wishes crown.

We saw a Wretch, with trait'rous Aid,
Our King's and Church's Rights invade;
    And thine, Fair Liberty!
We saw the Hero fly to War,
Beat down Rebellion, break her Spear,
    And set the Nations free.

Culloden Field, my glorious Theme,
My Rapture, Vision, and my Dream,
    Gilds the young Hero's Days:
Yet can there be one *English* Heart
That does not give thee, POYNTZ, thy Part,
    And own thy Share of Praise?

Nor is thy Fame to thee decreed
For Life's short Date: When WILLIAM's Head,
    For Victories to come,
The frequent Laurel shall receive;
Chaplets for Thee our Sons shall weave,
    And hang 'em on the Tomb.

EPILOGUE to TAMERLANE, *on the Suppression of the* Rebellion. *Spoken by Mrs.* PRITCHARD, *in the Character of the* COMIC MUSE, *Nov.* 4. 1746.

BRITONS, once more in annual Joy we meet
This genial Night in Freedom's fav'rite Seat:
And o'er the * two great Empires still I reign,
Of *Covent-Garden,* and of *Drury-Lane.*
But ah! what Clouds o'er all our Realms impended!
Our Ruin artless Prodigies portended.

    * The Two Great Empires of the World I know,
      This of PERU, and that of MEXICO.   *Indian Emperor.*

                                        Chains,

Chains, real Chains, our Heroes had in View,
And Scenes of mimic Dungeons chang'd to true.
An equal Fate the Stage and *Britain* dreaded,
Had *Rome*'s young Missionary Spark succeeded.
But Laws and Liberties are trifling Treasures;
He threaten'd that grave Property, your Pleasures.

    For Me, an idle Muse, I ne'er dissembled
My Fears; but e'en my Tragic Sister trembled:
O'er all her Sons She cast her mournful Eyes,
And heav'd her Breast more than Dramatic Sighs;
To Eyes well-tutor'd in the Trade of Grief,
She rais'd a small and well-lac'd Handkerchief;
And then with decent Pause—and Accent broke,
Her buskin'd Progeny the Dame bespoke:
" Ah! Sons, † our Dawn is overcast, and all
" Theatric Glories nodding to their Fall;
" From foreign Realms a bloody Chief is come,
" Big with the Work of Slav'ry and of *Rome.*
" A general Ruin on his Sword He wears,
" Fatal alike to Audience and to Play'rs.
" For ah! my Sons, what Freedom for the Stage,
" When Bigotry with Sense shall Battle wage?
" When Monkish Laureats only wear the Bays,
" * Inquisitors Lord Chamberlains of Plays,
" Plays shall be damn'd that scap'd the Critic's Rage,
" For Priests are still worse Tyrants to the Stage.
" *Cato,* receiv'd by Audiences so gracious,
" Shall find ten *Cæsars* in one St. *Ignatius:*
" And godlike *Brutus* here shall meet again
" His Evil Genius in a *Capuchin.*

    † The Dawn is overcast, the Morning lours,
      And heavily in Clouds brings on the Day,
      The great, th' important Day, big with the Fate
      Of Cato and of Rome.   CATO.
    * CIBBER preside Lord Chancellor of Plays.   POPE.
                                              " For

" For Herefy, the Fav'rites of the Pit
" Muft burn, and excommunicated Wit;
" And at one Stake We fhall behold expire
" My *Anna Bullen*, and the *Spanifh Fryar*.

" Ev'n †*Tamerlane*, whofe fainted Name appears
" Red-letter'd in the Calendar of Play'rs,
" Oft as thefe feftal Rites attend the Morn
" Of Liberty reftor'd, and WILLIAM born——
" But at *that* Name, what Tranfports flood my Eyes,
" What golden Vifion's This I fee arife?
" What Youth is He with comlieft Conqueft crown'd,
" His warlike Brow with full-blown Laurels bound?
" What Wreaths are thefe that Vict'ry dares to join,
" And blend with Trophies of my fav'rite *Boyn*?
" Oh! if the Mufe can happy aught prefage,
" Of new Deliv'rance to the State and Stage;
" If not untaught the Characters to fpell
" Of all who bravely fight or conquer well;
" * *Thou* fhalt be WILLIAM——like the laft, defign'd
" The Tyrant's Scourge, and Blefing of Mankind;
" Born, civil Tumult and blind Zeal to quell,
" That teaches happy Subjects to rebel.
" *Naffau* himfelf but half our Vows fhall fhare,
" Divide our Incenfe and divide our Pray'r;
" And oft as *Tamerlane* fhall lend his Fame
" To fhadow *His*, thy rival Star fhall claim
" ‖ Th' ambiguous Laurel and the doubtful Name. }

† TAMERLANE is always acted on the 4th and 5th of *November*, the Anniverfaries of King WILLIAM's Birth and Landing.

* *Tu Marcellus eris.* VIR.

‖ *Conditor Iliados cantabitur atque Maronis*
  Altifoni dubiam facientia Carmina Palmam. JUV.

An ODE to Sir C—— H—— W——s.

DEAR merry Knight, whose sportive Vein
Makes am'rous Duchesses complain,
   While Peers stand titt'ring by:
Now since you've fairly crack'd your Jest,
And *Pegasus* retires to rest,
   Permit me to reply.

And trust me, *Charles*, no real Muse
Such groveling Pertness e'er could use,
   To help a lame Invention:
Virgins are always something shy,
And Language that charms *H—b—y*,
   Their Lips disdain to mention.

But since you've found this easier Road
To furnish out a wanton Ode,
   I'll readily submit:
Where *Drury*'s Dames the Lays inspire,
Smut shall be stil'd Poetic Fire,
   And Bawdry shine for Wit.

Besides these Nymphs are ready still
Your every Pleasure to fulfil,
   And ne'er with Coyness teaze ye:
But thy *Apollo*'s tuneful Train,
Are skittish, fanciful, and vain,
   And oft refuse to ease ye.

Prudent thy Deed then, gentle Knight,
Such squeamish Goddesses to slight,
   Since *N—d—m*'s serve as well:
Their Inspirations raise the Song,
As loud, as lofty, and as long,
   As thy own Odes can tell.

How sweet thy Strains on Master *Prior*,
Of *Dublin* Town, Tar-Water 'Squire,
    When pleas'd thy Verse reveals
Each Female Fissure from below,
Whence fragrant Steams abundant flow,
    Resembling Carmen's Wheels!

Equal thine Odes, courageous Knight,
Where the fair Duchess feels thy Spight;
    For yielding to be bless'd:
How keen thy pointed Satire shines!
While Virtue swells the flowing Lines,
    In native Beauty dress'd.

Hence then, *Apollo*, with your Skill,
Your Nine, your Fountain, and your Hill,
    And learn your future Distance:
Without such Aids our Verses flow,
As *Charles*'s Strains and these may show,
    If N—d—*in* deigns Assistance.

But *Hussey*, frowning, shakes his Cane,
And *Charles* flies trembling o'er the Main,
    At *Berlin* long to tarry:
Oh GEORGE, if Pertness have the Power
To make *him* rise Ambassadour,
    Let *me* be Secretary!

VERSES written at BATH.

Inscrib'd to A—— H——, *Esq*;

AN ancient Sage, in Rules of Wisdom vers'd,
  Justly prescrib'd Self-Knowledge as the first.
But conscious Thou, what Penance it must cost,
To make Acquaintance with a Soul so lost,
Do'st still the salutary Science shun,
Which my officious Zeal, at length, makes known.

Scorn'd

Scorn'd by the Wife, detested by the Good,
Nor understanding aught, nor understood;
Profane, obscene, loud, frivolous, and pert,
Proud without Spirit, vain without Desert;
Affecting Passions, Vice has long subdu'd,
Desperately gay, and impotently lewd;
And when thy weak Companions round Thee sit,
For Eminence in Folly, deem'd a Wit!

A—— H——, *Esq; his Answer written by Himself.*

Whoe'er you are, who with such Warmth upbraid
Poor injur'd Virtue's unavailing Aid,
That preach Reflection to a Wretch undone,
And, whilst you lash my Folly, shew your own;
Know, that I pity your successless Zeal,
Nor form'd by Nature, nor inclin'd to feel;
I see myself; but to what Purpose see?
Deaf to all Truth and Sense, as Sense to me!
Still may you mark my Errors, still reprove,
As impotent in Hate, as I in Love:
I stand but singly, stigmatiz'd by Thee,
But Man himself is satiriz'd in Me;
I laugh at all your Vengeance can impart,
You'd change my Countenance, ere change my Heart;
Nor care I, by what Rules my Deeds you scan,
Alike the Reprobate of God and Man.

A DREAM.

Beneath a Myrtle Shade,
Which Love for none but happy Lovers made,
I calmly slept, and strait *Love* to me brought
PHILLIS, the Object of my waking Thought.
 Undrest she came, my Flames to meet,
 Whilst *Love* strow'd Flow'rs before her Feet,
Flow'rs, which so press'd by her, became more sweet.

From

   From the bright Vision's Head
A careless Veil of Lawn was loosely spread.
From her white Temples fell her shady Hair,
Like cloudy Sun-shine, not too brown or fair.
  Her Hands and Lips did Love inspire,
  Her every Grace my Heart did fire,
But most her Eyes, which languish'd with Desire.

   'O cruel Fair, said I,
' How long will you my Bliss and yours deny?
' By Love, this lonely melancholy Shade
' Was for Revenge of suff'ring Lovers made.
  ' Silence and Shade with Love agree,
  ' Both shelter you and favour me;
' You cannot blush, because I cannot see.

   " No, let me die, she said,
" Rather than lose the spotless Name of Maid."
Faintly methought she spoke, for all the while
She bid me not believe her, with a Smile.
  ' Then die,' said I: she still deny'd.
  " And is it right thus, thus, she cry'd,
" To use an harmless Maid?" and so she dy'd.

   I wak'd, and straight I knew
I lov'd so well, it made my Dream prove true.
Fancy, the kinder Mistress of the two.
Fancy has done what Phillis wou'd not do.
  O charming Nymph! see your Disdain;
  Whilst I can dream, you scorn in vain,
Asleep or waking you must ease my Pain.

AUSTRIA's DELIVERANCE.

To the Author's Friend in the Country.

Whether beneath some spreading Poplar laid,
You sigh to Zephyrs whisp'ring thro' the Shade;
Or wrapt in Thought along some silver Stream,
Indulge thy Love, and mourn the perjur'd Dame;
Shake off th' inglorious Burthen from thy Soul,
Shall Love's Delusions Virtue's Pow'r controul?
Rouze from thy Sloth, and hear the Muse who sings
The Praise of *Britain*, and the best of Kings.

Long had proud *France* beheld with envious Eyes
On *Britain*'s Arms the *Austrian* Eagle rise,
Her Schemes defeated, and her Troops repell'd,
Her Hopes of universal Sway dispell'd;
Yet forc'd to Peace, not daring to oppose
Or rouze the Fury of her pow'rful Foes,
In gloomy Care and Discontent she sate,
Watching to seize some happier Hour of Fate.

At length the wish'd-for Time she thought was come,
To strike the Blow, and finish *Austria*'s Doom:
Now *Charles* by Death was ravish'd from the Throne,
And left *Maria* envy'd, and alone:
Alone *Maria* stood, hemm'd round with Foes!
Bavaria's here, there *Prussia*'s Standard rose;
With these *Hispania*'s haughty Threat'nings join,
And all their Pow'rs, to ruin One combine;
While *France*, who long in treach'rous Silence lay,
Sprung forth to seize, and share th' expected Prey.

As some fierce Lion in the Hunter's Snare
Entangled, bears the complicated War,
Wounding and wounded, struggling to be free,
And more than Death disdaining Slavery:

Now

Now when his Hopes of Life are at an End,
Shou'd some amazing Aid from Heav'n descend,
Dissolve the Charm, and loose his cruel Ties,
With great Revenge upon his Foes he flies;
Tim'rous they run, or stand his Rage in vain,
Torn Limbs and mangled Bodies strew the Plain.

So Heav'n decreed; and mighty *George* arose,
And loos'd *Maria*'s Vengeance on her Foes.
Heaven's chosen Instrument, was *George*'s Arm;
And *Dettingen* beheld, dissolv'd the Charm.

But say, my Muse, what Numbers can display
The Thousand Wonders of that glorious Day?
Explore thy Magazine of Thought, and bring
Some Image worthy of *Britannia*'s King.
Oh set the mighty Hero in my View!
The highest Praise will be to paint him true.

Britannia's peaceful Shore behold him leave,
Resolv'd endanger'd Majesty to save;
Thro' Toils and Perils wing his eager Way,
Tho' few attend, impatient of Delay;
Tho' few attend, their honest Love he knows,
Nor fears to meet a Multitude of Foes.

He leads, and *Britons* follow to the *Mayne*,
Where *Gallia*'s num'rous Squadrons hide the Plain;
Her bravest Sons, and such as Fame must own,
Could yield to GEORGE and *Britain*'s Arms alone.

Ill-fated, perjured *Gallia!* canst thou dare
Again to meet thy Conquerors in War?
Hast thou forgot how *Blenheim*'s sanguine Plain,
Made *Isler*'s Waves roll purple to the Main?
Cannot thy Wounds scarce heal'd, at *Taniers* felt,
Or *Ramillies*, thy fierce Ambition melt?

Or can thy Hero, thy *Noailles* do more
Than poor *Tallard*, or *Villeroy* before?
Shall *Marlborough*'s Name affright the wounded Ear,
Yet GEORGE's Presence fail to make thee fear?
But soon thy rash Presumption thou shalt know,
And learn to tremble at the mighty Foe.

   Hark! the loud Cannons thund'ring from afar,
Begin to speak the Horror of the War;
In deep Array the boasted Strength of *France*,
Troops of bold Youths, in aweful Pomp advance;
Proud of their Numbers, they securely go,
And Thought already prostrate paints the Foe.
Unhappy Men retire ere 'tis too late,
Nor madly tempt the Malice of your Fate.
In vain hereafter shall all *Gallia* mourn,
And wish (alas, too late!) for your Return.

   For now the *Britons* kindling into Rage,
Rush to the Charge, and Lion-like engage.
The dreadful War in all its Fury burns:
Battalions give and meet Repulse by turns;
Each fights, as if to end the glorious Toil
Was his alone, and Worlds the Victor's Spoil.
See the brave Youths pierce thro' the hottest Fire,
And Crowds envelop'd in the Smoke expire.
Guns, Drums, and Trumpets rend the vaulted Skies,
And drown Ten Thousand bleeding Heroes Cries.

   'Twas then, great *Cumberland*, thy gen'rous Breast,
Amongst the fiercest Ranks of Danger prest.
Like the young Eagle's flam'd thy native Fire,
To imitate the Glory of thy Sire;
A Thousand winged Fates around thee fly;
A Thousand bleeding Victims round thee die:
Yet nought could stop the Fury of thy Speed,
Tho' *France* exulted to behold thee bleed.

                                                  You

You bled, great Prince! but yet how calm, how well
You bore your Soul, young *Fenelon* can tell,
When nobly pitying his illustrious Woe,
You in the Hero quite forgot the Foe.
High rag'd the furious Fight, they slay, are slain,
And vast promiscuous Carnage heaps the Plain:
Here *British* Troops victorions scour the Field;
And there to *Gallic* Numbers almost yield.
What Eye beholds the Wreck, and can forbear
To pay the Brave a tributary Tear?
With grief, illustrious *Honeywood*, I see,
The Patriot and the Hero fall'n in thee.
Here bleeding *Clayton* welters on the Ground,
And his brave Soul comes rushing thro' the Wound.
Oh cease, my Muse, such Horrors to pursue,
And chuse some Scene more pleasing to the View!

   Where now is GEORGE? behold the Hero near,
And *Gallia*'s Hopes soon chang'd to black Despair;
O'er all the Scenes of Death revolves his Soul,
And in one Prospect comprehends the Whole:
His Aids where wanted, timely interpose,
And turn the Tide of Battle on his Foes:
Himself amidst the thickest Dangers springs:
(Does Death revere the Majesty of Kings?)
Transported *Britons* view him with Amaze,
And only with redoubled Efforts praise:
Borne down at once by their impetuous Course,
The *Gauls* no longer can withstand their Force:
Broken and scatter'd o'er the Field they fly,
And pierc'd with Wounds behind, ignobly die.

   So some proud Oak, which eminently stood,
And shadow'd all the Plain, (itself a Wood!)
Laughs at the Fury of conflicting Storms.
Which Ocean, Earth and Heav'n itself deforms:
But shou'd the rapid Light'ning from above,
Shot from the flaming Arm of a *any foe*,

Dart

Dart on his Side, unequal to the Stroke,
Torn from the Roots, and all his Vigour broke,
Dying he falls, and o'er the Earth are spread
The hapless Honours of his blasted Head.

From Realm to Realm now flies the Victor's Fame;
And distant Foes grow Cowards at his Name:
The glorious Deed inspires his great Ally;
She springs to War, and all before her fly.
Nor longer now she guards a doubtful Throne;
Her Rivals learn to tremble for their own.

Such Joys great GEORGE's Friendship can bestow,
Then think what Blessings on *Britannia* flow.
So High he makes her Happiness arise,
Conquest and Glory are Her smallest Joys.
From Him Domestick Peace, Wealth, Freedom spring;
And all revere the Father in the King.

STELLA's DEATH.

A Pastoral Essay, writ in the Year 1744. *To a Lady.*

What is our Bliss, that changeth with the Moon;
And Day of Life, that darkens ere 'tis Noon?

PRIOR.

DAPHNE *and* GALATEA.

D. WHY loosely flow those Tresses of Despair?
    Why heaves that Bosom with unusual Care?
Can Love, fond Tyrant, lead the mazy Chace?
Or mourn'st thou dearer Friendship's lost Embrace?
G. The last, good *Daphne* —— yet my Presence leave,
Alone sad *Galatea* asks to grieve,
Unseen, unheard, to give the lab'ring Sigh,
And ope the tearful Sluices of the Eye.

D. And wouldest thou thy Pains from *Daphne* hide?
Shall *Daphne* meanly but thy Joys divide?
No, by the Nights in harmless Mirth we spent,
Whilst in the Folds our fleecy Care weer pent;
By all the soft and tender Things we said,
When late we trod the Thought-inspiring Shade;
By all our Hopes, by all our Loves and Fears,
I cannot, will not quit thee thus in Tears!

G. Too friendly Fair! tho' here 'tis mine to mourn,
'Twere Crime in thee to weep before thy turn;
Go then, nor know for whom I now complain,
Go, lest thy Lambkins call for Help in vain!
Death, cruel Death! his Shafts at random flings—
Alas, the dread Vicissitude of Things!

D. To me more sad thy trembling Accents seem,
Than the dull Murmur of the Wood-land Stream,
Than Winds that whistle thro' th' enchanted Dome,
Than Midnight Dirges round the dreary Tomb.

G. Peace, gentle *Daphne*! ——

D. —— —— —— Oh severe Request!
Can *Daphne* live a Stranger to thy Breast?
Toss'd like the Bark by Sorrow's doubtful Gale,
A World of Tears, a World of Pangs prevail,
The Rock beneath, the Tempest still behind,
Rise to my View, and gather in my Mind.

G. What else but Trouble canst thou hope below?
At best a darkling Labyrinth of Woe.
The Blaze may scorch thee, or the Floods o'erpow'r,
Nay, where thou stand'st may open and devour.

D. Forbid, ye Angels, what her Griefs impart,
And beam th' enliv'ning Rapture o'er her Heart!

G. Does genial Spring it's kindly Influence shed,
And call the slumb'ring Tendril from its Bed?
Gay Nature's Head the blushing Flow'r unfold,
Give the Blue Cast, or tinge it o'er with Gold?
Does the wide Wood a waving Green display,
And all the fair Expansion smile with Day?

F   Do

Do these, dear *Daphne*, bid thee bless thy Hour?
Thou dost but grasp a Vision for a Flow'r.
Death, clad like Winter, spoils the beauteous Scene,
The breathing Tendril, and the waving Green.
D. Dire Chance of Life! ———
G. ——————— Ah! what is Life indeed?
Approach yon aweful Monument, and read.
D. Peace to the Tomb! —— a peaceful Wish, or two,
Is all we can bestow,—— and all that's due.
Whate'er the Ashes——or of Age or Youth,
Whate'er th' Inscription——Flattery or Truth.
G. The Tale is *Stella*'s———
D. ————————— Heaven's! cou'd *Stella* die,
And I nor Balm, nor cooling Draught supply?
Where was I when the asking Glance she threw?
Where, when I shou'd have giv'n the last *Adieu?*
G. What Things were wanting to her Aid we brought,
The Couch we crouded, and the Look we caught;
For her unceasing importun'd the Skies,
And gently clos'd the dear-departing Eyes.
D. Was she not harmless as the harmless Dove?
Belov'd and loving as the Choirs above?
Form'd for Delight by Nature's happiest Care?
As Fair as Graceful, Elegant as Fair?
G. Less wish'd, less welcome was the dawning Day;
Less bright the Lilly in its best Array;
Less chaste the Whiteness of unsully'd Snows;
Less mild the balmy-breathing Breeze that blows.
D. Who cou'd like Her the Social Hour prolong,
Warm with a Smile, or rapture with a Song?
On golden Wings the blisful Moments flew;
Nor Summer's Heat, no Winter's Cold we knew.
G. 'Twas one bright Scene of Sun-shine in the Mind—
Alas, that now the sad Reverse we find!
On ev'ry hand cold sickly Damps invade,
And one dead Horror lengthens ev'ry Shade;

Whilst

Whilst all Despair, the dreary Scenes among,
Thames sorrowing rolls his drowzy Tide along.
D. Wide and more wide, ye Streams, your Woes declare!
G. Old *Ocean*, bear them fast as Waves can bear!
D. Attend and learn, ye Savage, to complain!
G. Bow down, ye Forests, with a Load of Pain!
D. The World before a greater Loss ne'er found.
G. The World before ne'er felt so great a Wound.

CHORUS.

Attend and learn, ye Savage, to complain,
And bow, ye Forests, with a Load of Pain!
The World before a greater Loss ne'er found,
The World before ne'er felt so great a Wound.

R.

The SWEET WILLIAM.

——————*Semper apud nos*
Munera sint Lauri, et suave rubens Hyacinthus ——

THE Pride of *France* is *Lilly* white,
The *Rose* in *June* is *Jacobite*,
The prickly *Thistle* of the *Scot*
Is Northern Knighthood's Badge and Lot;
But, since the DUKE's victorious Blows,
The *Lilly*, *Thistle*, and the *Rose*
All droop and fade, all dye away,
Sweet William only rules the Day—
No Plant with brighter Lustre grows,
Except the Laurel on his Brows.

That ever-living Wreath of Fame,
To spread and keep the HERO's Name.

BRITONS, the tarnish'd *Rose* detest,
And stick *Sweet William* in your Breast;
'Tis *English* Growth, of beauteous Hue,
Cloath'd like his Guards, in Red and Blue,
From *Parent*-root it Strength and Vigour drew.
'Tis full of Spirit, Bloom and Sweet,
Thence represents the DUKE compleat——
The factious *Rose* in Pieces tear,
And this more charming Nosegay wear:
Sweet William is the darling Theme,
'Tis this deserves the World's Esteem ——

A Knight of *Bath* on gaudy Days
The silver'd Star and String displays:
Let this fine *Flow'r* be ever worn,
And *William*'s Two * bright Days adorn:
The one to Life the HERO brought,
The next a glorious Conquest wrought ——

His *natal Day*, the Battle-Eve,
When *William's* Valour all retriev'd,
Shall *June*'s fictitious *Birth-day* sink,
And make both *Rose* and *Lilly* stink———

---

* The 15th of *April* was the Duke's Birth-day, and the 16th the Day of the Victory at *Culloden*.

An Appeal from the late DAVID MORGAN, *Esq; Barrister at Law, to the good People of* England, *against a late scurrilous Paper, intitled,* A faithful Narrative of the Wonderful and Surprising Appearance of Counsellor MORGAN's Ghost, *&c.*

Nos animæ viles inhumata, infletaque turba
Sternamur campis——— ——— VIR.

AFTER the painful and publick Death that I suffered upon *Kennington Common,* I did flatter myself that all Punishment upon Earth was at an End; but it adds to the Torments I now feel, to find my Persecution still carried on, and the little Character I left behind me, as an Author and Man of Parts, vilified and depreciated by a stupid nonsensical Speech printed in my Name, and said to have been delivered by me to my Brethren and Old Companions, the Independent Electors of the City of *Westminster.*

I don't deny in the least that I was at their Meeting, and that I made them a Speech; so far is true; but that I made *that* Speech, is false.

I had not been long in t'other World before I wished myself on Earth again. I asked Leave to return for one Night, which at first was deny'd me; but upon my saying, I only intended to go up to our Monthly Meeting, *Beelzebub* gave me Leave at once, and said, I could not go into better Company, and bid me desire them to return my Visit as soon as possible, for that he expected them all with Impatience.

Now to prevent all Misrepresentations that have been, or shall be made of my Journey, I will here set down every Particular that happen'd to me during my last Stay upon Earth, which I have made Oath of in the most solemn Manner before the Ghost of the late Justice *Hall,* and which my old Friend Alderman *B———r* has promised to get privately printed, and hawked about the Streets.

After I had gathered up my Limbs, and put on my Head, I began my Journey. It was natural for me to have come into the World at the Place I went out of it; but for some private Reasons, I had such an Aversion to the County of *Surrey*, and the Juries thereof, that I bent my Course quite another Way, and made my first Appearance out of *Fleet Ditch*. I did intend to have made my first Visits to the Lord May—r and Sir *John* B———d; but when I reflected on their late Behaviour, and how much I have been deceived in them, and hearing that they had both been to wait upon Prince *William* of *Hanover*, with his Freedom of the City of *London*, I resolved not to let them have the Honour of my appearing in their Houses, nor will I ever set the Ghost of my Foot within their Doors whilst I am a dead Man. My first Visit was therefore paid to that true Patriot Mr. Ald—n B——, to whom I had many Compliments and Services from the late Sir R———G———, Ald—n B———, and Ald——n P———s.

From thence I went to see that learned and worthy Gentleman, who sent the three loyal Lords that Plea which did them no Service. After that, I called upon a good Friend and Countryman of mine, who lately made so great a Figure in the *Middlesex* Grand Jury. As I was going out of his House, I met with the active Mr. C———, who asked me a great many Questions about the Devil, and desired me to tell him, that he was very sorry the Parliament sat so long, that he could not have the Happiness of seeing him at his House in the Country this Summer. His Friend Mr. S———n was with him; but upon hearing me name the Place from whence I came, he ran away with the utmost Precipitation. From thence I went through *Clare-Market* to make a Visit to my old Friend Orator H———y; but in crossing the Market, I was terribly frighten'd at a Face, which I was sure I had seen before, and upon on Recollection, knew him to be one of the Duke of *N*———'s Butchers, who was an Assistant to *Jack Ketch* at my Execution.

I found the Orator at Home, who seemed a little surprized to see me; but when I told him the Name of the Place from whence I was just arrived, he reply'd with a Smile, that he thought Hanging had spoiled People's joking; but at last, by a certain Smell I had about me, and some Secrets which I whisper'd in his Ear, I fully convinced him there was such a Place. Immediately upon this his Countenance alter'd; he turn'd pale, looked full of Horror, fell into an Agony, and dropped down before me. My Time being short, I did not stay to take Care of him, I knew I should soon see him again; either the next Time I came into the World, or when I went Home at Night.

I now resolved to go directly to the Club.—— As I walked along the Streets, I met Mr. *T*———— the Council, Mr. *R*———s the Sollicitor, Mr. *Mackdonald*, Mr. *Macpherson*, Mr. *Macgregor*, Mr. *Mackenzie*, Mr. *Cameron*, Mr. *Erskine*, Mr. *Frasier*, and Mr. *Murray*, all Gentlemen of unshaken Loyalty, and undoubted Affection to the Royal Family. I had not Time for much Conversation with them; so I only told them where I lived, that I was glad to see them, and that I hoped we should all meet together one Time or another.

Being arrived at the *Standard* Tavern, I went directly up into the *Club-Room*. The Confusion I put my Friends into, is inexpressible. Mr. *G*——— ran up the Chimney, and spoiled a new Suit of Cloaths, which his Taylor had trusted him for upon the Strength of his *Continuation of Rapin*. Mr. *J*———s was leaping out of the Window, when I catched him by the Skirt of his Coat and saved him. Upon which I thought his Friend Mr. *C*——— looked a little out of Humour, because it deprived him of his Fee for letting him Blood.

Mr.

Mr. *B———n*, the Grocer, fainted away; but I ran to him, and embraced him, which had the same Effect upon him as burning a Match under his Nose, and he immediately came to himself. Mr. *S———l*, the Woollen-Draper, jumped down all the Stairs at one Leap, ran into the Street without his Hat, and appeared no more among us that Night; but I have since heard that he was so frighten'd as not to know what he did, so he went directly to Sir *T———s D—— V——*, and took the Oaths. Mr. *Wh——d* and Mr. *C——y* were at first under great Astonishment; but upon perceiving that I had neither a Greyhound upon my Breast, nor a Writ in my Hand, they soon recovered themselves, and drank my Health very civilly in a Bumper. They then address'd themselves to the rest of the Company, desiring them to return to their Places, and pointed to Mr. *S———*'s empty Chair for me to sit down in, which I did; and after having drank to them all in a large Glass of Water (which was very acceptable to me) I spoke to them in the following Manner:

Friends, Countrymen, and Fellow Patriots,

IT is with the greatest Truth that I can assure you, that the Passions which govern Men while they are alive, attend them in the Grave; and tho' my being hanged prevents my being any longer an *Independent Elector*, yet I still have the Welfare of this honourable Society as much at Heart, as when I suffered with so much Constancy in it's glorious Cause.——— I suppose I now can be no longer suspected of want of Steddiness to your Interests; for tho' most of you have deserved it, as well as myself, yet I am the only one of this Club who have hitherto met with a just Reward. But don't despair---the Goodness of our Laws, the Justice of the Prince who now sits upon the Throne, and your own Merits, may in Time accomplish it.

The

The ancient and loyal Kingdom of *Scotland* will, I can assure you, ere long, furnish you with another Opportunity of exerting that Zeal, which you lately with such great Difficulty restrained; for tho' it is the Nursery, yet I hope it is not the Grave of Rebellion; and believe me, when I tell you, that at this very Instant Prince *Charles* is much stronger, and has more Followers with Him, than when He first landed in that Kingdom.

Sanguis Martyrum Semen Ecclesiæ, is a known and allowed-of Maxim in the Church; the Blood of Patriots is as strong, and as certain in the State. What may not we then expect from the Battle of *Culloden?* What a strong Party must arise from the Numbers which have since been destroyed all over the Highlands? and what Success may not our Sovereign promise to himself, from the general Devastation the Laws are now making among his Friends in *England?* Upon this Principle, Gentlemen, reflect with what Vigour you ought to go on.—— Are you, Mr. B———n, any longer afraid of the Gallows? Should you, Mr. J———s, be in the least sorry to be hanged—? Would not Mr. G———y rejoice at a Sentence of Death? And would not Mr. F———r, the Apothecary's Head, look down from *Temple-Bar* with Pleasure upon his Friends below? For my own Part, I am free to declare, that it is my stedfast Opinion, that if every Member of this Assembly were to be executed To-morrow, it would be the happiest Day, except that of *Culloden,* that *Great Britain* in general, or the City of *Westminster* in particular, ever saw.

And yet I must own, that when my Dead Warrant came down, I began to repent that I had joined his M——y's Troops so early, and that I did not follow your Advice, Mr. W————d, not to go into 'em till they were actually arrived in this City: but how soon was this Opinion altered, and with what Pleasure did I look Death in the Face, when I reflected how odious my Fate would make the Elector of *Hanover!* because his

meanes

meaneſt penſion'd Flatterers could not deny, but that his hanging me was an Attack upon the Law, which they have hitherto boaſted to have been the conſtant Rule and Meaſure of the Government.

But there is one Thing, Gentlemen, that ſits heavy upon my Mind, and for which you Mr. *J———s*, and you Mr. *W———d*, and you Mr. *C———y*, are in mine and in the Opinion of all our Friends below, very much to blame; you have been careleſs in your Province, and have neglected your ſeveral Duties, you have ſuffer'd our old Allies the Mob to return to their right Senſes. It is owing to you, and to you only, that they love and adore the Houſe of *Hanover*; that they look upon the Elector as the Father of his Country, and his numerous Offspring as their beſt Support. Why do they follow Prince *William* with Eagerneſs and unbeſpoken Acclamations, bleſſing the Ground he treads upon, and purſuing Him with the heartieſt Wiſhes for the Continuance of his Health, Happineſs, and Glory? How came you to let them learn his juſtly-acquired Title of their DELIVERER? And laſtly, what Madneſs poſſeſt you, when you ſuffered them to be convinc'd that their Religion and Liberties might be ſafe in the Hands of a free Parliament and a Proteſtant Prince!

How would you have laught at me formerly, if I had but ſuſpected that the City of *London* would have exerted itſelf in ſo many effectual Ways, as it has done, for the Support of our Enemies? How would Mr. *C———y* have ridiculed me, if I had propheſied that the Pariſh of St. *Martin's in the Fields* would have levied Men at their own Expence, for the Defence of the preſent Government? and what would Mr. *W———d* have ſaid to me, if I had told him St. *Paul's Covent Garden* would have raiſed Soldiers againſt their lawful P———? YET ALL THESE THINGS ARE SO.

Did not you promiſe me, Gentlemen, after the Battle of *Dettingen*, that the Deteſtation of the Name of
an

an *Hanoverian* would be general, and not admit of one Exception? Did not you assure me, that the Electoral Troops should never more be taken into *British* Pay? and notwithstanding all this, did not I live to see this Nation unanimously desiring not only to have them in their Pay, but to have them brought over, even into *England* itself, to put an end to that Struggle for Liberty which every one of you fomented, and I died for?

And now, Gentlemen, having laid before you the dismal Scene of our Affairs, I must tell you, that I am come armed with fresh Matter (false as the Place I am come from) for you to work upon: and unless my Lessons are diligently followed, and practised with Success, this Nation is ruined, and this Assembly no longer of any Effect——But so well laid is my Plan, that if it does not succeed, Lies must have lost their Force, and Scandal is no longer acceptable; Truth must prevail, and the *Hanover* Family be establish'd upon the *British* Throne till Time shall be no more.

Begin then with Prince *William*, (as you did with his Father after his late Victory over the *French*) by affirming that He was not at the Battle of *Culloden*, and that the Success of that Day was solely owing to the *Argyleshire* Men; that Highlanders only can deal with Highlanders; that the young *Hanoverian* was partial to the *Scotch* to the highest Degree; that He made a Treaty with his Ma———'s Garrison of *Carlisle*, by which they were to be considered as Prisoners of War; that he broke it afterwards in the most infamous Manner; swear that you have seen a Copy of that Treaty; insist upon it that the Numbers destroyed at *Culloden* were poor and ignorant, tho' brave Men, that meant no Harm to the Government, lay'd down their Arms upon the first Approach of the *German* Army, and were all murdered in cold Blood. That since, by Orders from above, Prince *William* has massacred every Woman and Child in the Highlands; that he spared none but such as were Subjects of the King of *France*; that he loves Foreigners, that he robs his own Soldiers of their Pay, that he sells all the vacant Commissions, that the Army detests him, and that He himself is a Coward.

On the other Side, Prince C——s's Character wants Support, and must be raised. Labour this Point, trumpet forth his Victories at *Preston-Pans* and *Falkirk*; in short, do for Him all you did for Ad——l V——n; for in his Case you convince the World, by your superior Abilities, that a Hero might be made without the help of Fighting.

But as *Englishmen* have long been frighten'd with the Power, Persecution and Cruelty of the Church of *Rome*, and as his R——— H——— has been suspected (without any Foundation, except his Education) of leaning towards that Religion, it is my Advice that you should confidently declare to the most Sincere, Zealous, and Devout of our High-church Friends (in order to ingratiate Him thoroughly with Them) that he is so far from being a *Roman* Catholick, that He is of no Religion at all.

It has been also insinuated, that the *Stuart* Family always affected Absolute Power, and that it is probable this young P——— would tread in the Steps of his Forefathers. The Answer to this is very short: Defy the most malicious of his Enemies to produce one Instance, before his late landing in *Scotland*, of his having exercised the least Degree of Arbitrary Power, or any other Power whatsoever since he was born. Paint him forth in the mildest Colours; declare that you are certain that he is of a sweet and gentle Disposition; that all the Acts of Barbarity committed by his Troops in *Scotland* or *England* were done without his Knowledge, and against his Consent; but above all, stiffly deny that he ever issued Orders to give no Quarter to the Troops sent against him; and knock any Man down, that presumes to say, that he ever agreed to murder all the *Eng-*
lish

lish Prisoners at *Inverness* the Day before the Battle of *Culloden.*

The next Thing you have to do, is, to point out the Advantages that will accrue to this Kingdom by the S———t Family's being restored to their Rights: And this may be done very briefly, by affirming, that if They were upon the Throne, *France* would immediately grant us a Safe and Honourable Peace; that the grievous Burthen of Taxes would at once be taken off; and that we should be eased of the heavy Load of the National Debt, by a Sponge.

These are the few Hints I had to throw out, which I now leave to your fertile Brains to improve; they are sufficient for this time; and when you have convinced the People of these plain Propositions, you may depend upon seeing me again, laden with fresh Instructions.

But should you fail in these first Attempts, which I think next to impossible, then all we have hitherto done is vain; vain was the *Westminster* Election itself! And Death having remov'd the Mists from before my Eyes, I now see clearly that that noble Struggle did not fully answer the Ends we designed it for; nay, that the Fall of Sir *R. W.* was not altogether so beneficial to the Nation, or to Ourselves, as we expected; and I am certain that Sir *Charles Wager* was as knowing, as brave, and as generous, tho' not so rich a Man as A———l V———n; that L———d S———n lives full as well, and is full as wise, as Mr. E———; and that L—d P———l is a very able and a very honest Man. I hope I shall be excused for mentioning these few Truths in this Company; which I should not have done, but that there are none here but Friends, all of whom (I am sure) would be ashamed to repeat them.

One Word more, and I vanish. ——— Since the late numberless Apostacies in all Degrees and Ranks of Men; since Deserters and Traitors rise up every Day in all Parts of these Kingdoms, so that it is almost impossible

ble to know whom to confide in, I am order'd to acquaint you, that H. M. looks upon the Independent Electors of this City as his ableſt, beſt, and ſureſt Friends; and into your Hands, and your Hands only, he commits the whole Management of his Affairs.—— Where elſe could he place them ſo wiſely? Where elſe could he place them at all?

This great Mark of his M———'s Confidence will, I hope, rouze up your dejected Spirits, inflame your drooping Zeal, revive your former Clamours to diſturb Society, to overturn the preſent Government, to reſtore your lawful K———, and in the End to aſcertain to you all the Rights and Privileges belonging to ſuch freeborn *Englishmen*.

I have now done my Part; I have explained your Duty to you, and thoſe Principles which I acted upon whilſt alive, and which I ſealed with my Blood.—— Go all of you and do likewiſe.

On a certain Methodist-Teacher *being caught in Bed with his Maid.*

' YOU a *Magiſtrate chief; his Wife tauntingly ſaid,
'   You a Methodiſt-Teacher! and caught with your Maid!
' A delicate Text this you've choſen to *handle*,
' And fine *holding-forth*, without Day-light or Candle!
   Quoth *Gabriel*, " My Dear, as I hope for Salvation,
" You make in your Anger a wrong Application;
" This Evening I taugnt *how frail our Condition*;
" And the good Maid and I were but at ——*Repetition.*

* He is Mayor of a certain Corporation.

On passing the Window-Tax.

JOVE said, *Let there be Light* —— and lo
  It instant was; and freely given
To every Creature under Heaven.
Says P————m, ' I'll not have it so;
' Darkness much better suits my Views,
' Let Darkness o'er the Land diffuse.
' Henceforth I WILL that all shall pay,
' For every Light, by Night or Day.'
He said —— and as he had been a God,
The —— Herd obey'd his Nod.

P————M *Defended.*

'TIS said that *Earth*, *Fire*, *Air* and *Water*,
  Compose this Universe of Matter;
And *Light*, Philosophers agree,
In Fire's a Part of Entity.
Then why this great *Complaint* of *P——m*,
Who spares *two Elements?*——Let's tell 'em:

Open your Door, or go without it,
And *Air* is *free*, you cannot doubt it:
Nay, in your Windows there are Cracks,
Where *Air* finds Passage —— *without Tax.*

Pure *Water* of the Brook, or Lake,
Each Passenger may *gratis* take.
'Twas all that *Nature* meant at first;
'Tis all she gives to *quench our Thirst.*
But if 'tis *mix'd* with Malt, or Berry,
Why then *you pay—for being merry.*

The

The Cenfure, therefore, can't be right,
Which blames the Charge on *Earth* and *Light* ;
For, fince the *Elements* are *Four*,
The 'Squire is kind to touch *no more*.

An EPIGRAM *on the* Life *and* Character *of* Cicero, *from Dr.* Middleton, *by* C———— C————, *Efq*; *Servant to His Majefty.*

*T*ULLY and *Colley, Cicero* and *Cibber*;
   Can Names be better match'd, or Verfe run glibber?
Great Cæsar's Servant, emulous of Praife,
Matchlefs in Profe, as matchlefs in his Lays,
Prefents the Publick with his humble Senfe
Of *Cicero*'s immortal Eloquence.
Fye! mix not *Tully*'s Name with fuch a Groom;
Nor ftain the facred Orator of *Rome*.
'Tis Nuts for *Colley*, (fneering Rogue) 'tis Fun,
To lullaby this Brat of *Middleton*:
Born weak and puling, now grown worfe and worfe;
Old Goody *Cibber*'s taken it to Nurfe.

A Tarpaulin-Opinion *upon fome new Promotions.*

*J*ACK reckons up the A————ls we have,
   And wonders what a Plague we mean by *new*?
Why, faith! half thefe might ferve, if half were *Brave*,
But twice as many Cowards are too few.

A Specimen of a BIRTH-DAY ODE.

RECITATIVE.

THE *Prince's natal Day* I foar tó fing,
  Sublimely foar! like *Colly* to the King:
At leaft, I ftrive as much as I am able
To *imitate* his great *Inimitable*.
But fordid Flatt'ry I have none, alack!
Becaufe I have no *Salary*——nor *Sack*.
'Tis *Truth* I fing, fuch Truth as will remain,
Whatever Prince may reign, or hope to reign.

AIR.

When Princes encourage,
  The Arts rife apace:
Then why does not our Age
  Advance into Place?
Alas, for this Reafon!
  No Premium for Wit ——
This cannot be Treafon
  I humbly fubmit.

That Paymafter LEWIS
  Did ne'er want his Lay;
And fure it moft true is,
  Who has it muft pay:
Elfe none will endeavour,
  No *Phœbus* will fhine,
But Odes will be ever
  Like *Cibber's* and mine.

One Thousand Seven Hundred and Forty Seven.

BRITONS, by all good Signs it does appear,
That FORTY SEVEN will be a saving Year:
The C———t begins, with condescending *Grace*,
And saves a World of *Men*, and eke of * Lace.
Pl—m--n, 'tis said, will follow the Example,
And P——— ns without Pl——s be less ample.

For C——— on *saving* does insist,
Thro' *Fleets*, thro' *Armies*, and the C——l L—ft,
Provence invaded, save *Sardinia*'s King;
And ev'ry *British* Muse shall Pæans sing,
If WILLIAM's Plan should happily advance,
And save us from the future Fear of *France*.

* The two Troops of Guards.

An EPITAPH *on a* VICE-A———L *lately dead of the* Gout.

    Hi motus animorum atque hæc certamina tanta
    Pulveris exigui jactu compressa quiescent.   VIR.

PASS o'er this Grave without Concern,
    Here lies Old *Vice* from *Head* to *Stern*;
Averse to strike a Blow in Fight,
Inaction was his chief Delight.
He quiet lies, as off *Toulon*,
Pacifick Son of old *Neptune*.
Death struck his Flag and laid him by,
As Hulks in Docks and Harbours lie,
Unfit for Sea, with *British* Fleet
To second Heroes, fight and beat;
Heroick only in a safe Retreat.

Though

[51]

Though Men of Valour merit Fame,
Less-Stock of Merit has no Claim.
No Wonder such in Battle flinch;
Can gouty Cripples stir an Inch?
Let none lament this *Tar* defunct
But *France*, and *Boccha Chica* Punk.

STANZAS of CONSOLATION, *written in the* Sternholdian, *or* C-bb—n *Stile*; to be said or sung by all whom it may concern.

COME, all ye Men of Pl--e or P--y,
 And eke ye Men of Hope;
Rejoice in this *illustrious* Day,
 The Ex———r soon will ope.
Come ye who v———e to fill the House,
 And ye who v——te therein;
From C———l down to C--*m*--*o*--*e*,
 Where *Duties* run full *thin*,

For why? the Lord of S———a saith,
 Your Wages shall be paid:
He long has try'd your stedfast *Faith*,
 And now expects your Aid.
Then till your Credit sinks anew,
 No *Comfort* need you lack:
The P — r his Tradesmen round may view,
 And C—ll—y drink his Sack:

GRACE

GRACE after MEAT; *Spoken extempore by a neighbouring* Gentleman *at the Table of a* MISER, *who, once in his Life, made a sumptuous Entertainment.*

THANKS for this Miracle; for 'tis no less
    Than to eat Manna in the Wilderness!
Where Hunger reign'd, there we have found Relief,
And seen the Wonders of a Chine of Beef.
Chimnies have smoak'd, that never smoak'd before,
And we have eat, where we shall eat no more.

Ex MARTIALE. *Epigram.* 1.

Applyed to G. *and* E. C———r.

SO like in Manners and in Lives,
    The worst of Husbands, worst of Wives;
It seems surprizing quite to me,
Two so well matcht should not agree.

An EPIGRAM.

On the very different Behaviour of the Earl of Kilmarnock, *and Lord* Balmerino, *and the Accounts of them at their Execution.*

KIlmarnock all Ice, *Balmerino* all Fire,
    Shall I censure the One, or the Other admire?
Both lost i'th' Extremes!—Why in Truth I think neither;
True Virtue is fixt, and inclines not to either:
Then cease your Contentions, 'tis plain on the Whole,
For as One was too Warm, was the Other too Cool.

TYBURN'S

TYBURN's *terrible Quarrel with* Tower-Hill, *about*
L——d L———T.

In Imitation of the Measure of the old Doggrel Ballad.

WHEN Libertine *Simon* was brought to Town,
   Soon after his Clans had met a Rout,
When Liberty rose, and Rebellion fell down,
   They say *Tower-Hill* and *Tyburn* fell ou .
Quoth terrible *Tyburn* to lofty *Tow'r-Hill*,
   Thy long'd-for Days are come at last,
And now thou wilt daily thy Belly fill
   With Lordly Blood, while I must fast.
More Rebel Peers will come to the Bar
   There to be cook'd and serv'd for thee;
Whilst I, that live out of Town so far,
   Must only be fed by Felony.
If Treason be deem'd the foulest Act,
   And dying be a Traitor's Due,
Then why should you all the Glory exact,
   You know he is fitter for me than you.
Then with compos'd and stately Face,
   Tow'r-Hill to *Tyburn* made Reply:
" Brother! be moderate in the Case,
   " Thou'lt have our Friend old Simon, not I.
" E'en take him, Tyburn, he's thy own;
   " Divide his Quarters with thy Knife,
" Who did pollute with Flesh and Bone
   " The Quarters of his Neighbour's Wife.
" He's in the Clan of scurvy Peers,
   " His Title doubted———take him thither;
" But he has been addled so many Years,
   " I fear he'll hardly hang together.
" Then never fear me that I will
   " Deprive thee on the fatal Day,
" 'Tis fit, they who their King would kill,
   " Should hang up on the King's Highway."

Then taunting *Tyburn* fill'd with Scorn,
  Made proud *Tow'r-Hill* this curst Reply,
" *So much rank Blood my Paunch will turn,*
" *Thou better hadst be sick than I.*"
Tow'r-Hill with this began to fret,
  And *Tyburn* look'd quite grim with Spleen,
And as sure as a Club they both had met,
  Had not good *London* step between.

METHUSELAH.

An exact Copy of the Letter wrote by Lord L———T *to his Royal Highness the Duke of* C—————D. *Dated at* Fort-William, June 12, 1746.

SIR,

THIS Letter is most humbly addressed to your Royal Highness, by the very unfortunate SIMON Lord F———R of L———. I durst not presume to sollicit or petition your Royal Highness for any Favour, if it was not well known to the best People in this Country attached to the Government, such as the Lord President, and by those that frequented the Court at that Time, that I did more essential Service to your Royal Family in suppressing the great Rebellion in the Year 1715, with the Hazard of my Life, and the Loss of my only Brother, than any of my Rank in *Scotland*; for which I had three Letters of Thanks from my Royal Master, by the Hands of Earl *Stanhope*, then Secretary of State; in which his Majesty strongly promised to give me such Marks of Favour, as should oblige all the Country to be faithful to him; therefore the gracious King was as good as his Word to me; for as soon as I arrived at Court, and was introduced to the King by the late Duke of *Argyle*, I became, by Degrees, to be as great a Favourite as any *Scotchman* about the Court; and I often carried your Royal Highness in my Arms in the Parks of *Kensington* and *Hampton-Court*, to

hold

hold you up to your Royal Grandfather, that he might embrace you, for he was very fond of you and the young Princesses. Now, Sir, all that I have to say in my present Circumstances, is, that your Royal Highness will be pleased to extend your Goodness towards me, in a generous and compassionate Manner, in my present deplorable Situation; and, if I have the Honour to kiss your Royal Highness's Hand, I would easily demonstrate to you, that I can do more Service to the King and Government, than the destroying an hundred such old, and very infirm Men like me, passed Seventy, (without the least Use of my Hands, Legs, or Knees) can be of Advantage in any Shape to the Government.

Your Royal Father, our present Sovereign, was very kind to me in the Year 1715. I presented on my Knees to his Majesty a Petition in favour of the Laird of *M'Intosh*, to obtain a Protection for him, which he granted me, and gave it to *Charles Cathcart*, then Groom of his Bedchamber, and ordered him to deliver it into my Hands, that I might give it to the Laird of *M'Intosh*. This was but one Testimony of several Marks of Goodness his Majesty was pleased to bestow on me while the King was at *Hanover*; so I hope I shall feel, that the same compassionate Blood runs in your Royal Highness's Veins.

Major-General *Campbell* told me, that he had the Honour to acquaint Your Royal Highness, that he was sending me to *Forto William*, and that he begged of your Royal Highness to order a Litter to be made for me to carry me to *Fort Augustus*, as I am in such a Condition, that I am not able to stand, walk, or ride. I am, with the utmost Submission, and most profound Respect,

Sir,

Your Royal Highness's most obedient,

and most faithful humble Servant,

The D-ke of C————D's most gracious Answer to Lord L————T's Address. By Way of Epigram.

YOU *nurs'd* me, and *buss'd* me, and *hugg'd* me, 'tis true,
　　When I was but a Babe in a Coat;
But now I'm grown *big*, and as *bulky* as You,
　　You would, if you could, cut my *Throat*.
Yet, waving all this, if indeed you'll repent,
　　Tho' you have prov'd such a wicked old *Tartar*,
Let the *Pope*, your good Friend, but make you a *Saint*,
　　I'll promise to make you a *Martyr*.

A Modern VISIT.

A Rap at the Door; when forth from her Chair
　　Flounces Madam, bedizen'd with much Cost and Care.
John, is not that Coach, which stands at the Door,
The Dutchess of *Basto's*?—Nay, it is, I am sure;
Therefore step to her House, (it is scarcely a Mile,)
And say I'm hard-by, and have sent you the while
To know if her Grace is at home, and alone,
And if my Lord *Whistle* to *Ilanders* be gone;
And don't you forget to ask after *Jannet*,
Her favourite Dog—and be back in a Minute.
Then up Stairs she stamps, and bawls out aloud,—
I hope, Sir, your Lady has not got a Croud;
If she has—Oh! my Dear, what, quite all alone?
Why sure ev'ry Mortal is gone out of Town:
I thought I shou'd never have seen you again.
Have you heard of the News that's just come from *Spain?*
They say the Queen's dead;—and 'tis certain the King
Will march back to his Convent;—and that till the Spring
The Camp will not form.—I some way feel very odd—
Do you know for a Truth that our King goes abroad?—
　　　　　　　　　　　　　　　　　　　　　　And

And so Mrs. *Cibber*'s return'd to the Stage!—
I wish the Directors wou'd *Handel* engage.—
I'm quite in a Rapture with sweet *Montichelli:*—
I wonder what's come of poor, dear *Farinelli!*—
He ne'er will return, I very much fear.—
Oh! pray have you ever seen *Garrick* play here?
Pray give me Permission to mend up your Fire.—
Lord! how strangely I look!—But have you heard
    from the 'Squire
Since he went out of Town?—You seem grave, Lady
    Betty—
I think Green and Gold upon Slippers looks pretty;—
Of Damask, or Velvet, which best do you like?—
Oh! my Nephew at last is to carry a Pike.—
I thought last Night's Party wou'd never have ended:
From such stupid Mortals may I be defended!
Did you mind how she look'd when she said she renounc'd,
And how, when the Rubbers was over, she flounc'd?—
I thought my good Lady, as it then was so late,
Might have had the good Manners to have ask'd us to
    eat:—
And her Sister, for Breeding so vastly admir'd;—
But where little is given, there is little requir'd.—
I'm sure those that mind them have but little to do.—
By the way, how goes Matters 'twixt *Bellmour* and you?
I thought long ere this to have given you Joy:—
Now really, my Dear, I think you're too coy.
I'll swear he's the handsomest Man in the World.—
Lord! your Hair, my dear Child, is most frightfully
    curl'd:—
But here comes more People; my Dearest, adieu:
I hope I shall see you, when you have nought else to do.

A Letter from a French *Secretary to a* Dutch *Minister, literally translated in* Prose, *and fairly represented in* Doggrel.

SIR,

THE King has commanded me to write to your Excellency on the Subject of the Situation in which Prince *Edward* and his Party find themselves since the *Advantage* which the Troops of the King of *England* gained over them on the 27th past. All *Europe* knows the Ties of Kindred which subsist between the King and Prince *Edward:* And besides, that young Prince unites in himself all the Qualifications which ought to interest in his Favour those Powers, who esteem and cherish *Valour and Courage*; and the King of *England* is too just and impartial a Judge of *true Merit*, not to respect it, *even when it is found in his Enemy.* The Character also of the *Britannick* Nation cannot but inspire every *Englishman* with Admiration for a *Countryman of theirs,* so distinguished by his Talents and his heroic Virtues.

All these Reasons, Sir, should naturally ensure the Fate of Prince *Edward*; and it may be expected, at the same Time, from the Moderation and Clemency of the King of *England*, that he will not permit the utmost Severity to be exercised on those Persons, (of whatever Condition *or Sex* they be) who, in these Circumstances of Trouble and Confusion, have followed those *Standards* which lately fell before the *English* Arms commanded by the Duke of *Cumberland*.

However, Sir, as in the first Motions of a Revolution, Resentment and Revenge are sometimes carried to such Excess, as in more peaceable Circumstances would not take Place; the King thinks he ought, on this Account, to prevent (as much as in him lies) the dangerous

dangerous Effects of every too severe Resolution which his *Britannick* Majesty may take.

It is with this *so just and so decent View*, that the King has commanded me, Sir, to demand of your Excellency, that you would write to the *English* Ministry, and represent to it, with all possible Force and * *Unction*, the Inconveniencies that will infallibly result from every violent Enterprise against Prince *Edward*.

The *Law of Nations*, and the particular Interest which his Majesty takes in this Prince, are Motives which will *probably* make an Impression on the Court of *London*: And his Majesty hopes he shall find none but *noble and magnaminous* Proceedings from the King of *England* and the *English* Nation: And that *all those who, in this last Instance, have attached themselves to the House of* Stuart, will have nothing to do but to praise the Generosity and Clemency of his *Britannick* Majesty.

But if, contrary to all Hopes, any Attempt be made on the Liberty of Prince *Edward*, or the Lives of his Friends and Partisans, it is easy to foresee what a Spirit of Animosity and Fury may be the fatal Consequence of such Rigour; and how many innocent Persons on each Side may, for the Remainder of this War, *fall the sad Victims of a Violence*, which can only serve to sharpen and irritate the Malady, and assuredly cannot at all *edify Europe*.

Nobody *more properly than you*, Sir, can give their due Weight to all these Reasons: Your Equity and your Love of Peace will suggest to you, on this Occasion, what is best to be said on so interesting a Subject.

Your Excellency will of yourself perceive that there is not a Moment's Time to be lost, in writing to the Ministers of the King of *England*; and I hope you will

---

* The *French* Term *Onction*, has chiefly been used among Divines. A Preacher that moves the Passions strongly, is said (among those Mysticks) to preach with *Unction*. Just as the *Method is* to say a Man preaches or prays with *Power*.

be so kind as to communicate to me the Answer you shall receive on their Part, that I may give an Account thereof to the King, who, in Consequence, will take such Resolutions as his Majesty shall judge proper for his Glory, and the Dignity of his Crown. He sincerely desires that the King of *England* may give him nothing to follow but Examples of *Humanity, Sweetness, and Greatness of Soul.*

     I am, Sir, &c.

           D'A———n.

The same VERSIFIED.

SIR,

BY my Monarch's Command I have ta'en Pen and Ink,
To give you to know what we both of us think
Of the Pickle in which is Prince *Ned, alias Charly,*
Since the Drubbing, Duke *Will* lately gave him so fairly.
All *Europe* well knows of the Kindred and Kindness
That subsist 'twixt our Monarch, and P. *Edward's* Highness:
Besides that the Prince, (Oh! the precious young Elf!)
All those Qualities rare does unite in himself,
Which so wond'rously take with all Princes in our Age,
Who love Courage and Valour, and—*Valour and Courage :*
And K. G. being himself a just Judge, needs must own him
A Prince of *vast Merit, who hopes to dethrone him.*
The Character too of the Nation *Britannic,*
(Now their Spirits are up, and they're out of their Panic)
Is such, that each *Englishman* must set a Value on
This their Countryman *Scot—who was born an Italian.*

These *so natural* Reasons must needs, without doubt,
Secure the Prince *Edward,* and his whole Rabble Rout,
           And

[61]

And the *Clement* K. G. muſt forgive all the Ninnies,
(Not only the *Jockeys*, but alſo the *Jennys*)
Who from *Cumberland*'s Valour did fairly run off, in
Th'Adventure of *Standard with Crown and with Coffin*.
And ſince, after all their Confuſion and Pother,
They have miſs'd of the one, he'll e'en let 'em miſs t'other.

Our Maſter howe'er, (if he can) thinks it proper
To prevent all the dangerous Effects of the Rope here;
'Cauſe he often, *full wiſely*, has made Obſervation,
That in Times when Rebellion's on foot in a Nation,
The Government's much more inclin'd to apply it,
Than when Matters go forward in Peace and in Quiet.

'Tis with this View alone—(Oh! *how juſt and how decent!*)
This Letter, dear Sir, is by Order to thee ſent,
To command thee to write to the Duke of N———,
And ſend him a Copy of this in the Parcel.
And be ſure that you labour and drudge in this Function,
Till you *ſweat* like a Bull—then inform him *with Unction*,
That from Shoulders ſo princely to take off the Head,
    wou'd
Prove a great Inconvenience, be ſure, to P. *Edward*.
K. G. can't but know, that the great *Law of Nations*
Allows of *Rebellions*, if we call 'em *Invaſions*;
And our Monarch's Attachment to the Houſe of the
    Stuarts
Is a Motive *moſt likely* to influence the true Hearts
Of magnanimous *George*, and of each noble *Briton*,
Theſe *Rebels* not to hang or behead, but have Pity on.
Thus, their Pardons obtain'd, they'll have nought—
    that they'll tell ye on,
But his Praiſes, from henceforth—*till another Rebellion:*
But if, contrary to all this well-grounded Aſſurance,
Our peerleſs Prince *Edward* ſhould get in vile Durance;
Or Attempts ſhould be made on the Heads of his Party,
B-l-m-r-no, L-v-t, K-l-m-rn-ck, Cr-n-rty,

It

It then will appear, with what Rage and what Fury
Grand Monarques can hang up Folks *without Judge or*
 Jury.
While Rack, and while Gibbet, while old Rope, and
 new Rope,
A full evil Example shall set to all *Europe.*
For we own, *spite of Popery*, on this sad Occasion,
Persecution tends not unto Edification.

To give proper Force to this *new sort* of Reason,
For pard'ning of Traytors, and praising of Treason,
Your Excellence best can tell how: for no such Man
To do Work like this, as a *frenchify'd Dutchman.*

There's no Time to be lost—make what Haste then
 you can, Sir,
And send me with Speed what they give you for Answer,
That the King may such Measures pursue when he
 knows,
As for the Honour of *France* he shall judge *a-propos.*
He sincerely desires from the King of *Great Britain*
An Example (*and truly he much wants a fit one*)
Of Humanity, Sweetness, and Greatness of Soul,
Good Subjects to cherish, and Traytors controul.

The END *of* NUMBER IV.

Foundling Hospital
FOR
W I T.

Intended for the
Reception and Preservation of such Brats of WIT and HUMOUR, whose Parents chuse to drop them.

NUMBER V. To be continued Occasionally.

CONTAINING,

1. The Litchfield Defeat.
2. The Answer.
3. Ode to *P. Y—ke*, Esq;
4. *Richmond*, a Vision.
5. *Bergen-op-zoom*, a Ballad.
6. *Balaam* and *Palaam*.
7. Green-Room Scuffle.
8. Epistle from *G. Hind*.
9. Hymn for the 9th of *Oct*.
10. Advice to the *French* King's Painter.
11. Lamentations of *Lewis* XV.
12. On the Tax on Coaches.
13. Ode to Sir *C-- H-- IV.--*
14. *Diggon Davy* and *Colin Clout*.
15. An Apology.
16. Downfall of *Westminster* Bridge.
17. Plot and no Plot.
18. *Bœotia*.
19. *Europe* in Masquerade.
20. Speech of King *Harry* the Ninth.

With many other Curious Pieces, some of which never before printed.

By TIMOTHY SILENCE, Esq.

LONDON.
Printed for W. WEBB, near St. Paul's, 1764.
[Price One Shilling.]

Where may be had any of the preceding Numbers.

THE *Litchfield* Defeat	3
The Answer	6
Ode to *P. Y——ke*, Esq.	8
Richmond, a Vision	10
Rape of *Bergen-op-zoom*, a Ballad	13
The Fool against the Ass	16
Green Room Scuffle	19
Epistle from *George Hind*, Clerk of the Parish of M—rd—n in *Dorset*, to the absent Vicar Mr. ——	22
A Hymn for the 9th of *October*, 1746	25
Advice to the French King's Chief Painter	27
The Lamentations of *Lewis* the Beloved	28
The Second Part	29
Upon a Tax on Coaches	ib.
Thought on the late Expedition	31
To the Genius of *Britain*	ib.
An Anatomical Epitaph	32
Part of a Letter from a Gentleman who had lately visited *Norfolk*	33
The Heroism of *Lewis*	53
Europe in Masquerade	36
An Ode to Sir *C--- H--- W---*	37
A Pastoral	38
On Miss *Madan*	41
To Lady *Winchelsea*	ib.
Her Ladyship's Answer	42
New Night Thoughts on Death	43
An Apology	45
Lines spoken by a Sailor	46
Britannia revived	47
A Whimsical Receipt	ib.
In Honour of the first of *March*	48
The Downfall of *Westminster* Bridge	ib.
Plot or no Plot	54
Bœotia	56
King *Harry* the IX. Speech to both Houses of Parliament	61

THE
Foundling Hospital
FOR
WIT.

NUMBER V.

The LITCHFIELD DEFEAT.

GOD prosper long our noble King!
   Our Lives and Safeties all,
A woeful *Horse-Race* late there did
   At *Whittingdon* befal.

Great B————d's Duke, a mighty Prince!
   A solemn Vow did make,
His Pleasure in fair *Staffordshire*,
   Three Summer's Days to take,

At once to grace his Father's Race,
   And to confound his Foes:

But ah! (with Grief my Muse does speak,)
   A luckless Time he chose.

For some rude Clowns, who long had felt
   The Weight of *Tax* and *Levy*,
Explain'd their Case unto his G——ce,
   By Arguments full heavy.

"No G———w'r, they cry'd! no Tool of Power!
   At that the E—l turned pale :———
"No G—w'r, no G—w'r, no Tool of Power!
   Re-echo'd from each Dale.

Then B———d's mighty Breast took fire,
   Who thus enrag'd, did cry,
"To Horse, my *Lords*, my *Knights*, and '*Squires*;
"We'll be reveng'd, or die.

They mounted straight, all Men of Birth,
   Captains of Land and Sea;
No Prince or Potentate on Earth,
   Had such a Troop as he.

Great Lords and Lordships close conjoin'd
   A shining Squadron stood:
But to their Cost, the *Yeoman Host*,
   Did prove the better Blood.

"A G—w'r, a G—w'r! ye sons of Whore,
"Vile Spawn of *Babylon!*
This said, his G———ce did mend his Pace,
   And came full fiercely on.

Three Times he smote a sturdy Foe;
   Who undismay'd reply'd,
"Or be thou *Devil*, or be thou D———ke,
"Thy Courage shall be try'd.

The Charge began; but on one Side
　　Some Slackness there was found;
The smart Cockade in Dust was laid,
　　And trampled on the Ground.

Some felt sore Thwacks upon their Backs,
　　Some, Pains within their Bowels;
All who did joke the R——l Oak,
　　Were well rubb'd with its Towels.

Then Terror seiz'd the plumed Troop,
　　Who turn'd themselves to Flight;
Foul Rout and Fear brought up the Rear:
　　Oh! 'twas a piteous Sight!

Each Warrior urg'd his nimble Steed;
　　But none durst look behind;
Th' insulting Foe, they well did know,
　　Had got them in the Wind;

Who ne'er lost Scent until they came
　　Under the Gallow-Tree:
" Now, said their Foes, we'll not oppose
" Your certain Destiny.

" No farther help of our's ye lack,
" Grant Mercy with your Doom!
" Trust to the Care o' th' three-legg'd Mare;
" She'll bring you *All* safe home.

Then wheel'd about, with this loud Shout,
　　" Confusion to the R——p!
Leaving each Knight to mourn his Plight,
　　Beneath the triple Stump.——

Now

Now Heav'n preserve such Hearts as these
  From secret Treachery!
Who hate a *Knave*, and scorn a Slave,
  May such be ever *Free!*

The ANSWER.

GOD prosper long great GEORGE our King,
  His Friends, both great and small,
Confound all those, that are his Foes;
  A Curse upon them fall.

Great B——D's D——e, a Man of Fame,
  A solemn Vow did make,
That with the *St--ff--d* Rebels he
  A hunting Day would take,

And try to quench rebellious Flame,
  Which then did rage so high,
That in the Face of Church and King,
  They now began to fly.

In borrow'd Dress of Highland Lads,
  Which they that Day put on;
O! had it been Two Years ago,
  They dar'd not so have done.

Since the Pretender he was beat,
  They've lived in Peace and Wealth,
But now quite cloy'd with Luxury,
  Refuse God's saving Health.

A Tool

A Tool of *France*, cry'd they, we'll have,
  To Priests we'll give the Power;
A Romish Pope! a Romish Pope!
  They bellow'd for an Hour.

Then B——D's zealous Breast took Fire,
  And loudly thus did cry,
To Horse! to Horse! from Lord to 'Squire;
  Revenge the Church, or die.

For Church and State none could be found,
  Save those with this brave D——e,
Who gallantly did mount their Steeds,
  And Sword in Hand they took.

No false Pretender, cry'd they, we'll have,
  Nor *Belial*'s Power we'll own;
God prosper long great GEORGE our King,
  Long may he grace the Throne.

Great GEORGE's Name, like Thunder, struck
  Those Rebels to the Heart;
Ah! did not he once set us free,
  Let's gratefully depart.

But *Beelzebub*, through Clyster-Pipe
  Some *Endor*'s Milk did give;
Saying *Children dear, suck Righteous Blood,*
  The Priest can you forgive.

Those Tools of crafty Papist Priest
  In white Cockades and Plads,
Through Doctor P——'s foul Advice
  Have made them Iron Rods;

Which

Which they upon their brawny Backs
    One Day may chance to feel;
For no Pretender's Force can stand
    The Protestant's good Steel.

For they like *Tyler* and *Jack Straw*,
    Will make a fearful End,
Unless that with Proverbial Scourge,
    We give them Grace to mend.

But if that we do Mercy shew,
    When they for Mercy cry,
Like Blood-hounds they will thirst again,
    And drink kind Mercy dry.

Great God, preserve true Protestants
    From Papist Tyranny;
From all *French* Power, if we unite,
    We shall be ever free.

An ODE *to the Honourable* PHILIP Y--KE, *Esq;*
    Imitated from HORACE, *Ode* XVI. *Book* II.

FOR Quiet, Y——KE, the *Sailor* crys,
    When gathering Storms obscure the Skies,
        The Stars no more appearing:
The *Candidate* for Quiet prays,
Sick of the Bumpers and Huzza's
        Of blest Electioneering.

Who thinks that from the Sp—k—r's Chai
The Serjeant's Mace can keep off Care,
        Is wond'rously mistaken.
Alas! he is not half so blest,
As those who've Liberty and Rest,
        And dine on Beans and Bacon.

Why should we then to *London* run,
And quit our chearful Country Sun,
    For Bus'ness, Dirt and Smoke?
Can we, by changing Place and Air,
Ourselves get rid of, or our Care?
    In Troth 'tis all a Joke

Care climbs proud Ships of might'est Force,
And mounts behind the Gen'ral's Horse,
    Outstrips Hussars and Pandours;
Far swifter than the flying Hind,
Swifter than Clouds before the Wind,
    Or C—pe before th' Highlanders.

A Man, when once he's safely chose,
Should laugh at all his threat'ning Foes,
    Nor think of future Evil.
Each Good has its attendant Ill;
A Seat is no bad thing —— but still
    Elections are the Devil.

Its Gifts, with Hand impartial, Heaven
Divides —— To ORFORD it was given,
    To die in full-blown Glory;
To B—th, indeed, a longer Life,
But tho' he lives —'tis with his Wife,
    And shun'd by *Whig* and *Tory*.

The Gods to you with bounteous Hand,
Have granted Seats, and Parks and Land;
    Brocades and Silk you wear;
With Claret and Ragouts you treat;
Six neighing Steeds with nimble Feet,
    Whirl on your gilded Car.

To me they've given a small Retreat,
Good Port, and Mutton (best of Meat)
    With Broad-Cloth on my Shoulders;
A Soul that scorns a dirty Job,
Loves a good Rhyme, and hates a Mob;
    I mean —— that an't Freeholders.

RICHMOND, a VISION.

IN that soft Season, when the blushing Rose
    Cheer'd by the Sun's invigorating Ray,
Begins it's fragrant Beauties to disclose,
    And all things own the genial pow'r of *May:*
When Sleep had lock'd each careless Limb to rest,
    And only Fancy waking, gently strove
To drive each fiercer Passion from my Breast,
    Ambition, Envy, Jealousy and Love;

In thought along *Thames'* winding Shore I stray'd
    Amid the verdant Scenes of silent *Ham:*
Where on the Margin of the Stream was laid
    Beneath a spreading Elm, a mourning Dame.
Before her Feet a Cypress Wreath was thrown,
    Her Hair neglected and dishevell'd hung;
Her Eyes suffus'd with Tears still faintly shone,
    And plaintive Accents trembled on her Tongue.

I saw, I wonder'd, and with Awe drew near,
    When gently raising her dejected Head,
She wav'd her Hand. Approach, my Son, nor fear
    To hear the Story of my Woes, she said.
See'st thou yon lofty Hill's extended Side,
    Whose waving Top o'erlooks the ample Plain?
(Whence, erst more happy, I beheld with Pride
    An hundred Villas grace my wide Domain)
                          There

There long embower'd the Dryad of these Woods,
    I saw my Lawns extend, my Forests rise,
While *Thames* roll'd pleas'd his tributary Floods,
    And Nature strove with Art to please my Eyes.
Here laurell'd Valour found a Place of Rest,
    Here hoary Statesmen sought the peaceful Grove,
Here tender Passions warm'd each youthful Breast,
    And Nuptial Virtue was the Meed of Love.

And shall these Scenes polluted Pleasures hide?
    Shall Rapine here conceal its hated Head?
Shall the proud Gamester here in Triumph ride,
    And the pale Coward boast of Fields he fled?
No more the Soldier feels a gen'rous Heat,
    His Country's Groans no more the Statesman move,
Ev'n Pride can stoop to league with mean Deceit,
    And frighted Virtue flies the Name of Love.

When royal *Richmond* flesh'd from *Bosworth*'s Field
    Had sheath'd the Sword of civil Rage in Peace,
With me he hung his consecrated Shield,
    And hop'd to rest in not inglorious Ease;
Alike in Council as in Arms rever'd,
    Severe in Justice as in Manners plain,
Thro' rough Rebellion's Storms secure he steer'd,
    And growing Arts adorn'd his rising Reign.

When great *Eliza* filled *Britannia*'s Throne,
    And *Spain* with Terror heard her from afar,
She forc'd the boasting Pride of Man to own
    Wisdom and Courage might become the Fair:
Form'd by her Manners, each attendant Maid
    Thought Modesty the Dress of Woman-kind;
To comely Neatness due Observance paid,
    But labour'd only to adorn the Mind.

When frolick *Charles* to *Windsor*'s regal Site
   Transfer'd the Scenes of Luxury and Love,
I envy'd not the Monarch's loose Delight,
   For *Temple* study'd in my sacred Grove.
There, whether *Europe*'s Fate requir'd his Aid,
   Or milder Labours eas'd his civil Care;
Retir'd from Noise he met th' *Athenian* Maid,
   And ev'ry Muse, and ev'ry Grace was there.

But where are all these boasted Glories now?
   Where Arts, where Learning, Modesty and Truth?
See! Spleen and Av'rice mark each Aged Brow,
   See! frontless Impudence the Badge of Youth.
No ****'s Example makes the Subject wise,
   No Laws restrain the Bad, protect the Good;
The num'rous Guilty join to shelter Vice,
   And vaunting Folly pours her whelming Flood.

Thro' Pleasure's Maze the beardless Stripling flies,
   Or sinks supine in useless Indolence;
Too proud to learn, too empty to be wise,
   He screens in Laughter the Defects of Sense.
If haply Beauty deck the Virgin's Face,
   Her wanton forward Mien, her vain Attire,
Defeat the Passion she attempts to raise,
   And check the Transports which her Eyes inspire.

Incens'd, not warn'd by Beauty's frail Decay,
   The waning Matron seeks the Aid of Art;
In aukward Affectation vainly gay,
   Still hopes new Conquests, still would fire the Heart,
Or pale o'er Midnight Lamps, where Discord reigns,
   She sits attentive on the various Game:
While Fraud and Malice shake their galling Chains,
   And rankling Scandal blasts the fairest Fame.

But

But *Jove* no longer bears the guilty Scene,
  The lifted Bolt already fills his Hand;
His Brow 'midſt mingled Terrors ſtill ſerene,
  Determines Vengeance on this fated Land,
She ſaid—loud Thunder ſhook the trembling Ground,
  Swift thro' the murky Air the Light'nings gleam,
Amaz'd I ſtarted at the ſolemn Sound,
  And dread the Fate portended by a Dream.

A BALLAD on the RAPE of BERGEN-OP-ZOOM.

HAN'T you heard of a Fortreſs, renowned in Fame,
Poſſeſs'd by a Lady, *Batavia* by Name,
Who's the Pride of all *Flanders* for Beauty and Bloom,
What Place can compare with ſweet *Bergen-op-Zoom*?

When the * Count firſt drew near, and with Pleaſure beheld
Her lovely fine Towers ſurveying the *Scheld*,
'Twas diverting to ſee how himſelf he did plume,
With the Thoughts of ſubduing ſweet *Bergen-op-Zoom*.

Tho' ſtrong by its Site, as by Nature befriended,
With Rav'lins, and Baſtions, and Curtains defended,
He began his Approaches, yet ſtinted for Room,
In Hopes to be Maſter of *Bergen-op-Zoom*.

In vain he her Out-works did often aſſail,
Tho' always repuls'd, yet he ſcorn'd to turn Tail:
But his Onſets renewing, he ſtill did preſume
By Degrees to prevail o'er ſweet *Bergen-op-Zoom*.

" If

* Lowhendahl.

"If to me, fair *Batavia*, said he, you'll refign,
"All Acts of Hoftility I fhall decline;
"Tho' with Cannon and Mortar prepar'd I am come
"To batter in Breach your lov'd *Bergen-op-Zoom*."

To this fhe replied, "Brifk Soldier, forbear,
"I never will buy a Ceffation fo dear:
"Her Maiden-head * fhe fhall convey to her Tomb;
"No Favour expect then from *Bergen op-Zoom*.

"Tho' fo much renown'd for your Prowefs in War,
"And taking Forts larger than mine is by far,
"Do the worft that you may with your Cannon and Bomb,
"You fhall ne'er have the Keys of my *Bergen-op-Zoom*."

When he found that Perfuafions were ufed in vain,
He try'd if by Art he the Fortrefs could gain:
He faid he'd retire, and fhortly march home,
Nor think more of ftorming her *Bergen-op-Zoom*.

The Lady believ'd him, yet ftill kept her Eyes
Upon all his Motions, for Fear of Surprize:
Thus unactive, a while did his Vitals confume,
Impatient to enter her *Bergen-op-Zoom*.

At length as one Morning the Walls he did fcour,
He fpy'd a fmall Sally-port open before,
When ftrait rufhing forward, he quickly made Room,
And thus got Poffeffion of *Bergen-op-Zoom*.

The Lady furpriz'd, to call-out did begin:
But alas! 'twas too late when the Hero was in,

Who

* This is a Term apply'd to *Bergen* by the *Dutch*, on Account of her never having been taken before, though three Times befieged.

Who ravish'd with Joy, cry'd in rapturous Fume,
O! the lovely!——the charming!——sweet *Bergen-op-Zoom!*

He erected his Standard the Rampart upon,
Yet she had the Courage to pull it thrice down;
And had she persisted, without Beat of Drum,
She might have recover'd her *Bergen-op-Zoom*.

But such was her Fluster in that fatal Hour,
To make more Resistance she had not the Power;
While the Count of a Courtier the Air did assume,
And thus he addres'd her in *Bergen-op-Zoom*.

" Fair Lady, said he, tho' by Art I have gain'd
" What perhaps from your Coyness I ne'er had obtain'd,
" I shall always regard my Success as your Boon,
" And be kind, for your Sake, to your *Bergen-op-Zoom*.

" If you keep but your Promise, Lady *Batty* reply'd,
" To obey your good-Pleasure shall still be my Pride:
" Nor shall I henceforward repent of my Doom,
" But freely surrender my *Bergen-op-Zoom*."

The FOOL *against* the ASS.

Cudgel thy Brains no more about it, for your dull Ass will not amend his Pace by Beating.
          HAMLET.

To the FOOL.

Dear Cousin,

OF all Politicians who have ever appear'd in Print, a certain Four-footed one, who for about six Weeks has exhibited his Weekly Performances, is certainly the most extraordinary.

When I talk of a Four-footed Politician, it may perhaps set your Readers in Amaze, and wonder what kind of an Animal I mean; but their Admiration can't last long, because the Author I refer to has not only placed his own Picture in the Frontispiece of his Paper, but has labour'd hard in his Weekly Lucubrations to convince the World of what they knew long before, *viz.* That he is an *Ass*.

It is not, indeed, the Nature of every Beast of his Species to be so ingenuous: Attempts have been formerly made by some of his Race (stupid as they are by Nature) to impose upon the World under various Pretences; as the *Ass* who put on the *Lion*'s Skin, &c. And indeed our Author, in his Time, has been a little gamesome in this Respect; for if Fame says true, he formerly put on the long Robe, and appear'd at the Bar, and might have pass'd for an excellent Lawyer if he had held his Tongue: He has since aped the Poet, and now puts on the Politician; and if he had never set Pen to Paper, he might have been esteem'd both; but the Misfortune of all *Asses* is, they discover themselves by their Braying.

I would by no Means be thought to despise any Animal on Account of its Species, neither is an *Ass* so contemptible as some may imagine; for though their modern Employment consists chiefly in drawing Sand-Carts, carrying Earthen-ware and Brick-dust, yet Time has been, when they have carried Kings and Prophets on their Backs; and I believe it is recent in some of our Memories, that *Asses* have been in the Service of P—— M———s.

I can't think but there is some Resemblance between the Story of *Balaam* and his Ass, and the Story of *Palaam* and his Ass.—*Balaam* was a Prophet,—*Palaam* a P— M—; but no body ever suspected *Palaam* to be either a Prophet or a Conjurer. ——*Balaam*'s Errand was to curse the People—*Palaam*'s only to rifle them by Taxes, and afterwards to introduce a Banditti of Foreigners to cut their Throats: A very pretty Employment truly! Upon these laudable Expeditions up mount *Balaam* and *Palaam*, on their Asses; and speed them well say some.

Now Balaam *was riding on his Ass, and his two Servants were with him.*—Now *Palaam* was riding on his Ass, and a Minority of common Pensi—ers were with him. —— An Angel stands in the Way for an Adversary against *Balaam*. —— L—nd—n and W—st—m—ster, Guardians of the Liberty of *Britain*, stand in in *Palaam*'s Way for Adversaries against him.—*But* Balaam *was blind, and did not see the Angel.*—*Palaam* both blind and deaf, and will neither see the Friends of Liberty, nor hear the Groans of a distress'd Country. —— *Balaam*'s Ass, at the Sight of the Angel, goes out of the Way.——*Palaam*'s Ass never kept

in any one Way, and therefore was called a Rigler.
―― *Balaam* smites his Ass to turn her into the Way.
――― *Palaam* first tickles and then pricks his Ass.
――― I will promote thee unto very great Honour, I will do whatever thou sayest unto me.

When Balaam's *Ass saw the Angel, she fell down under* Balaam. ―― When *Palaam's* Ass saw the Metropolis of this Kingdom determin'd to assert the Birthrights of *Englishmen*, it chagrin'd him not a little, and down came *Palaam* and his Ass.—*Balaam* is soon enrag'd, and says to his Ass, *Would there was a Sword in my Hand, for now would I kill thee.* —— Says peevish, fretful *Palaam* to his Ass, Would the Liberty of the Press were destroy'd, and that I did not need thee to scribble for me, then would I starve thee. —— Says *Balaam's* Ass to its Master, *Am I not thine Ass, upon which thou hast ridden ever since I was thine unto this Day: was I ever wont to do so unto thee?* ——Says *Palaam's* Ass to its Master, *Am I not thine Ass, thy Pimp, thy Drudge, and thy Tool? Have I not prostituted my Understanding, Conscience, Education and Character to Thee? Was there ever any mean Action, any base Design, in which I ever fail'd thee? Have I not gone through Thick and Thin for thee at the Bar, on the Stage, and in the Press?*

Balaam's Eyes are open'd, and he sees the Angel. —— The Lord open the Eyes of *Palaam*, to see the Iniquity of his Doings, and turn his Heart from destroying his Country!

Balaam returned to his Place, and so must *Palaam* return to his Place. —— But what Place? That Place which is prepared for those that are Enemies to Millions.

What became of *Balaam's* Ass after this Affair, History does not inform us. But what will become of *Palaam's* Ass, if Politicks should fail? Why, if it is capable of nothing higher, it may get its Bread by crying *Great News in the* London *Evening* Post. I am,

Dear Cousin,

Thine eternally,

SLABBER BIB.

The GREEN-ROOM SCUFFLE: Or Drury-Lane in an UPROAR.

To the Tune of *Gossip Joan*.

YE *Peers,* ye *Cits,* and Beaux,
    Who haunt *Pit, Box,* and *Gall'ry,*
Your Persons to expose,
    And shew your *Wit* and *Raill'ry,*
        Little Boys!

Ye *Lads,* that Soldiers are;
    Ye gen'rous *keeping* Cullies;
Who, with lank Face and Shape
    At home set up for Bulllies,
        From *Quib'ron:*

Mourn, mourn your late Disgrace,
    That shut ye from *behind,* Sirs!
For *there* we know's a place,
    Where you much Sport may find, Sirs,
        The *Green-Room.*

ROXANA

ROXANA, on the Stage,
    Wou'd but appear a *Baby*,
Shou'd she with KATE engage;
    Yet she's Nought to a Lady
                        Called PEGGY.

Of late these *Nymphs* fell out,
    And had a dismal Scuffle;
D——gl——s, who loves a Rout,
    Ne'er met with such a Ruffle
                        From the D——

KATE, who was long ill-us'd,
    Depended on her *Merit*,
But PEG, by all abus'd,
    Said, She had only *Spirit*,
                        Pretty Girl!

None knew from whence it rose,
    But 'twas about their *Duty*:
To rise by *Wit* one chose,
    And t'other by her *Beauty*:
                        Both are Vain!

Who can describe the Airs,
    The Green-Room Girls befitting,
The Pride and pleasing Leers
    When they're each other twitting?
                        Artful Nymphs!

Hear the loud Storm ascend!
    Oh! cruel to your Hearing!
Their diff'rent Voices blend,
    And HOTSPUR interfering,
                    Poor B——rr——y!

PEG, in a Taste polite,
    At once began the Battle:
Says she, " You may be right;
    " But this is Tittle-Tattle,
                      Red-Fac'd B—ch!"

Now bristles bonny *Kate*;
    All ready, fierce and fiery,
" Such BRIMS (cries she) I hate——
    " Cou'd DAVEY e'er admire Ye?—
                      PROSTITUTE!

" My Beauty me defends,
    Cries *lovely pretty* PEGGY;
Whilst you abuse your Friends;
    And so — no more — I beg you ——
                      HELL'S DUCHESS!

Up starts a *grey-hair'd Sage* ——
    Says *Kate*— " 'tis most provoking!
" Why should you rule the STAGE?
    Mind *Building, Pimping, Joaking,*
                      Old STAGE-GOAT!

From this, sad Work ensued:
    Old LIMPO got a Slap, Sir:
Which he return'd; quite rude!
    And fell'd an *harmless Chap*, Sir,
                      Sad JEMMEE!

" My Child shant be abus'd,"
    Says limping am'rous S——y;
" Though POLLY me refus'd——
    Shou'd you,—The Devil's in ye,
                      Saucy *Peg*!

                      Oh

Oh L—cy! then beware
    How you such *Belles* do trust to;
For, tho' they speak you fair,
    They treat you as a Busto,

                      Players All!

An EPISTLE from George Hind, *Clerk of the Parish of* M——rd——n *in* Dorset, *to the absent Vicar Mr.*———

Measter, an't please you, I do zend
    These Letter to you as a Friend;
Hoping you'll pardon the Inditing,
Becaz I am not uz'd to writing;
And that you will not take unkind,
A Word or zo, from poor *George Hind*.
For I am always in the Way,
And needs must hear what People zay;
First of the House they make a Joke,
And zwear the Chimnies never smoke.
Now the Occasion of these Jests,
As I do think, were Zwallows Nests;
Which chanc'd but t'other Day to val
Into the Parlour, Zut and aal.
Bezide the People not a few,
Begin to grumble much at you,
For leaving of them in the Lurch,
And letting Ztrangers serve the Church,
Who are in heast to go agen,
Zo we han't zung the Lord knows when.
And for their Preaching (I do know
As well as most) 'tis but zo, zo.
Zure if the Call you had were right,
You'd not vorsake our Neighbours quite:

                        But

But I do vear you've zet your aim on
Nought in the World but vilthy Mammon.
The People, when the Church is o'er,
Do goo a Straggling o'er the Moor,
A Zundays there is zuch a Hooting!
And the young 'Squires do goo a zhuting.
If I had never learn'd a Letter,
I think that I could tell 'em better.
But it don't matter when I talk
To them, or any other Volk:
Of all I zay they take no heed,
Meafter, 'twou'd grieve you if you zee'd.
The Boys are come to zuch a Pafs,
They've broken ev'ry Pane of Glafs.
If you do go the Orchard round,
There's not a Quodling to be found.
I think there's not a Soul that's living
Minds the Commandment againft thieving.
Before they're ripe, the Walnut-tree
Has not a Walnut you can zee.
Now thefe the Boys cou'd never get,
Becaz they have no Kernels yet;
Zome fay, that in a zartain Place,
They've pickled them to put in Zauce;
I'm fure to zave them I was willing,
Zome Years they've yielded vorty Shilling;
I'm zorry I'm to write a Letter,
Zo full of News that is no better;
But 'twou'd difpleafe you to conceal
Whatever happens, good or ill.

Zo I will tell you one thing more,
Which when I zee'd did grieve me fore.
The Pars'nage Houfe, that look'd fo tight,
Upon the Roof is naked quite:

The

The Wind has ſtript the Thatch away,
Zo it rains in both Night and Day.
Theſe Things unto my Mind did bring,
The Zong of *Deb'rah* which we zing,
Againſt a Man (as we read there)
" *The Stars did in their Courſes war:*
But God forbid that zuch Diſaſter
Shou'd e'er befal my Rev'rend Meaſter.
Zo hoping that I han't been rude,
I think 'tis time for to conclude,
Deſiring you will ſtill be kind
To M————rd————n, your Friend *George* H————d.

 P. S. This at the Ale-houſe in our Town,
On Zunday Night I did write down:
And Mrs. *M—rt—m—r* do join
Her humble Zervice, Zir, to mine,
Wiſhing, if it ſo pleaſe the Lord,
That you to us may be reſtor'd.
I for my part wou'd quit the Place,
To have you come again in Peace:
And if the Buſhop wou'd conſent
When I from *M————rd————n* Clerkſhip went,
At * *M————dd—ngt—n* to make me Curate,
I'd do the Duty————juſt at your Rate,
Nor aſk you more than half the Price,
Which wou'd another Man ſuffice———
Bezide that I could teach the Ringers,
And be a Meaſter to the Zingers;
So you'll conſider my Requeſt,
And God direct you for the Beſt.

* A Town in *Wilts* where the Vicar reſided.

A

A HYMN *for the* 9th *of* October 1746, *being the Thanksgiving Day for the Victory over the Rebels at* Culloden.

COME, *Britons*, in triumphant Songs
    Your thankful Voices raise,
Come, sound with thrice Ten-thousand Tongues,
    Your great Deliv'rer's Praise

'Twas not our Gen'rals, or their Might,
    Our Strength or Skill in Arms,
'Twas God that put our Foes to flight,
    And hush'd our dread Alarms.

Victorious do we sheath the Sword,
    And sing beneath our Vine?
Thine is the gen'rous Vintage, Lord,
    The glorious Conquest thine.

Tho' *Rome* and *France*, of bloody Fame,
    Were ready to devour,
Thine Arm their sanguine Hopes o'ercame,
    And bury'd in an Hour.

In vain they new Rebellions try,
    To fix the slavish Chain;
The Sons of Murder faint and die,
    And thirst for Blood in vain.

O let our Isle now rest secure
    Beneath thy shelt'ring Hand,
Our lov'd Tranquillity restore,
    And guard the peaceful Land.

Let civil Feuds from *British* Ground
    Henceforth be banished far,
Nor one rebellious Breath be found
    To wake the Trump of War.

So vain *Pretenders* shall repine,
    And still be forc'd to own
That Heav'n itself, with Arms divine,
    Protects the *British* Throne.

Avis à Monsieur de *** *Premier Peintre de sa Majesté tres Chrétienne, pour representer dans son vrai jour Gloire du Roi son Maitre, & le bonheur de ses Sujets & de ses Alliés.*

PEINTRE, pour bien tracer la gloire de la *France*,
Montre moi d'un grand Roi seulement l'apparence;
Fais le voir entouré d'orgueil de trahison;
Regnant comme un tiran, rongé par l'ambition;
Montrez-y des traitez, la bonne foi trahie,
Le crime soutenu, la justice bannie;
Fais le environné d'un peuple malheureux;
Des esclaves rampants, qui se croyent heureux,
Des hommes nez sans coeurs, des gens foibles & laches,
Qui cherissent le lien, qui au joug les atache;
Fais voir dessous ses loix, son pays abatu,
Son commerce ruiné, son negoce perdu;
A ses vastes projets, éleve un *Mausolee*,
Et represente en pleurs l'*Europe* desolée;
Pour finir, fais y voir se fiant trop a lui,
Le *Genois*, l'*Espagnol*, le *Bavarois* detruit;
Mais arrête--il te faut, pour embellir l'ouvrage,
Le parsemér de feu, du sang & du carnage;
Et ecrire en grand mots, a la gloire des lys,
Ces sont ici les faits du monarque *Louis*.

A. G. FOURNIER *de Pezenas*.

ADVICE

ADVICE to the FRENCH KING's *Chief* PAINTER, *how to represent in its true light, the Glory of his Master, and the Happiness of his Subjects and his Allies.*

PAINTER, display in honour of the State,
  A Monarch only in Appearance great:
Swoln with Ambition, let the Tyrant stand,
With Pride and Treach'ry plac'd on either Hand:
In scraps let broken Treaties strew the Ground,
Here Vice exulting, and there Justice bound:
Fill his throng'd Levee with a wretched Croud,
Mean sneaking Slaves, of fancied Blessings proud,
A dull, tame Race, whom nothing can provoke,
Fond of the Chains that bind them to the Yoke.
Stript by his Laws, present the Country bare,
And ruin'd Commerce sinking in Despair.
By his vast Projects a *Mausoleum* raise,
On *Europe*'s Ruins to record his Praise.
And last—Examples of too easy trust,
Paint *Genoa, Spain, Bavaria,* in the Dust.
Yet hold.—The Work demands one Height'ning more;
Let all with Fire and Blood be sprinkled o'er;
And write beneath, in Gold, distinct and plain,
These are the Symbols, LEWIS, of thy Reign.

The LAMENTATIONS of LEWIS the Beloved, his People, for the Loss of his Ships.

By a Young GENTLEMAN of the NAVY.

MARS, O God of War, why hast thou turned thy Back upon us, and why fightest thou for our Enemies?

How is my *Glory* fallen! my *Diamonds* and my *Rubies* are no more!

Instead of being *August*, how I am Crest-fallen!

Where is now my *Invincible*?

Thou, *Panther*, hast been worried by the *British* Mastiffs?

Thou, O *Ambuscade*, hast been taken in a Snare!

The *Serieux* is now serious enough, but 'tis otherwise * with my Enemies.

The *Subtile* is subtile in vain!

And the *Vigilant* shall be watchful against me!

What can I do without thee, O *Mercury*? my Sore runneth and is incurable!

O *Jason!* *Britain* has thy Golden Fleece!

L'Etoil, my *Morning Star* is vanished in a Blaze! [Burnt.]

Medea the *Sorceress* has forsaken me, the *Solebay* is returned to her own Home, for which my Heart mourns in secret, and *L'Ardent* fires me with Rage.

* The Name is changed by the Lords of the Admiralty.

The SECOND PART.

In a Complaint *to Monsieur* Maurepas.

O My Renown! [*Le Renommé*] *Maurepas*, is fled, and I fear is come upon me.

O *Terrible!* my Governor *Conflans* is in the Hands of mine Enemies!

The *Severn* is returned to its ancient Course.

Neptune is gone over to the Hereticks!

George has Possession of the *Trident*, and commands the Ocean!

The Rascals pay no more Respect to the † *Fierce* grand *Monarque*, than they did to the Boy *Charles*, whom they sent packing out of *Scotland*.

|| *Le Castor* has a Malevolent Influence upon my Maritime Affairs, and *I am stung to the Heart by the* Hornet ‡.

Upon the TAX *on* COACHES, &c.

BEfore *Bohemian Anne* * was Queen,
Astride their Steeds were Ladies seen;
And good Queen *Bess* to *Paul*'s, I wot,
Full oft aside has jogg'd on Trot:
Beaus then could foot it thro' all Weather,
And nothing fear'd but wear of Leather.

† *Le Fougueux.* || The Name of a Star. ‡ Retaken.

* Consort to King *Richard* II. who first taught the use of a Side Saddle to our *English* Ladies.

But now (so Luxury decrees)
The polish'd Age rolls on at ease:
Coach, Chariot, Chaise, Berlin, Landau,
(Machines the Ancients never saw)
Indulge our gentle Sons of War,
Who ne'er will mount Triumphant Car.
The Carriage marks the Peer's Degree,
And almost tells the Doctor's Fee;
Bears ev'ry thriving Child of Art :——
Ev'n Thieves to *Tyburn* claim a Cart.

 O cruel Law! replete with Pain,
That makes us use our Legs again;
Or, half our Pair oblig'd to lack,
Bids us bestride the other's Back.
A Shilling Stage would suit with many,
Who cannot reach an Eighteen-penny.
Rock must enhance the Price of Pills,
Or drive again one Pair of Wheels,
The Graduate will be to seek,
Who mounts his Chariot twice a Week:
For if the Hackney-men should grumble,
I fear our *Phaëton* must tumble.
O cruel Law! to raise the Fare
Of Christmas Turkey, Chine, and Hare;
The Vails or Wages to retrench
Of Country Serving-man or Wench,
Who twice a Year ride up and down,
Betwixt their native Place and Town;

 O cruel Tax! who must not say,
While only those who will—need pay.

Thought on the late Expedition.

Cornwall, Dec. 19. 1746.

WHY our Forces miscarried, the Wonder is out,
 Your last Magazine has clear'd up the Doubt.
At *Boca*'s Command, the Commander gave Orders,
Weigh Anchor, my Boys, quit the *French* and their
 Borders;
We've Cattle enough, fresh Victuals in plenty,
And if we should Fight, my *Boca* will * faintie:
If more Reasons you'd have, Sir, I think you a blunt
 Ass;
" *Sic volo, sic jubeo, sit pro ratione voluntas.*"
          J. L.

To the GENIUS *of* BRITAIN.

GEnius of *Britain*, spread thy Guardian Wing
 O'er thy lov'd Isle, and round thy fav'rite King,
One sacred † Life now rescue from the Grave,
Since saving one, thou may'st an Empire save.
Oh! pour in *Britain*'s Wounds the healing Balm,
Smooth her rough Passions, and her Discords calm.
Give her (nor oh! the pious Wish disclaim!)
Or War with Triumph, or a Peace with Fame.
Her sacred Rights still teach her to defend,
And scorn that Foe, she cannot make a Friend.
Where-e'er her Cannons roar, or Crosses fly,
Plant Dread and Flight, and each pale Terror nigh.

  * Our Country Dialect.
  † The Duke.

Let *Gallia* tremble, and let *Bourbon* fear,
When glorious *William*'s conqu'ring Troops appear.
Touch ev'ry Heart with Thirst of honest Praise,
And Love of Honour more than Length of Days.
With Courage let her awe, with Virtue—charm,
Each Realm that courts her Smile, or slights her Arm.
Not fond of Peace, if Peace would but inslave;
Nor dreading War, if War alone can save.

An Anatomical EPITAPH *on an* Invalid.

Written by * HIMSELF.

HERE lies an Head that often ach'd,
   Here lie two Hands that always shak'd;
Here lies a Brain of odd Conceit,
Here lies an Heart that often beat;
Here lie two Eyes that daily wept,
And in the Night but seldom slept;
Here lies a Tongue that whining talk'd,
Here lie two Feet that feebly walk'd;
Here lie the Midriff and the Breast,
With Loads of Indigestion prest;
Here lies the Liver, full of Bile,
That ne'er secreted proper Chyle;
Here lie the Bowels, human Tripes,
Tortur'd with Wind and twisting Gripes;
Here lies that livid Dab, the Spleen,
The Source of Life's sad Tragic Scene,
That left Side Weight that clogs the Blood,
And stagnates Nature's circling Flood;

* The Learned, Facetious and Rev. *Wm. Goodwin*, late Fellow of *Eton* College, and Vicar of St. *Nicholas* in *Bristol*, who dy'd in *June* last, and left several other Pieces of the like kind.

Here lie the Nerves, so often twitch'd
With painful Cramps and poignant Stitch;
Here lies the Back oft' rack'd with Pains,
Corroding Kidneys, Loins, and Reins;
Here lies the Skin *per* Scurvy fed,
With Pimples and Eruptions red.
   Here lies the Man from Top to Toe,
That Fabrick fram'd for Pain and Woe;
He catch'd a Cold, but colder Death
Compress'd his Lungs, and stopt his Breath;
The Organs could no longer go,
Because the Bellows ceas'd to blow.
   Thus I dissect this honest Friend,
Who ne'er till Death was at Wit's end;
For want of Spirits ere he fell,
With higher Spirits let him dwell,
In future State of Peace and Love,
Where just Men's perfect Spirits move.

Part of a Letter from a Gentleman, who had lately visited N—f—k, *to his Friend.*

WE saw Sir *Andrew*'s, but Ld. *W—poole*'s first.
   At both, we felt the Calenture of Thirst:
At both, we sought in vain our Throats to cool:
Dry was *the Fountain*, and as dry *the Poole!*

Heroïsme de Louis XV. *sur le Combat, qui s' est donne pres de Village nomme la* Val.

HORS de danger sur un haut mont,
Louis, a l'abri du cannon,
Se servant de longue lunette,
De loin voit, sans emotion,
L'acharnement de l'action,
Et des alliés la retraite.
Morbleu, dit on, comment cela ?
Quoi ! voir un combat sans se batre ?
C'est faire honte a *Henri* Quatre.
Mais arretés. —— Voici le cas,
Qui doit d'abord leur ton rabatre :
Quand Louis a l'armée va,
Ce n'est que pour voir combat,
Mais nullement pour y combatre.

REMARQUE.

Quand la *France* jadis, avec un cœur *Gaulois*,
Scavoit, sans s' avilir, obéir a ses rois,
Chez soi elle prenoit ses fameux captaines,
Tel que le grand *Conde*, *Montmorenci*, *Turenne*;
Mais rampante aujourd' hui, sous le joug de *Bourbon*,
A sa honte fait choix pour heros d'un *Saxon*.

The Heroism of Lewis XV. *at the late Battle of* Val.

ON a Hill, from Danger free,
   Mighty Lewis mounted see;
With his Glass (not Sword) in Hand,
(To survey, who should command.)
There at Ease, without Emotion,
Sees of Subjects Blood an Ocean;
Sees the dreadful Battle rage,
Friends and Foes by turns engage;
Safely keeping there his Seat,
'Till the Enemies retreat.
  Morbleu! you cry, how see this Sight!
His Subjects Fighting, and not Fight!
Why 'tis enough to bring Disgrace
On the Fourth *Harry*'s fighting Race.
  But soft and fair—the Case is this,
Hear, and you'll think it not amiss.
Who does all he design'd—does right;
He came to *see*—and—not to *fight*.

REMARK.

When the *French* heretofore, like the *Gauls* whence
    they spring,
Were Subjects submiss, but not Slaves to their King;
Of themselves, they could boast, were the bravest of
    Men,
Such as *Conde* the Great, *Montmorenci, Turenne:*
By the Yoke of the *Bourbons* now crush'd past Relief,
To their shame! from the *Saxons* they borrow a Chief.

EUROPE in MASQUERADE:

Or the ROYAL FARCE.

THE States, at laſt, with one accord
Have made themſelves a Sovereign Lord.
For Public good?—Be not miſtaken,
It was to ſave their own dear Bacon.
The King moſt Chriſtian does his Work;
By leaguing with the Heathen *Turk*,
The haughty *Turk*, and *Kouli Kan*,
Are Friends or Foes, as ſuits their Plan;
The *Ruſſian* Lady plays her Game,
As fits her Intereſt or Fame.
You've ſeen two Curs for Bone at *Bay*,
A third has run with it away;
Juſt ſo the *Pr—n* ſlily watches,
While others fight, the Prey he ſnatches;
At Home behold a mighty Pother
Friends worrying Friends, and Brother Brother,
Puſhing and elbowing one another.
To *Weſtminſter* but turn your Eye,
And the whole Myſt'ry you'll deſcry,
The Independents there you'll ſee
Bawling aloud for Liberty;
But if you follow in the Dance,
They'll lead you blind to *Rome* or *France*.

An ODE to Sir C—— H—— W———s.
Occasion'd by seeing an ODE inscrib'd to L———d
C———d.

WHO's this? what! *H——y* the LYRIC?
    Changing his Note to PANEGYRIC,
        In fearful Dread of Fighting?
But 'tis in vain; for *H———y* swears,
If * *Cynthius* won't, he'll lug your Ears,
        And make you leave off writing.

Think you, because you ba—ly fled
To *Sax——y* to hide your Head,
        On Odes you still may venture?
Or wipe off Scandal left at Home,
By meanly dawbing him, in whom
        All Commendations center?

No; *St———pe* chuses thy Abuse,
Detesting such a filthy Muse,
        Whose very Praise is Satire;
For well he knows the worthless *K———t* is
Just such another as *Thersites*,
        For Bulk, Abuse, and Stature.

If charg'd with Courage Man should be,
(Like Powder in Artillery,
        Proportion'd to the Barrel)
Can'st thou, a *Blunderbuss* so large,
With scarce a *Pocket-Pistol*'s Charge,
        Presume to bounce or quarrel?

        * *Cynthius aurem vellit & admonuit.*

Then quit these dangerous, trifling Lays,
With low Abuse, or empty Praise,
   'Tis Nonsense all and Folly;
Or if you will be writing Odes,
Which ev'ry Mortal here explodes,
   Write Birth-day Odes for *Colley*.

There may you stretch Poetic Wing,
Sing Peace, or War, GOD BLESS THE K——G,
   And all his Measures praise;
Then, should old *Cy—er* chance to dye,
And *H———y* lets you come and try,
   Perhaps you'll get the Bays.

A PASTORAL.

DIGGON DAVY, *and* COLIN CLOUT.

Dii meliora piis, erroremque hostibus illum. VIRG.

Beneath an Hawthorn-bush, secreted Shade,
  The Herdsman *Diggon* doleful ply'd his Spade;
The deep'ning Grave conceal'd him to the Head,
Near him his Cow, his fav'rite Cow, lay dead:
When o'er the neighb'ring Stile a Shepherd came,
The Herdsman's Friend, and *Colin* was his Name:
Touch'd with the Sight, the kind and guileless Swain
Sigh'd, shook his Head, and thus express'd his Pain.
              COLIN.
How! *Mully* gone!—the sad Mischance I rue!
Ah! wretched *Diggon*, but more wretched *Sue*!
              DIGGON.
How could I hope, where such Contagion reigns,
Where one wide Ruin sweeps the Desart Plains,
                          Where

Where ev'ry Gale contains the Seeds of Death,
That *Diggon*'s Kine should draw untainted Breath?
Vain Hope, alas! if such my Heart had known,
Since *Mully*'s gone, the last of all my own.
No more shall *Susan* skim the milky Stream,
No more the Cheese-Curd press, or churn the Cream,
No more the Dairy shall my Steps invite,
So late the Source of Plenty and Delight:
Thither no more, with *Susan*, shall I stray,
Nor from her cleanly Hands receive the Whey.
Sad Plight is ours! nor ours alone! for all
Mourn the still Meadow and deserted Stall.

COLIN.

But have you, *Diggon*, all those Methods try'd,
By Book-learn'd Doctors taught, when Cattle dy'd?
Or, tho' no Doctor's Remedies prevail,
Does the good Bishop's fam'd Tar-Water fail?

DIGGON.

Each Art I try'd, did all that Man could do;
Med'cines I gave, like Poison Med'cines flew:
The Bishop's Drink, which snatch'd me from the Grave,
Giv'n to my Cow, forgot its Pow'r to save.
The dire Disease increas'd by swift Degrees,
'Till Death freed *Mully*; Death, which all Things frees!

COLIN.

I wou'd not, *Diggon*, now your Grief renew,
Yet wish to hear her Sickness trac'd by you,
How first it seiz'd her, and what change its Rage,
Relentless, wrought in each successive Stage.

DIGGON.

Dejected first she hung her drooping Head,
Refus'd her Meat, and from her Pasture fled;
Then dead and languid seem'd her plaintive Eye,
Her Breath grew noisome, and her Udder dry.

Erit

Erst sweet that Breath as Morning Gales in *May*,
And full that Udder as of Light the Day.
Scorch'd with perpetual Thirst short Sighs she drew,
Furr'd was her Tongue, and to her Mouth it grew:
Her burning Nostrils putrid Rheums distill'd,
And Death's strong Agonies her Bowels fill'd;
Each Limb contracted, and a Groan each Breath,
Lost Ease I wish'd her, and it came in Death:———
Cast out infected, and abhorr'd by all,
See how the Useful, and the Beauteous fall!
Not ev'n her Skin, when living sleek and red,
Can aught avail me, *Colin*, now she's dead.

COLIN.

May Heav'n relenting, happier Days bestow,
Suspend the Rod, and smile away our Woe!
But if in Justice for our Crimes we smart,
If with Affliction Heav'n corrects the Heart,
'Tis ours, submissive, to receive the Stroke,
Since to repine is only to provoke.

DIGGON.

Hard is the Task from Murmurs to refrain;
Ev'n Blessings past increase the present Pain.
Once in these Vales my lowing Herds were fed,
My Table Plenty crown'd, and Peace my Bed,
My jocund Pipe then tun'd to am'rous Lays,
A Kiss repaid me for a Lover's Praise.
Blest Times, farewel! no more those Herds are found,
No more my Table is with Plenty crown'd;
No more my Bed the Sleep of Peace bestows,
No more my jocund Strain melodious flows;
A Lover's Praise a Kiss rewards no more,
Joy spreads his wanton Wings, and leaves the Shore.
Pale Want remains with all her meagre Train,
And only Sighs are echoed o'er the Plain:
Far hence I'll fly, this rustic Garb forego,
And march in red, a Soldier, to the Foe;

The

The *French*, whose Bosoms Popish Plots conceal,
My Hand made heavy by Distress, shall feel.
On *Flanders* Plains I'll lose domestic Care,
Desp'rate thro' Want, and mighty thro' Despair.
And there, if Heav'n at length my Labours crown,
I'll *Sow* false *Frenchmen*, and I'll *Reap* Renown.
Susan, farewel —— —

COLIN.

Zooks! yonder o'er the Mead
The Squire's curst Mastiff scours with headlong Speed,
See how my Flock in wild Confusion flies—!
S'lud, if I catch him, by this Hand he dies.

On *Miss* MADAN, *after hearing repeated*,

' *If to her Share some Female Errors fall,*
' *Look on her Face, and you'll forget them all.*
POPE's Rape of the Lock.

IN Nature 'twas kind, by the Charms of a Face
To hide Faults which would else the fair Female
  disgrace;
But why did the Goddess such Beauties reveal
In *Madan*, who ne'er had a Fault to conceal?

To Lady WINCHELSEA, *occasioned by four Verses in the*
RAPE of the LOCK.

By Mr. POPE (*not in his Works.*)

IN vain you boast Poetic Names of yore,
  And cite those *Sapphos* we admire no more:

N° V.   F   Fate

Fate doom'd the Fall of ev'ry Female Wit,
But doom'd it then when first *Ardelia* writ.
Of all Examples by the World confest,
I knew *Ardelia* could not quote the best:
Who, like her Mistress on *Britannia*'s Throne,
Fights and subdues, in Quarrels not her own.
To write their Praise you but in vain essay;
E'en while you write, you take that Praise away:
Light to the Stars the Sun does thus restore,
And shines himself, till they are seen no more.

Lady WINCHELSEA'*s Answer.*

Disarm'd with so genteel an Air,
    The Contest I give o'er;
Yet, *Alexander*, have a care
    And shock the Sex no more:

We rule the World our Life's whole Race,
    Men but assume that Right;
First Slaves to ev'ry tempting Face,
    Then Martyrs to our Spite.

You of one *Orpheus* sure have read,
    Who would like you have writ,
Had he in *London* Town been bred,
    And polish'd too his Wit.

But he, poor Soul, thought all was well,
    And great should be his Fame;
When he had left his Wife in Hell,
    And Birds and Beasts could tame.

Yet vent'ring then with scoffing Rhymes
    The Women to incense;
Resenting Heroines of those Times
    Soon punish'd his Offence:

And as the Hebrus roll'd his Scull,
    And Harp besmear'd with Blood;
They clashing as the Waves grew full,
    Still harmoniz'd the Flood.

But you our Follies gently treat,
    And spin so fine the Thread;
You need not fear his aukward Fate,
    The Lock won't cost the Head.

Our Admiration you command,
    For all that's gone before;
What next we look for at your Hand
    Can only raise it more.

Yet sooth the Ladies, I advise,
    (As me to Pride has wrought)
We're born to Wit, but to be wise,
    By Admonition taught.

New NIGHT-THOUGHTS on DEATH.

A PARODY.* By Mr. WH****.

O Night! dark Night! wrapt round with *Stygian* Gloom!
Thy *Riding hood* opaque, wrought by the Hands

* On the first Night-Thought.

Of *Clotho* and of *Atropos*:—those Hands
Which spin my Thread of Life!—so near its End.
Ah wherefore, silent Goddess, do'st thou now
Alarm with Terrors?—Silence sounds Alarms
To me, and Darkness dazzles my weak Mind!
Hark! 'tis the *Death-watch! Posts* themselves can speak
His aweful Language.   Stop, insatiate Worm!
I feel thy Summons:—to my Fellow-worms
Thou bidst me hasten!—I obey thy Call,
For wherefore should I live?—Vain Life to me
Is but a tatter'd Garment,—a patch'd Rag,
That ill defends me from the Cold of Age.
Crampt are my Faculties; my Eyes grow dim;
No Music charms my Ear, no Meats my Taste;
The Females fly me—and my very Wife,
Poor Woman! knows me not! ——

   Ye fluttering, idle Vanities of Life,
Where are you flown?—The Birds that us'd to sing
Amidst my spreading Branches, now forsake
The lifeless Trunk, and find no Shelter there.
What's Life?--What's Death?--thus coveted and fear'd.
Life is a fleeting Shadow;—Death no more!
Death's a Dark-Lantern, Life a Candle's-end .
Stuck on a Save-all, soon to end in Stink.
The Grave's a Privy; Life the Ally green
Directing there—where chance on either Side
A sweet-briar Hedge, or Shrubs of brighter hue
Amuse us, and their treach'rous Sweets dispense.
Death chaces Life, and stops it ere it reach
The topmast Round of Fortune's restless Wheel.
Whee!! Life's a Wheel, and each Man is the Ass
That turns it round, receiving in the End
But Water, or rank Thistles for his Pains!
And yet, *Lorenzo*, if consider'd well,
A Life of Labour is a Life of Ease;
Pain gives true Joy, and Want is Luxury.

                             Pleasure,

Pleasure, not chaste, is like an Opera Tune,
Makes Man not Man, and castrates real Joy.
Would you be merry? search the Charnel-house,
Where Death inhabits,—give the King of Fears
A Midnight Ball, and lead up *Holben*'s Dance. *
How weak, yet strong; how easy, yet severe,
Are Laughter's Chains! which thrall a willing World.
The noisy Ideot shakes her Bells at all;
Nor e'en the Bible, or the Poet spares.
Fools banter Heaven itself, O *Young*!—and thee!

An APOLOGY.

Zealous for *Truth*, and careless of *Applause*,
We find *no Fault* while *Britain* has no *Cause*.
St——f——n, we know, are necessary Things
To *please* the *Worst*, and *serve* the *Best* of Kings:
But under the best King we must *complain*,
If all *his Virtues* and his *Views* are *vain*:——
Vain for this Reason—that the Courtier-strife,
Is, who shall best succeed in *private Life*;
Av'rice and *Pride* extinguish Thirst of *Fame*;
This wants a *Fortune*, that a *Titled Name*:
Not C——chmen from the *Charge* exempted are,
Who *Market* for the *Mitres* they would *wear*.
'Tis *Private* all;—the *Public* is no more!
Hence *Britain*'s *Arms prevail not*, as of yore;

---

* Alluding to twenty Emblematical Representations of the *Progress of Death*, painted on the Walls of a Church at *Basil*, called *Holben*'s *Dance of Death*, which shew the masterly Invention of that celebrated Genius.

Hence

Hence grow *new fruitless Debts*, the *old unpay'd*;
Hence all our *Schemes* and *Counsels* are *bet*———'d;
Hence *Projects* are essay'd by *Means unfit*,
And *Subject* rises for—SARCASTIC WIT.

A Sailor in his Majesty's Sloop the Tartar, *being sentenc'd to the Cat-o'nine-tails, spoke the following Lines to his Commander.*

BY your Honour's Command,
  An Example I stand,
Of your Justice to all the Ship's Crew:
  I am *hamper'd* and stripp'd;
  And if I am whipp'd,
'Tis no more than I own is my Due.

  In this scurvy Condition,
  I humbly petition
To offer some Lines to your Eye:
  Merry *Tom*, by such Trash,
  Once avoided the Lash,
And if Fate and you please, so may I.

  There is Nothing you hate,
  I'm inform'd, like a Cat;
Why, your Honour's Aversion is mine:
  If Puss with one Tail,
  Can so make your Heart fail,
O! save me from that which has Nine.

Note, *He was pardon'd, and is now Boatswain of a Capital Ship.*

BRITANNIA *revived*; *the Hint suggested by Mr.* R. Y.

HER Lance inverted, Head reclin'd,
   As late *Britannia* pensive sate,
Revolving in her anxious Mind
   The Woes of her declining State;
Fame in her rapid Flight drew near,
   And sounding loud from ev'ry Tongue,
Hawke! Anson! Warren! in her Ear,
   The Genius rouz'd, depress'd so long.
If *Anson, Warren, Hawke*, she said,
   Now rising with a sprightly Bound,
Are known to Fame, my laurell'd Head,
   With pristine Glory shall be crown'd.
No more I'll sigh, no more complain,
   My ancient Rights at length restor'd,
Restor'd my Emp're o'er the Main,
   And dreaded round the Globe my Sword.

A Whimsical RECEIPT, *perfectly in the Modern Taste.*

TAKE a Tory that measures two Yards in the Waist,
That can drink up a Gallon of Wine at a Feast;
Who stands up for the Church, tho' a Place he ne'er enters,
And heartily damns the whole Sect of Dissenters:
Who has Faith and Religion as far as the Names,
And believes in the Creed that was taught by King *James*:
In a Word, who holds Conscience and Truth at Defiance,
And is never sincere, but with Rogues in Alliance.
                        When

When you've found out the Man, which I think will
　　　be soon;
For it cannot be long if you know the Half-Moon;
You must take out his Brains (if he's any to spare)
For his Guts are enough, if they fill but the Chair:
Stuff his Head, when it's empty, with Pride and Conceit,
And a thorough Dislike to the Measures of State;
With a Hate of the Whigs, and a Passion for Gold,
And the Hopes to be fam'd for a Knave when he's
　　　old:
This observ'd with Exactness, let him never be sober,
And he'll make a good Dish t'wards the End of *October*.
　　　　　　　　　　　　　　　　　　C. B.

In Honour of the first of MARCH.

WHEN good St. DAVID, as *old Writs* record,
　　　Exchang'd his *sacred Crosier* for a *Sword*;
Nor *Drum* nor *Standard* kept his Men together;
Each *smelt* his Neighbour's *vegetable Feather*:
In *Heart* and *Stomach stout*, they turn'd not Crupper;
The *Foe* their *Breakfast* was; the *Leek* — their *Supper*.

The Downfall of WESTMINSTER BRIDGE.

I Sing not of Battles, nor do I much chuse
　　With *too many* Vict'ries to burden my *Muse*:
I sing not of Actions that rise to Renown;
But I sing of a monstrous huge *Bridge* tumbling down.
　　　　　　Derry down, down, hey derry down.

The

The Work of *nine* Summers, the Toil of *nine* Years,
Supported by *Commons* as well as by *Peers*:
And by *Peers*, I assure you, so firm and so good,
That, unlike to most others, they were not of Wood.
      Derry down, down, &c.

They were fram'd, as to all it is very well known,
Of large massy Blocks of good *Portland Stone*:
For *Stone*'s in such Vogue universal of late,
That—his *Grace*'s Support upholds K—g, Church.
 and State.   *Derry down, down, &c.*

But our *Constitution* how firm must it stand,
When hard *Stone*'s the Upholder of all the Land?
Tho' e'en *Stone* itself, to *Time* must give way,
Or *Westminster*-Bridge had not fall'n to this Day.
      Derry down, down, &c.

Come, Muse, sing the Cause, and set forth the Man,
The *Great Architect!* that projected the Plan;
Who first built a *Bridge*—O forbear now all Laughter!--
And sought a *Foundation*—almost nine Years after.
      Derry down, down, &c.

I've heard much Talk of building *Castles* in *Air*,
Tho' in troth, I ne'er yet could perceive any there;
But his *Genius* and *Parts* must put all to a Stand,
Who endeavour'd to build a *Bridge* on a *Quicksand*.
      Derry down, down, &c.

Who founded huge *Piers* on a Bed of soft Clay,
With a *Quicksand* beneath, that would surely give way:
Tho' clumsy the Work, it surpriz'd all the Town;
But much more surpriz'd, when its *Weight* brought it
 down.   *Derry down, down, &c.*

Now it was in those Days, that were ne'er seen be-
    fore,
When most *Knaves* were grown *rich*, and most *honest*
    Men poor;
Then, whoe'er crost the *Thames*, must certainly ferry,
Either in the Horse-boat, or else in a *Wherry*.
      Derry down, down, &c.

A long Time for the first they were oft forc'd to stay,
The Passage was dang'rous—and for both they must
    pay:
Thus these *Evils* affected all those that crost o'er,
Both the *Peer* and his *Miss*,— and the Squire and his
    W—re.   *Derry down, down, &c.*

These *Griefs* to remove, now all Parties consult,
And of their wise Counsels this was the Result,
"That a *Bridge* should be built, to pass over the Water,"
But how?—or by whom?— it was not much matter.
      Derry down, down, &c.

The first they referred unto a Committee,
Who brought it about, in spight of the City;
The latter they heeded not,—so it were done,
—Whether by a *Hod-Carrier*, or a *B———n*.
      Derry down, down, &c.

O, *B———n!* pardon the Use of your Name,
On a Subject inferior by much to your *Fame*;
Your *Fame*, which shall last long as *Inigo Jones*,
Whilst others decay, like their Mortar and Stones.
      Derry down, down, &c.

Now, tho' in a *Bridge* all Parties concurr'd,
Yet on the *Piers* they a long while demurr'd;
          But

But at length they decreed them of Stone—By're *Lady*,
They'd too many wooden ones amongst them already.
Derry down, down, &c.

But then for the *Arches*, so stately and thick,
Were they to be Wooden, or to be of Brick?—
Of neither, in Troth — for 'tis very well known,
That all public Works should be fashioned of *Stone*.
Derry down, down, &c.

The *Arches* and *Piers* were thus quickly set out,
And the *Bridge*, so design'd, must be soon set about;
But the *Money*—Gadzooks—must be had first of all,
Or else this fine *Bridge*, e'en in *Embryo* must fall.
Derry down, down, &c.

Therefore, that *Delay* might create no Vexation,
They resolv'd the Expence should be paid by the Nation;
Tho' the Benefit of it reach'd but to two Counties,
It should be at the Cost of the whole Kingdom's Bounties.
Derry down, down, &c.

And now that the Money be levied straightway,
They instantly set the whole *Nation* to play;
The *Game*, altho' old, yet most happily took,
'Twas call'd——*Who will prick in my Lottery Book?*
Derry down, down, &c.

The Cause why this Game had just now such Success
Is soon to be told——tho' not easy to guess:
Fortune's known unto *Whores*, and to *Bastards* to fly,
And all to her Favours their Rights would fain try.
Derry down, down, &c.

A Penny by Chance's worth a Pound got by Care,
And all were in such haste the Dame's Favours to share,
That the Cit left his Counter, the P—r left the Court,
And immediately all to *Change-Alley* resort.
Derry down, down, &c.

The *Sharpers* relinquish'd their Cards and their Dice,
To juggle with Tickets, at a very high Price:
The *Jockeys* forsook too their *Newmarket* Race,
With *Jews* and *Stockjobbers* *Change-Alley* to grace.
Derry down, down, &c.

Both *Porters* and *Carr-men* thus left off to ply,
That with other Fools they their Luck now might try:
E'en *Milkmaids* and *Sweepers* put in for their Shares
Of *Fortune*'s kind Favours—with *Garters* and *Stars*.
      Derry down, down, &c.

No Diſtinctions, at preſent, divided Mankind;
And *Fortune* makes none:—for you know ſhe is blind.
But the Wiſe and the Fooliſh, the Honeſt and Knave,
All ſtrove that ſome Share in the *Game* they might have.
      Derry down, down, &c.

Thus public *Vice* it ſaved private Men's *Purſes*,
And the *Bridge* it was founded on the Oaths and the Curſes
Of all the Advent'rers on whom Fortune ſhould frown,
Enough of all Reaſon—to ſink a *Bridge* down.
      Derry down, down, &c.

The Money thus rais'd, they ſtraight ſought for a Man,
That of this great Work ſhould ſketch out the *Plan*;
And he muſt be a Man—that could *Bridges* erect,
A Free Maſon—at leaſt—and a good *Architect*.
      Derry down, down, &c.

Such ——— was: —— and a Peer of nice Taſte,
And he was the Perſon they pitch'd on at laſt:
For Building—his Fame it was very well known,
As old * *Sarah*, if living, would honeſtly own.
      Derry down, down, &c.

But, alas! ſince ſhe's dead, all that now can be ſaid,
Is ——he built her a *Houſe* —— and for it ſhe paid;
But the *Price* matters not:—'twas enough to be ſure,
From *building* more Houſes the *D—ſs* to cure.
      Derry down, down, &c.

Its Name I've forgot; but at preſent ſhall call
It, only for Rhime ſake, by *W—don Hall*.
A Houſe moſt commodious!—and ſurely it ought,
As it coſt dear in Building—tho' †cheaply 'twas bought.
      Derry down, down, &c.

* *Late Dowager D—ch—ſs of Marl—gh.*
† *Being Part of the forfeited Eſtates of the South-Sea Directors, became a cheap Purchaſe.*

         Now,

Now, fraught with *Fools Pence*, our Builder defigns
The *Plan* of the Work, with *Circles* and *Lines:*
But what furpriz'd all *Connoiffeurs* of the Nation,
He never once thought to infpect the Foundation.
      Derry down, down, &c.

Howe'er he went on, and erected his Piers,
That, to look at, would laft fome hundreds of Years;
His Arches were turn'd; and the Work almoft done,
When alas! the fine *Bridge* it began to fink down.
      Derry down, down, &c.

How chanc'd this Difafter? Why thus, as fome fay,
The Arches were fix'd on a Bed that gave Way;
But others declare 'twas *Thames'* Anger and Spite,
That damag'd the Work——Who knows which is
  right?   *Derry down, down, &c.*

His Paffage, the *God* being vex'd to fee crofs'd,
Moft furioufly foam'd, and his Waves about tofs'd;
But yet all his *Foam* and his *Rage* were in vain,
For the *Bridge* ftood up firm, and was like to remain.
      Derry down, down, &c.

With Rage almoft fpent, he look'd down in the Water,
And faw the Bridge preffing of *Ouze*, his black Daughter;
He refcues the Girl from the Ravifher's Arms,
When down finks the Bridge —— and the Town fore
  alarms. *Derry down, down, &c.*

My L——d, when he heard it, he rav'd, ftorm'd
  and fwore,
That he'd ne'er undertake to build a Bridge more,
Till firft that he knew on what Foundation it ftood,
And never to build on a foft ouzy Mud.
      Derry down, down, &c.

Take Warning, ye *Builders* and *Architects* all,
How Bridges ye build, left down they fhould fall;
And on this L——d's Method, pray never rely,
But be fure, the firft Thing —— the *Foundation* to try.
      Derry down, down, &c.

         And

And thou great *Architect*, O! project not in vain,
To prop up what's finking; but let it remain;
Left that a Jeft—you become to the *Town*,
When, even at laft, your fine Bridge is quite down.
                          Derry down, down, &c.

Perhaps, that in finking, of Years half a Score
It may take ere it reaches the Bottom, or more:
When you, for your Comfort, may chance to be *rotten*,
If not fo already—and all quite forgotten.
                          Derry down, down, &c.

But however that be, e'en let it decay;
And continue to *fink*—till it *finks* quite away:
Of G——t B——n's Follies we've enough yet in fight,
Altho' you and your *Bridge* were in *Thames* plung'd
         down right.   *Derry down, down, &c.*

PLOT *or* NO PLOT. *Or Sir* WILLIAM *and his* SPY *foiled: A new* BALLAD.

YE Lords, and ye Commons, give Ear to my Ditty,
    While I tell of a Plot lately hatch'd in the City.
You have heard how a Mountain once brought forth
    a Moufe.
Such a Labour I fing —— No Offence to the H——.
                                    Derry down.

A Sett of *True Britons*, who've ne'er fold a Vote,
And fcorn'd for Court-Favour to alter their Note,
Met together at Dinner, as thinking with Reafon,
Roaft Beef in *Old England* cou'd ne'er be deem'd Treafon.
                                    Derry down.

Tho' they met, as they tell you, no Mifchief intending,
Yet the Proof of the Pudding is found in the fpending;
For as Children are frighten'd with Tales of a Ghoft,
So our Courtiers they're fcar'd with the Sound of a Toaft.
                                    Derry down.

Nor

[55]

Nor think this Alarm of our Miniſtry ſtrange;
For who knows what's meant by the *Royal Exchange?*
Then the Words *abſent Stewards* ſmell ſtrong of rebelling,
Since to make 'em High-Treaſon—wants only the Spelling.   *Derry down.*

Sir W———m ſuſpecting ſome horrid Deſign,
That endanger'd his Place and the Proteſtant Line,
Diſpatch'd a Court-Engine, whoſe Ear and whoſe Eye
Might remark what was doing—ſome call him a *Spy*.
                                                                                                Derry down.

But ſome, who were ſurely no Friends to the Crown,
Not liking the Face of our Spy, knock'd him down:
The Knight ſore enrag'd at this cruel Diſaſter,
Thought a Plot for his Noddle would prove a good Plaiſter.   *Derry down.*

Beſides, as he held, in ſuch dangerous Times,
For *Tories* to eat and to drink were high Crimes;
So no Meal-Tub or Harlequin Puppy before,
Produc'd ſuch a Plot as this Dinner, he ſwore.
                                                                                                Derry down.

To the H———e he complain'd then, and ſtraight was appointed
To ſearch out this Scheme 'gainſt the Lord's High Anointed;
But like *Scrub*, when his Plot he reveal'd to Friend *Martin*,
Knowing not what to make on't, he thought made it certain.   *Derry down.*

For ſo cloſely theſe *Tories* their Projects had ſmother'd,
That the more he enquir'd the leſs he diſcover'd:
So finding not one Wrinkle more in his A———,
The H———e all concluded this Plot but a Farce.
                                                                                                Derry down.

Our Stateſman then cry'd, ſince we've made ſuch a Pother,
And this Plot's too young, let us cook up another;
For altho' our Knight's Credit has chanc'd to miſcarry,
Sure all will believe *Honeſt Gentleman Harry.*
                                                                                                Derry down.

BŒOTIA; a *POEM*. *Humbly Addressed to his Excellency* PHILIP *Earl of* CHESTERFIELD. *By the Rev.* WILLIAM DUNKIN, D. D.

AS late I mus'd upon the Fates
   Of various Monarchies and States,
The Revolutions on this Ball,
The Rise of Empires, and their Fall,
Ambition, Power, Pleasure, Strife,
And all the splendid Woes of Life,
The solid Views and watchful Schemes
Of Men appear'd as empty Dreams;
While Indignation fill'd my Mind,
I sigh'd in Pity to my Kind,
Till sunk in Meditation deep,
Insensible I fell asleep,
As if repos'd to rest: yet fraught
With active, visionary Thought,
Transported beyond Seas I stand
On fam'd BŒOTIA's magic Land,
When, lo! a *Theban* Bard appear'd,
Serene his Front, and sage his Beard:
A circling Crown of Bays he wears,
That dignifies his hoary Hairs;
One Hand compos'd his loose Attire,
And one sustains an ancient Lyre.
He meek salutes me with a Smile,
Descending to familiar Stile:
While at his graceful Stature high,
Majestic Mien and Eagle Eye,
As smitten with religious Awe,
I stood abash'd, and would withdraw.
   Approach, he says, and lend an Ear,
Nor Danger from *Amphion* fear.
The pious Bards, who till these Glebes,
Or live within the Walls of *Thebes*,
Are ever hospitable found;
For here you tread on Classic Ground.

                       Each

Each Guest, (and be it long our Boast)
Shall find an easy chearful Host.
All Men who breathe *Bæotian* Air,
But chiefly Strangers, are our Care.
Contented with our present Store,
We seek from Providence no more,
On Nature's Bounty freely live
Unbounded, and as freely give.
To *Phœbus* we devoutly true,
The Rust of Lucre never knew,
No Passion, but his purer Flame;
No Lust, but that of honest Fame.
   Those Walls, that Citadel, which shrouds
Its Head imperial in the Clouds,
To letter'd Eyes distinctly shine,
And own their Architect divine,
From Harmony such Beauty springs,
I touch'd the Silver-sounding Strings:
The Rocks began to move enorm,
And roll'd spontaneous into Form.
   Bæotia, memorable long
For valiant Deed and lofty Song,
In Tears had utter'd her Complaints,
That she condemn'd to sad Restraints,
Despis'd, neglected, and opprest,
Should ever stand a public Jest.
But *Jove*, in Pity to her Cries,
That often rent the distant Skies,
At length amidst the grand Affairs
Of high *Olympus*, hears her Pray'rs,
Assenting to her Wishes, nods,
And thus harangues the frequent Gods.
   To each of you, ye sacred Pow'rs,
Who share with me these blissful Bow'rs,
My Substitutes, I have assign'd
Some Province over human Kind.
Triumphant *Mars* conducts the Race
Of quiver-bearing hardy *Thrace*. -

N° V.   H   *Tarentum*

Tarentum and *Sidonia*'s Coast
Through you their distant Commerce boast,
O *Neptune*, who the Realms divide,
To bless them with a golden Tide.

 Thee *Lemnos* hails, *Ætnean* Sire,
Array'd with Majesty of Fire,
To forge against the bold Revolts
Of Rebels my terrific Bolts,
That, from this Arm indignant hurl'd,
Shall blast the Tyrants of the World.

 You, goodly *Bacchus*, Foe to Care,
And that thy Sister, *Venus* fair,
Controul the *Cyprian* Nymphs and Swains,
And bind your Slaves in Silken Chains.

 Gay *Pan*, attended by the Fauns,
And Satyrs dancing o'er the Lawns,
Attunes the rural Reed, and roves
Licentious through *Lycean* Groves;
Or gently waves with aweful Hand
His Crook, the Scepter of Command,
To teach the tender bleating Breed
Amid the verdant Vales to feed,
Or lead from nightly Wolves and Cold
His fleecy Subjects to their Fold.

 You *Pallas*, in Perfection born,
With Arts divine your Sons adorn,
And wide through *Attica* rever'd,
Protect the Towers, which you rear'd.

 And yet behold a Nation, known
For old Allegiance to my Throne!
For me their choicest Victims feed,
And Hecatombs unnumber'd bleed:
To me with reverential Vow,
Their blameless Priests obedient bow,
And pour unsparing at my Shrine
Libations of the purest Wine.

 If Virtue claims a just Reward,
Bœotia merits my Regard:

But

But she, renown'd of old for Arts,
Accomplish'd Heads and martial Hearts,
Is now become the Ridicule
Of each unbred, unletter'd Fool.
But *Phœbus* thou, my Son sublime,
Revisit this unhappy Clime.
To thee I delegate my Might,
Thou genial God of Wit and Light.
There exercise thy guardian Sway,
Though Demigods lament thy Stay.
   Thy Beams shall banish black Despair,
And purify the grosser Air.
Each pleasing Attribute is thine,
Thou, skill'd in Pharmacy divine,
Shalt all her Perturbations calm,
And give to ev'ry Wound a Balm.
   Thy Quiver, with becoming Pride
Suspended by thy regal Side,
Such as adorns the Virgin Queen,
Shall teem with Darts and Arrows keen,
Though none, but Animals malign'd
By Vice, and preying on their Kind,
Shall ever from Experience know
The feather'd Vengeance of thy Bow.
   Go then—nor shalt thou go alone,
Astrea shall support thy Throne,
Nor shall she blush again to see
The World, when countenanc'd by thee;
Her shall the never-failing Horn
Of Plenty, Joy, Content adorn,
While she, by passing Crouds ador'd,
Shall poise the Scales, and wield the Sword.
   Thy Brother *Mercury* shall deign
To lead the Graces in thy Train,
And they to mortal Eyes reveal
Their Beauties half, and half conceal.
   The Muses should obey thy Call,
But they in Thee are center'd all.

Then shall *Bœotia*'s Offspring rise,
To lift her Glories to the Skies,
Thebes rival *Athens* in her Charms,
And shine in Arts, as well as Arms.
 Already she thy Presence waits,
See rushing through her crouded Gates
Her Poets, each with Rapture led
To bow to thee the laurel'd Head!
Thy great Example shall inspire
Their Souls with more exalted Fire,
And teach the Druids of the Grove
To celebrate thy Father *Jove*.
That lenient and enchanting Hand,
Whose melting Modulations bland
Infernal Anguish could assuage,
Yet crush'd the baneful *Python*'s Rage.
But there no Pest, in Volumes roll'd,
With flaming Crest of scaly Gold,
And forky Tongue, awakes our Fear,
Or darts Defiance at thy Spear.
 Vertumnus at thy Sight renews
The Beauties of a thousand Hues,
And rich *Pomona*, who had pin'd
So long by wat'ry Clouds confin'd,
Thy Radiance blushing to behold,
Displays her vegetable Gold,
While yellow *Ceres* through the Land
Invites the lusty Reaper's Hand.
 Bright Liberty like this above,
Which know no Bands, but those of Love,
Establishes her Empire now,
And Peace extends her Olive Bough.
 Bœotia cherish'd by thy Rays
Begins a Course of *Halcyon* Days,
While many troubled Nations round,
Excited by the brazen Sound
Of horrid War, with *Stygian* Breath
Spread Ruin, Rage, and mutual Death.
 So *Delos*, which had stray'd, before
Latona sanctify'd her Shore,

Confess'd the present God in you,
And first a firm Foundation knew,
While other Isles no Rest could gain,
Toss'd through the wide *Ægyptian* Main.

 He said: Away the Vision flies;
I sudden starting in Surprize,
Was 'waken'd by the glad Uproar,
That CHESTERFIELD was safe on Shore.

King Harry *the Ninth's* SPEECH *to both* Houses *of* P———T.

My Lords and Gentlemen,

IT is with particular Pleasure that I meet this new P—m—t, which I have called much sooner than was expected, purposely to oblige our *good Friends*, and *faithful* Allies, the S—tes-G—l of the united P—v—n—s; and to evince them, and all *E—pe*, of the entire Dependence that I have upon the Affections of my *People*; nor do I in the least doubt, but that you are met together with a full Resolution, of giving me your Advice and Assistance, with that *Unanimity*, as will afford the World convincing Proofs of your Duty and Fidelity to me, your *particular Regard* for the Interest of the *D—h*, and your ardent Zeal for the common Cause. As such your Proceeding must add vastly to the Weight and Credit of our Affairs Abroad, in the present *Crisis*, and effectually support the tottering Greatness of our *trusty* Friends, and ancient Allies, the *H—ders*, so it will be no less destructive to those Designs, that our Enemies may have formed against the public Welfare, and particularly against the Peace and Tranquillity of these Kingdoms, by convincing them of your being thoroughly determined, vigorously to support such Measures as I shall find necessary to be taken, in order to obtain a *lasting*, *safe*, and *honourable* Peace for ourselves, and our *Allies*, which has all along been the sole Point that I have had in View.

 With much Concern I must acquaint you, that our *Endeavours* on the *Continent* this Summer, have not been attended with such *Success*, as I could have wished for; owing to the want of *Vigour* in our Allies, and the *Deficiency* of those *Troops* which they brought into the Field; whereby my Subjects have been left to signalize themselves against an almost *innumerable Host* of *Enemies*. As these Things ever furnished Matter of Complaint during the last War, so it will be almost impossible to remedy them in this; any otherways than by taking a greater Number of their *Forces* into our Pay, and by enlarging their several *Subsidies*. Tho' by this means we shall in a manner take the whole *Burthen* of the *War* upon our own *Shoulders*, it may perhaps be better for us, at the present Juncture, so to do, than to rely as hitherto, on those Powers, whose *Cowardice*, *Treachery*, or *Weakness*, may so far prevent them from assisting us to *Distress* the *Enemy*, as rather to become an *Annoyance* to ourselves. And indeed, tho' I have made use of the utmost Efforts in my Power, to *spirit* up and *invigorate* our *Allies* to be sanguine in the common Cause; yet the *Quotas* which they have hitherto furnished, either in Men, Money, or *Valour*, have been very inconsiderable, when compared with what my People have always cheerfully and readily contributed towards carrying on this *just* and *necessary* War.

I have lately, in Conjunction with our true and steady *Friends* and *Allies*, the *St———s·G————l*, entered into a Treaty of *Subsidy*, for the March of forty thousand *R———ns*, to the Assistance of the allied Army, which have been hitherto, tho' often promised, so long retarded; and may again meet with such fresh Obstacles, as will prevent their setting out, should you hesitate a Moment upon enabling me to make good the Engagements I have entered into on this Occasion. I shall order a Copy of this Treaty to be laid before you; and am thoroughly persuaded, that you will readily contribute to the Promotion of an Affair, so exceeding *beneficial* to the Support of the *Common Cause*, in the present necessary Juncture.

Tho' this Treaty that I have concluded, has already given some Umbrage to the King of *P——a*, and perhaps may afford him more; especially, as I have not as yet been able, notwithstanding my continuing to exert my most earnest Endeavours, to prevail with him to enter into any Measures with the *Allies*, for restraining and subduing the exorbitant Power of *France*: I would therefore strongly recommend it to your Consideration, to find out some effectual *Method* of bringing that Prince over to our Interests; by enabling me to make him such an extraordinary Allowance, as may satisfy his most lucrative Views, and far exceed any Offers that *France* or *Spain* are capable of affording him: and this I would the more zealously commit to your Care, as his Alliance would be more valuable to us, than that of any other of the *G—rm—ic* Body, excepting the House of *A··a*.

Our good Friends and Allies, the *D—h*, have lately come to a Resolution of considerably enlarging the Number of *Swiss* Troops already in their Service, and of taking several more Regiments of them into Pay in Conjunction with *Great Britain*, that they may be able, if there be Occasion for them, to take the Field early next Spring: tho' whether the Influence of *French* Councils may not prevent this necessary Step from taking Place, I am unable to ascertain as yet; but I firmly rely on your timely *Support*, at all *Events*, on this and every other Occasion.

As our Enemies seem to afford us some very specious Hopes

of their being ready once more to embrace Peace, and establish the so-much-wish'd-for *Tranquillity* of *Europe*; so I have given my *Ministers* proper *Instructions* for attending the *Congress*, that is to be held this Winter.—But should this prove to be only an *Artifice*, to prevent our having a sufficient Number of Forces in Readiness against the next Spring; I shall endeavour to elude such a *Design*, by continuing in the mean time to *Negotiate* for such Troops as are to be obtained; that the *Allied Army* may be able to enter the Field early, and to act offensively next Season.

Should any unforeseen Accidents again prevent the *Ru—ns* from joining our Army, or frustrate my acquiring those Troops for the Service of the Public, which I am at present doing my Endeavours to obtain; even then I do not despair, with the Assistance of my *loving People*, of gaining sufficient Succours from the remotest Parts; and in order to be prepared against all Events, I shall cause immediate Application to be made on this Account to the *Sophi* of *Persia*, as soon as the Succession to that Kingdom shall be settled. The Force that I may expect from thence, together with those that I shall sollicit from the *Cham* of *Tartary*, the Kings of *Bantam*, *Siam*, and the *Great Mogul*, will be rather more than sufficient for making Head against the Enemy; especially, as with Troops of the latter, I expect to receive a considerable Number of *Elephants*, furnished with well-fortified *Castles* on their *Backs*, which *Moving Forts* will be a great *Annoyance* to the *French*, and afford them sufficient *Diversion* from making such dreadful Havock as they have lately done, with the most *impregnable* Places in the *N—lands*, and *United P—ces*.

The Behaviour of the *D—h* Forces, during the last *Campaign*, and their negligently suffering several of their most important Places to be *surprized* by the Enemy, needs *no Apology from me*; as it is impossible to imagine that either the *St—s G--n--l*, or the *St—dh—r*, were acquainted with, or gave their Assent to any such base and treacherous Proceedings; and I do not doubt, but *their speedy bringing* the Offenders to *Justice*, and punishing of them in as severe a Manner, as *they have already done all such as have been hitherto detected of either* TREACHERY *or* COWARDICE, will sufficiently manifest the Innocence and Integrity of those that preside at the Head of Affairs, amongst our ancient *Friends* and *Allies*.

The extraordinary Success which has attended my Fleet must have greatly weakened both the naval Strength and Commerce of our Enemies; and I shall not fail of profiting myself to the *utmost*, of those *Advantages* that I have already received therefrom; being fully determined to be more attentive to this important Service, *than I have hitherto been*: and as our good Friends the *H—rs* have not succoured me as yet, with such a sufficient Number of *Ships*, as is necessary for the Support of our Dominions on the Occasion; I shall directly apply to the several Governments of *Lapland*, and *Greenland*, in order to obtain from thence, such naval Supplies of *Canoes* and *Men*, as may compensate for the Deficiencies of our Allies in that Article.

Gentlemen of the H—e of C—s,

The great Facility with which you have carried your Elections, almost without Opposition, throughout all Parts of the *Kingdom*, particularly in *Surry* and *Sussex*, affords me fresh Proof of the *good Disposition* of *my People*, in the Choice of their Representatives.. The *many* Considerations that I have already mentioned, are so necessary for our own Preservation, the Support of our Allies, and the Maintenance of the *Protestant* Cause, that I doubt not, you will grant me such a Supply, as shall be amply sufficient for all those *good* Purposes, that I have undertaken. The *proper Estimates* shall be laid before you: and I rely the stronger on your succouring of me with *suitable Grants*, as there are so many amongst you, that either in their *Civil* or *Military* Capacities, are sure *to benefit by the public Supplies*; and whose *Interest* in this Point, is always the same with, and inseparable from, *mine*. I must acknowledge it is with the greatest Regret, that I am obliged to lay any extraordinary Burthens upon my People; but hope that they will consider the immediate Necessity thereof, for the Support of the public Credit, in this critical Conjuncture.

My L—s and G—tl—n,

As I have fully explained to you my Views and Intentions, so I need not urge any thing farther, to induce you to afford me a vigorous Support; and it is with great Satisfaction I am able to acquaint you, that the *Money* granted by *Parliament* for the effectual carrying on the War, has been so well bestowed, as to retain the King of S——a hitherto entirely to our Side; where he is likely to remain stedfast, as long as you shall continue to support him with fresh and ample Subsidies. And also to keep the *Empress* Queen in Possession of more extensive Territories, maugre the Endeavours of her Enemies, than *what she is able to maintain.*

As there was never more Occasion for your acting with Vigour, Unanimity, and Dispatch, than in the present Juncture, when the Eyes of the whole World are fixed upon your Proceedings; so it is on this that I rely, for supporting the Honour of my C—n, the Well-being of my K—d—ms, the *Avarice* and *Indolence* of our Allies, and for restoring our *Neighbours* to that Degree of P—de, A—g—ce and Inf—l—ce, which they formerly enjoyed.

FINIS.

THE
Foundling Hospital
FOR
W I T.

Intended for the

Reception and Preservation of such Brats of Wit and Humour, whose Parents chuse to Drop them.

NUMBER VI. to be Continued Occasionally.

CONTAINING,

1 The Court Ballad on Dr. C—s Sermon.
2 The embarrassed Knt. to Sir C. H. W—s.
3 A congratulatory Ode to the D. of N—le on his going to H—r.
4 A new Ballad on Sir Billy Tinsel, L— M—.
5 Sir W—m St—pe's Speech on the Buckingham Bill, &c. &c. &c.
6 Isis, an Elegy, to the Gentlemen of Ox—d.
7 Advice to Mr. L—g—n the dwarf Fan-Painter, at Tunbridge Wells.
8 The Bottle-Conjurer.
9 To the Independent E——s of W——r.
10 Odes, Rhapsodies, &c. on the Peace.
11 A reduced Office's Complaint.
12 Petition of Justice B—d—n's Horse to the D. of N——le.
13 On the late M—rt—l Bills.
14 A Fable to the E—l of G—lle.
15 Filch at the Gallows.
16 Prologue and Epilogue spoke by Prince George, &c.
17 Account of Sieur Rocquet.
18 A Ballad on B—n and W—r.

With many other Curious Pieces, some of which never before printed.

By TIMOTHY SILENCE, Esq;

LONDON:

Printed for W. Webb, near St. Paul's. 1749.
[Price One Shilling and Sixpence.]
Where may be had any of the Preceding Numbers.

CONTENTS.

C———t Ballad on Dr. C—b—'s Sermon. Page 1
The Embarrassed Knt. an Ode inscribed to Lord C———d. 3
A Congratulatory Ode to the D—e of N——— on his Travels. 5
A new Ballad on Sir Billy Tinsel, L——M——. 7
An Ode to Lord G———r. 12
Sir W—S—pe's Speech. 14
A Speech without Doors, in Answer. 21
Richard White-Liver's Speech. 30
Dick Green's Speech. 35
Isis, an Elegy. 40
A Character of Baron Mountney. 44
A Reflection. 44
Advice to Mr. L—g—n the Dwarf Fan-Painter. 45
Humorous Pieces on the Bottle Conjurer. 49 to 52
An Epitaph on Moll Batchelor. 53
A Sneer on the Independent Electors of W———r. 53
A Song by a Lady. 54
Odes, Rhapsodies, and Songs on the Peace. 55 to 60
A Reduced Officer's Complaint. 61
Verses on a Grumbling Politician about the K— S—h 63
England's Alarum-Bell. 64
A Letter to Miss Jenny * * * * 67

The

CONTENTS.

The Petition of Juſtice Boden's *Horſe to the Duke of* Newcaſtle.	68
A Dream.	69
Epitaph on John Trotplaid, *alias* J— F—g.	69
On the late M—rt—l *Bills.*	70
A Fable to the Earl of Gr—nv—le.	70
The Inſcription on the Inner-Temple Gate.	73
Anſwer to Ditto.	73
Filch at the Gallows.	73
An Epigram on a diſconſolate Tutor, inſcribed to B—	74
Miſs L—tt—r *to* C——F—	75
Verſes on the Report of the Britiſh *Fleet being to be ſent into the* Baltick.	76
Verſes on the Report that Sir Peter Warren, Hawke, *and* Vernon, *were to be made Peers.*	76
Prologue and Epilogue ſpoke by Prince George, *Princeſs* Auguſta, *and Prince* Edward.	77
Cato *to* Portius.	79
An Account of Sieur Rocquet.	81
No Peace for the Wicked, a Ballad on the Battle between B——n *and* W——r	83
On ſeeing the Workmen employed upon the Preparations for the Fire-Works *in the* Green-Park, *on Sunday laſt.*	87
On oppoſing the late Mutiny and Deſertion Bill.	87
Epigram, occaſion'd by a Religious Diſpute at Bath.	87
Pantine. *In Part an Imitation of the* 8*th Satire of the Firſt Book of* Horace.	88
On admitting Soldiers, under Arms, into St. Paul's, *on the Thankſgiving-Day.*	90
On the Thankſgiving, and the Jubilee Ball that is to follow it.	90
A Pindarick Ode upon Oddities. *Extempore.*	90

THE

THE
Foundling Hospital
FOR
W I T.

NUMBER VI.

To the Reverend Dr. C———— *on his Excellent Sermon preached before his* M——y.

Dear Doctor,

AT the Request of several very young *Gentlemen* and *Ladies*, and some very elderly Ones, who never heard the *like*, the following Scrap of Poetry, far short of your Desert, is dedicated to you, for enlightening their Understanding, heightening their Imaginations, touching their Passions, and tickling their Pulse,

By your humble and obliged
JOSEPH.

The C——t Sermon. *A new Ballad.*

YE Beaux and ye Belles, both in Court and in City,
    Your Attention I beg to my comical Ditty,
And of a ſtrange Sermon you'll preſently hear,
Such as never before reach'd his M———'s Ear.
      Derry down.

Young *Joſeph* that Youth of moſt innocent Life,
Who was tempted and teaz'd by old *Potiphar*'s Wife,
A Prieſt (who for want of Promotion was vex'd)
Revengefully choſe for his Subject and Text.
      Derry down.

Quoth the Doctor in Dudgeon, I'LL GIVE IT the C--t?
And tho' to a Man they are fond of the Sport,
I'll ne'er mince the Matter, but loudly proclaim,
Of whoring, and wenching, the Sin and the Shame.
      Derry down.

So ſaid and ſo done, up the Roſtrum he mounted,
And every ſly Sinner confoundedly hunted;
Told the Girls when their Pulſe and their Paſſions
  were high,
What they long'd to be at if young Fellows were nigh.
      Derry down.

He told them ſuch Paſſions were rais'd by bad Books,
And warn'd them of leering and languiſhing Looks,
And, as if from Experience, enlarg'd on the Sin
Of bewitching young *Joſephs*, and drawing them in.
      Derry down.

Of Venereal Diſorders very groſly he prated,
And in innocent Minds odd Ideas created;
Put the Thing in young Heads like an ignorant Elf,
Which is very well known to breed faſt of itſelf.
      Derry down.

If

If *Misaubine*, L—w—n, or *Rock* had been there,
Heard of Poxes in Pulpits, 'twould have made them all stare,
And have wickedly thought, by his choice Terms of Art,
That under the *Rose* he had felt all the Smart.
Derry down.

Such Subjects with Decency Teachers should touch,
Lest in speaking too plain, they should publish too much,
And the Truth of the old Woman's Proverb declare,
Who never had search'd, if she ne'er had been there.
Derry down.

Of Discourses like these, ye C—t Preachers beware,
And think *Covent-Garden* the properer Air;
In the Hundreds of *Drury* there build up a Stage,
To preach Bawdy, and lash all the Whores of the Age.
Derry down.

And now I have done, as you'll think it high Time,
With the Doctor, the Sermon, and whimsical Rhyme,
May the B—ps be made of such Parsons as these,
Then they'll never preach more, nor the C—t will displease.
Derry down.

The EMBARRASS'D KNIGHT. *A* SATIRE.

Occasion'd by seeing an Ode inscrib'd to Lord Ch——d.

Formidine fustis
Ad bene dicendi redactus.

WHO's this? what! *Ha*—y the LYRICK?
   Changing his Note to PANEGYRICK,
  In fearful Dread of Fighting?
But 'tis in vain; for *Hu*—y swears,
If *Cynthius* won't, he'll lug your Ears*,
  And make you leave off writing.

* *Cynthius aurem vellit et admonuit.*

Think you, becaufe you ba—ly fled
To *Sax—y* to hide your Head,
    On Odes you ftill may venture?
Or wipe off Scandal left at Home,
By meanly dawbing him, in whom
    All Commendations centre?

No; *St——pe* chufes thy Abufe,
Detefting fuch a filthy Mufe,
    Whofe very Praife is Satire:
For well he knows the worthlefs K—t is
Juft fuch another as *Therfites*
    For Bulk, Abufe, and Stature.

If charg'd with Courage Man fhould be,
(Like Powder in Artillery
    Proportion'd to the Barrel)
Can'ft thou, a *Blunderbufs* fo large,
With fcarce a *Pocket-Piftol*'s Charge,
    Prefume to bounce, or quarrel.

Then quit thefe dangerous, trifling Lays,
With low Abufe, or empty Praife,
    'Tis Nonfenfe all, and Folly;
Or if you will be writing Odes,
Which ev'ry Mortal here explodes,
    Write Birth-day Odes for *Colley*.

There may you ftretch Poetick Wing,
Sing Peace, or War, GOD BLESS THE K—G,
    And all his Meafures praife;
Then, fhould old *Ci—er* chance to dye,
And *Hu—y* lets you come, and try,
    Perhaps you'll get the Bays.

A Congratulatory ODE, *most humbly inscribed to the* STATESMAN *on his* TRAVELS.

By JOSHUA JINGLE, Esq; *Poet-Laureat to the* Pelemites, Selemites, *and other great Personages*.

Si PROCERES *peccant,* ── ──
Exemplo et sceleri pœna paranda duplex.

OLD *Eng*—*d* mourns her past Disgrace,
   Sad Fate of her unhappy Race,
     By Gibbets, Goals, and Axes;
Th' inglorious Slaughter War has made,
Her rising Debts, her sinking Trade,
     Her Places, Pensions, Taxes.

Cross'd with such Cares, press'd with such Pains,
What Wonder if she thus complains,
     Tells thus her dismal Story;
In hopes some wise, some Patriot Chief,
Some Statesman born for her Relief,
     Might yet retrieve her Glory?

But *Holly* of her C—ll's Head,
Having o'ercome his Water-dread,
     Thro' foreign Realms is running;
Some Strangers stare to see his Plate,
More smile at his projected Pate,
     Pate unaccus'd of Cunning.

Possess'd of Posts, and Power at Home,
Oh! why should mighty *Holly* roam,
     And leave O—*d Eng*—*d* weeping?
'Twas—Truth to say—because afraid,
Had others gone, or had he staid,
     He was not sure of keeping.

                         This

This flip'ry Tenure calls him forth,
At more Expence than quell'd the North,
    So late in Life to travel;
At mighty Feasts, of mighty Things,
With Princes set, expecting Kings,
    To talk—and Plots unravel.

Not *Gallic* Plots, for *Gallia* now
As *Holly* thinks is forc'd to bow
    By his superior Knowledge;
Alas! in Politics how mad!
And yet no Blockhead when a Lad,
    At *W*—— or College.

For these high Meals, this foreign Praise,
What mighty Sums did some Folks raise,
    And what is more amazing,
My L— too as well as He,
Must go in Triumph over Sea;
    To set the World a Gazing.

Happy if their own private Store,
Acquir'd by wiser Folks before,
    These Projects only troubled;
But ours, they'll measure by his Sense,
Compute our Wealth by his Expence,
    And then our Tribute's doubled.

New Treaties from these Feasts shall spring,
New Princes gain'd, perhaps a K—
    More Schemes for *Europe*'s Quiet;
Hence daily new Demands may rise,
New Quota's, Loans, and Subsidies,
    Sharp Sauce to *G——n* Diet.

                              Thus

Thus the young Squire his Wealth bestows
On home-spun Feasts and tawdry Cloaths,
    On Horses, Hounds, and Harlot;
Until Mamma to mend his Taste
Sends him to cross the *Alps* in haste
    With some *Bear-leading* Varlet.

Thus tutor'd NUMPS grows worse and worse,
False Taste acquires, what greater Curse!
    Brings home a Race of Vipers;
And on his new Refinements bent,
In twice five Years th' Estate is spent
    On Panders, Pimps, and Pipers.

Sir BILLY TINSEL. *An Excellent New* BALLAD.

To the Tune of the Abbot of *Canterbury*.

A Story I'll tell you, a Story so merry,
    But not of the Abbot of *Canterbury*,
For of *London* I sing, and of *London*'s L—d M—y--r:
Attend then, I pray you, my Ditty to hear.
                      Derry down, &c.

This City, saith *Stow*, in his *Annals* of old,
Had its Mayor, call'd *my Lord*, with his Chain of pure Gold,
And to add to the Dignity during the Year,
His Lordship is plac'd in a great Elbow-chair.
                      Derry down, &c.

In the Times of our Fathers, great Men of Renown
Were advanc'd to this Honour, for Merit well known,
But Merit, of late Years, but seldom is seen;
There's few that possess it but old fashion'd Men.
                      Derry down, &c.

But I pray now, good People, from this don't infer,
That I mean to reflect on our new-made L—d M—r:
His Merits are great, and his Virtue's are known,
And his Zeal for K—g H——y's as warm as his Gown.
Derry down, &c.

His Youth at *Emanuel, Cambridge,* he spent:
To study Divinity was his Intent:
And to read o'er the Fathers resolved was he,
In hopes my Lord Bishop one Day for to be.
Derry down, &c.

Aspiring his Genius, sublime were his Parts,
To gain a Reward, which he thought his Deserts
Gave him Title to think of, by Study and Care:
At last, at a Distance, he ey'd a great Chair.
Derry down, &c.

But mark! a Beer-brewer of Eminence great
From this earthly Climate one Day did retreat;
To a buxom brisk Widow, the Care of his Beer
He bequeath'd, with a Fortune of Hundreds a Year.
Derry down, &c.

Not long ere our Student from College to Town,
To visit this Widow, and make her his own,
Came and told the fair Lady he well understood
How to manage her Cask, and her Beer when 'twas brew'd.
Derry down, &c.

So smart and so smug our young Lover appear'd
With modest Assurance (for nothing he fear'd)
He attack'd the blyth Widow with man-like Address,
And she soon condescended his Wishes to bless.
Derry down, &c.

Exalted in Splendour, he soon sally'd forth,
And thro' the whole Ward gave Proofs of his Worth:

The

The good Alderman dy'd; and to keep up the Spirit,
To succeed him they thought that young *Billy* had Merit.
Derry down, &c.

To oppose ministerial Jobs, and Excise,
And other such Maxims more wicked than wise,
The new chosen Alderman firmly engag'd,
Which the Grief of the Citizens somewhat assuag'd.
Derry down, &c.

Soon after Sir *Robert*, whose Zeal, and whose Cares
For this City and Nation appear'd by his Tears,
Dy'd; and made in the Senate a Vacancy: Where
Zealous C—lv—t was chose in his Room to appear.
Derry down, &c.

For some Time he adher'd to his Promise and Trust,
And oppos'd all those Measures that deem'd were unjust;
'Till one Day he chanc'd to step over the Way,
And Compliments great to K—g H—r—y did pay.
Derry down, &c.

Great H—r—y, surpriz'd by our Senator, bow'd,
And told him his Merit had long been allow'd
By the K—g and his Courtiers, and fear'd not one Day
He'd approve the good Precepts of Vicar of *Bray*.
Derry down, &c.

The Senator stopp'd and Obeysance low made,
Whatever good Sir, of Excises I've said,
And otherwise Measures propos'd by the Crown,
Or their Ministers, formerly to me unknown;
Derry down, &c.

Your Honour's great Wisdom convinces me clear,
I have been mistaken; and now I do swear,
That no Measures e'er can be safely pursu'd
But those which your Honour shall think to be good.
Derry down, &c.

N° VI.   C   Such

Such Marks of Converſion his **Honour** approv'd,
And thenceforth his *truſty*, he ſtil'd him *belov'd*,
And aſſur'd him, the City by him ſhould obtain
Many Things that before they'd apply'd for in vain.
Derry down, &c.

Thus advanc'd to high Favour in *H—r—y*'s Eſteem,
Soon after by Title a Knight he became,
Sir *Billy* then ſtrutted in lac'd Coat moſt fine:
But ſome thought 'twas nought but his *Tinſel* did ſhine.
Derry down, &c.

At length it fell out, that our City diſtreſs'd,
And by Fall of our Trade, their Revenues decreas'd,
To aſſiſt them in S—n—te a Motion was made,
And a Bill order'd in for to grant what was pray'd.
Derry down, &c.

The Bill was committed, in order to paſs,
All things were prepar'd, and withdrawn was the Mace,
When Sir *Billy*, uncall'd for, jump'd into the Chair,
Which cauſ'd great Confuſion 'mong thoſe who met there.
Derry down, &c.

Then down came the Sp——r, ſaid, Sirs, What d'ye mean?
Such Diſorders amongſt you I never have ſeen:
'Till Sir *John,* for to quiet the Noiſe did declare,
None more fit than Sir *Bill* for a Cypher was there.
Derry down, &c.

Thus adorned with Dignity, Title, and Cloaths,
Did the Knight ſhew the City by whom he was choſe,
How well he could manage Debate in a Chair,
In hopes that one Day he might be their L—d M—r.
Derry down, &c.

The Time came about, the Election drew near,
The Freemen were ſummon'd each one to appear
In

In *Guildhall*, to chuse a chief Magistrate, who
Was to govern the City the Year to ensue.
Derry down, &c.

Sir *Billy* was talk'd of as next to the Chair,
But some thought a Courtier not fit to come there;
This frighted the Knight, who with Haste and full Speed
Hy'd away to K——g H——y, for his Aid he had need.
Derry down, &c.

His Honour receiv'd him with Favour and Grace,
And promis'd Excisemen, and Postmen, and Place,
Should attend with their Mobs, to huzza and proclaim
The new Merit due to his C——lv——rt's great Name.
Derry down, &c.

Accordingly rang'd and drawn up on the Day,
Dissenters of all kinds, and Placemen for Pay,
Cry'd aloud, We'll have C——lv——t to be our L-M-r,
For K——H——y a Convert doth now him declare.
Derry down, &c.

Sir *Bill* was then chose, and being chain'd and full dress'd,
Toward the Hall he stept forward, and thus he express'd
To the Commons, My Friends, not my old ones I mean,
But my new leagu'd Allies, and my P--b--m's true Men,
Derry down, &c.

Since you now elected have me to the Chair,
I'll in few Words inform you what sort of a M——r
You shall have for the Time I am destin'd to be
Of this City chief Magistrate, of which you're free.
Derry down, &c.

And first I think proper to you to declare,
No Alderman's fit to be President here,
That his Honour's wise Measures shall aim to disturb,
Or in Zenith of Power shall attempt him to curb.
Derry down, &c.

Tho' lately some Magistrates, such as *W—B—n*,
Did with others in Closets and Chambers convene,
T' oppose vile Corruption, and against it they roar'd,
Yet I hope they will always by you be abhorr'd.
Derry down, &c.

I, during the Time I shall reign in this Place,
Will obey my *K—H——y*, and honour his *Grace*;
Such *Par nobile fratrum* before we ne'er saw,
To you I'll commend 'em, and beg to withdraw.
Derry down, &c.

Now here ends my Ditty: I've only to pray,
That the Citizens may, on next *Michaelmas* Day,
Examine and prove first the Man they shall choose,
And not trust to such as have Treasury Views.
Derry down, &c.

An ODE *for the* 23d *of* September 1747.

FOR the Glory of *Kellum*
 Let's record upon Vellum
What Hirelings ascended his Booth;
 When at a late Race
 Stood each impudent Face,
Foes to Honesty, Virtue, and Truth.

 The foremost in Power,
  Was treacherous *G———r*;
Tho' inferior in Title and Birth,
 To his Grace, the first Lord
 Of the maritime Board,
Whose Element shou'd be the Earth.

Next

Next these might you veiw
    A Champion or two,
Who came there to embellish the Scene,—
    With a Badge on their Side
    Of Corruption and Pride,
But not of a Heart brave and clean.

    A new Senator grim
    Yet stately and trim,
As the Statue of *William* the Third;
    With his Brother the Tar,
    Whose Success in War
An illegal Election procur'd.

    Poor Sir *Richard* was near
    The disconsolate Peer,
But durst not adventure to run;
    For when lately he struggl'd
    And cheated and juggl'd,
His Prize was a base wooden Spoon.

    Two Brothers conspire,
    The Lord and the 'Squire,
To advance their Patron to Fame:
    But alas! nor the Mint,
    Nor all that is in in't
Can consecrate such a damn'd Name.

    One Baronet more
    Must not be pass'd o'er,
Whose Merit so great, that his Praise
    (Cou'd a Poet be found,
    For Invention renown'd)
Shou'd be sung in *Homerian* Lays.

For Manners polite
This *Hibernian* Wight
Has ta'en many a Tour from Home:
A Man of his Letters
May calumniate his Betters;
'Tis the Fashion of *France*, *Spain*, and *Rome*.

In the Rear of this Herd,
Some vile Fellows appear'd,
All bedaub'd with political Mire;
An Attorney with Face
Of *Corinthian* Brass,
Whose Trade is to Cozen and Hire.

But whilst we disdain
To put on the Chain,
Prostitution must bid us adieu;
We'll defy all their Wiles,
Their Threats and their Smiles,
And be steady to *Bagshot* and *Crewe*.

The Original SPEECH *of Sir* W—M St—PE, *On the first Reading of the Bill for appointing the Assizes at* Buckingham, Feb. 19, 1748.

Mr. Sp——r,

IF I did not think I could prove, that this Bill is the errantest *Job* that ever was brought to P—rl—t, I would not give the House the Trouble of hearing me. But why do I talk of Proofs; when there is a known Course of Law for appointing Assizes all over *England*? If one particular Town applies to P—rl——t to desire the Monopoly of the Assizes in their County, is there any Courtier who has so little of the Country-gentle-

man

man in him, as to want to be told that such a Monopoly, exclusive of the other Towns of the County, is a Job? Or will Courtiers be fond of such a Bill only because it is a Job and a Monopoly? But, Sir, this Exclusion is actually going to be inflicted on the County of *Buckingham*; and here let me condole with that unhappy, rather that blinded County, who neglected to choose *two Gentlemen* of such Power and Interest, that I am persuaded they will have more Votes in this House to-day, than they would have had at the general Election in the whole County in question, if they had done it the Honour to offer themselves for Representatives. It is the Power and Interest of those *Gentlemen* that I am afraid of, not of their Arguments; and they will have Occasion for both the former, to balance the Weakness and Ridiculousness of the latter. And to shew you, Sir, how sensible they are of the Frivolousness of the latter, I could recapitulate such Instances of intriguing for Votes, as no Man would believe, who does not know those Gentlemen. Conscious of the Badness of their Cause, they have employed every bad Art to support it, and have retained so much of their former Patriotism, as consisted in blackening their Adversaries, and acquiring Auxiliaries. They have propagated such Tales, that Men have overlooked the Improbabilities, while they wondered at the Foolishness of them; and they have solicited the Attendance of their Friends, and of their Friends Friends, with as much Importunity as if their Power itself was tottering, not the wanton Exercise of it opposed. The only Aid they have failed to call in, was Reason, the natural but baffled Enemy of their *Family*. A Family, Sir, possessed of every Honour they formerly decried, fallen from every Honour they formerly acquired. A Family, Sir, who coloured over Ambition with Patriotism, disguised Emptiness

by

by Noise, and disgraced every Virtue by wearing them only for mercenary Purposes. A Family, Sir, who from being the most clamorous Incendiaries against Power and Places, are possessed of more Employments than the most comprehensive Place-Bill that ever was brought into P—rl—t would include; and who to every Indignity offered to their R—l M—r have added that greatest of all, Intrusion of themselves into his Presence and Councils; and who shew him what he has still farther to expect, by their scandalous Ingratitude to his Son. A Family, Sir, raised from Obscurity by the Petulance of the Times, drawn up higher by the Insolence of their b—g Kinsman, and supported by the Timidity of two M—rs, who, to secure their own Persons from Abuse, have sacrific'd their own Party to this all-grasping Family, the elder ones of which riot in the Spoils of their T———y and P———s, and the younger———

(Here being called to order, he proceeded as follows) Sir, I am sorry to have offended the Gentlemen, when I thought the greatest Compliment I could pay them, as no Man can imitate them without giving up his Understanding or his Character, was to follow their Example. They introduced and cultivated the Use of personal Invectives, and they must be very tender, very sore indeed, Sir, when they would abolish the Practice. But as they have corrected me for imitating them, I shall now do quite the contrary from what I ever saw them do, and oppose this Bill from Reason and Argument; and of all the Bills I ever saw, the Opposition to this has the least Occasion to combine personal Odium with it to discredit it.

We were told, Sir, that Applications for similar Bills have been often made, and the Suit granted, but the Bill afterwards rejected: that sometimes Bills of the same Nature have even passed this House, and not

met

met with their Fate till at a subsequent Tribunal. These were Reasons I own for permitting the Introduction of the Bill as far as Precedent should reasonably operate; but on summing up the Accounts even of Precedent, I apprehend they will bear Evidence against passing the Act: For thus it stands; parallel Bills have been brought in; have sometimes scrambled through here, but have extorted the united Assent of the Legislature—how often? twice, Sir, say the ingenious Advocates for the Bill. Of that twice, once was as long ago as the Reign of *Harry* the IVth, and the other was so far from being a Case in Point, that it is directly contradictory. So far was the Parliament from pinning down the Assizes to one Town in *Cornwall*, that it left two Towns open for them to appoint the Assizes at either, Consequently there being but these two Cases pretended, where such a Bill has pass'd, the more Precedents there are for such a Bill being brought in, the more Precedents there are for throwing it out.

Another Reason for appointing the Assizes at *Buckingham* is its being the County-town; a Reason only fit to captivate the Imagination of an Antiquarian; if a County-town was always the most conveniently situated for the Concerns of the whole County, or always the best accommodated with every thing necessary for holding the Assizes, it might carry a Plausibility of Argument; but *Buckingham* having been proved by the united Voice of the Gentlemen of the County to be destitute of these Advantages, and *Aylesbury* appearing to be characterized by them, the Arguments summ'd up in the magic Term County-town, seem to have no more Weight than two Words without a definite Meaning can give them; which can be none here, as I am sure we are not in this Case, what we are sometimes denied to be, a Court of Judicature, for Jargon is not our Language. But the Gentlemen seemed sensible that no Stress would be laid upon Words of no Meaning, and therefore soon dropp'd this Topic, to flourish on others of equal Importance, and equally elucidated. They harangued out of the Petition, which having been coined in their own Mint, could lend no more Weight than it had received from them. For, Sir, what were the fundamental Arguments that produced the Petition, and that are to support the Bill? Why the great Concern the Town of *Buckingham* is under for losing the Assizes, and a Design of preventing these two dangerous Rivals from being played against one another. These were the Parents of the Bill. A constant, settled, uninterrupted Course of holding the Assizes there for a prodigious Length of Time, for no less than four and twenty Years, nay, and even before the Date of that very distant Period, some respectable obsolete Instances of their having been held there too; this great Prescription is to support the Bill; and if it were possible to want any additional Strength, besides these notable Arguments, and the whole Force of the M——ty, and the Drawcansirism of their well-worded Champion, the House has had a formal Assurance that there will be a better Goal built at *Buckingham* than there is at present at *Aylesbury*, where with all the undenied Advantages of Situation and Convenience, with a Goal and Town Hall already built, it is said there is less Attendance at the Assizes than at *Buckingham*.

To these Arguments, momentous as they are represented, no Answer need be given but what they carry along with them; foolish Reasons confute themselves. I can grieve, Sir, that the good Town of *Buckingham* should be concern'd; I can tremble at the Apprehension of two such potent States as *Aylesbury* and *Buckingham* entering into Competition for Power; I can contract such a Respect for venerable Custom,

Cuſtom, as to think four and twenty Years ſuch a Duration of Empire, that the Scepter cannot be raviſh'd from *Buckingham* without a Violation of all Antiquity; and I can think that a future Goal more accommodated for Reception, is an Object that ought to ſtrike the *preſent P—rl—t*; for as to the greater or leſs Attendance, I apprehend it depends on the different Seaſons of holding the Aſſizes; becauſe though we have been aſſured, that ſome Gentlemen muſt go fifty Miles to *Buckingham*, whereas the greateſt Diſtance from *Ayleſbury*, is not half the Number; yet I believe many would go fifty Miles in Summer, ſooner than twenty-five in Winter. By retaining the Aſſizes at *Ayleſbury*, no-body will go above twenty-five at any time. But, Sir, I ſhall not dwell on theſe Arguments, becauſe I ſhall hardly convince any Man who can ſhut his Eyes againſt the Conviction of the Map, nor in the Map itſelf will *Ayleſbury* appear the beſt ſituated, to any Man who looks there only for Stowe. For *Ayleſbury* I am ſure I have no particular Partiality; I never got a Vote there, that I did not pay for.

But, Sir, though I can accompany the Petitioners in all their Griefs and Fears, and Promiſes, yet I cannot get over one Objection, which ſtrikes me, as the very ſerious Point on which this whole Debate ought to turn. And that, Sir, is the great and unprovoked Injury which this Bill will offer to the whole Bench of Judges, whoſe Privileges will be violated, and even the Prerogative of the Crown infringed through their Sides. But though we know by Experience, how roughly *theſe Gentlemen* handle the Crown, whenever it ſuits their own Views, yet I ſhould hope the P—rl—t would not lend their Sanction to this Inſult on the Judges. When the Legiſlature has been ſo provident, as to eſtabliſh their Charges for Life, that they may execute their great and weighty Duties unſubjected to any Menaces of Power, or Appetites of Interest, I should hope no Man would consent to lop a Power, merited by Age, Experience and Abilities, entrusted by the whole Constitution, and a Check on all other Power, as theirs alone exists by, and is inseparable from the Execution of the Laws. Were there as many Cousins as there are Judges, and all chosen for *Buckingham*, I should hope the venerable Dignity of those Sages would save them from being sacrificed to the Clamours and Brigues of so importunate a Race. If the Bill passes, the Judges will no longer have the free Option, which they have in other Counties, of appointing the Assizes; and surely there is no Cause why these worthy Persons should lose a Privilege, which it is not pretended they have abused, only to favour the Petitioners in acquiring a new Privilege, much less supported by any Argument, than any old Privilege that I ever heard of. For, Sir, I repeat it again, there is not the Shadow of an Argument offered to support this Request. No Hardship is inflicted on *Buckingham* in taking away the Assizes, the original Hardship was to *Aylesbury*, from whence they were removed by a former Judge, to cultivate a Family-Interest in the present petitioning Town, which *these Gentlemen* having undermined by *their superior Merit*, it surely may be allowed to another Judge to remove the Assizes back to their former Situation; and if four and twenty Years are such a prodigious long Term, why then *Buckingham* has enjoy'd a Privilege wrested from *Aylesbury*, for a prodigious long Season. But the real Hardship is on the Judges, who are to suffer for the Competition between these two Towns. I cannot look on it, Sir, as personal to the great and learned Man, who made the last Removal; it is only incidental to him when he goes that Circuit, but all his Brethren and Successors are complicated with him for no Fault of theirs. It was said, that no Censure

sure was laid on that great Person for this Removal; I am amazed the Gentlemen should be so cautious, it is not the first Time they have censured a Chief Justice for doing what he has a legal Right to do, nor is this the first Attack made on the learned Profession by a *certain Family*; but though they can influence Court-Martials to execute their Piques and Prejudices, I hope the P—rl—t will have more Sense and Resolution, than to be the Tools of so hot-headed a Faction, and when their Drudgery *nemini obtrudi potest*, I hope if they are at last forced to resort to us, we shall have Spirit enough to preserve our own Dignity, and to refuse to be the Agents of their Jobs, and the Instruments of their Malice, and as all Parties have already been, the Dupes of their self-interested Politicks.

A S P E E C H *without Doors, in Answer to a supposed Speech within; on the Merits of the Great Cause of* Aylesbury *versus* Buckingham.

Hear both Sides

An old Maxim in Law.

SIR,

IT is a common, but a just Observation, that tho' *wise* Men are sometimes obliged to make, yet it is only those who are *otherwise*, that take a pleasure in printing and publishing long Speeches.——— Speeches that perhaps were never spoke at least in an Assembly, where Indecencies like those contained in the Paper before me, would undoubtedly have drawn the Resentment of every man of Honour, who considered the dangerous Consequence of divulging such scurrilous Invectives amongst the licentious Populace.—But what the P—t *would not* hear, it seems the People *must*, and what you were there stopped from uttering, by being called to *Order*, must now be trumpeted abroad,

as

as if it had been really pronounced, that the *Aylesbury* Faction may admire your *Eloquence*, and the cheated *Crowd* may applaud your *Courage* for naturalizing the Language of *Billingsgate* in St. *S—ph—*'s Chapel, and degrading the H— of C—s, some twenty Degrees below those polite Persons, who usually, about the same Hour of the Day that your Oration is supposed to be spoken, assemble at *Rag-Fair*.

But, Sir, if you took this Method with a View of receiving *no Answer*, you shall be quickly made sensible of your Mistake. We have smarted sufficiently by the Mischiefs that have attended these sort of *Mob Declamations*, and therefore it is fit that an *Antidote* should be exhibited as soon as *Poisons* of this Sort are thrown abroad.——— I shall confine myself intirely, Sir, to what I find in your admirable Oration, and shall refute whatever wears the least Colour of *Argument*, adding now and then a Remark upon your ill Language, without following your *Example*; because I think it base to abuse a *Gentleman*, or to supply the Want of *Reason*, with *Ribaldry*, which is the great Merit of your Performance.—A Performance, Sir, as much below your *Parts*, as it is inconsistent with your *Education*; a Performance to which you stooped, that you might be upon a *Level* with your *Party*; a Performance only comparable to another Piece of dry, obscure, unintelligible *Irony*, that has been cried up for *Wit* by those, who if they had had any, must have known it to have been as full of *false Humour* as yours is of *false Argument*.

But to come to the Point.———

You set out, Sir, with foul Language and false Facts, at a Time, you say, that the Bill you oppose is the erranteſt *Job* that ever was brought into P———t; you say that you can *prove* it, but immediately after you dispense with that, and say very cavalierly, that it needs *no Proof*—very arch and conclusive truly! But, Sir, I take it to be *no Job*, and I will prove it to be none.—For, Sir, those to whom you attribute this *Job*, did no more than their Duty, as *Members* for the *Corporation* they represent, which conceiving itself aggrieved, had recourse to P——t for Relief, and to them for their Assistance. — This, Sir, was a rational, a legal, and a proper Method; and to call this a *Job*, or to upbraid the Gentlemen who promoted it, for what they were bound to do in the Discharge of their Trust, was affronting them, insulting the H——, and offering a *high Indignity* to the C———s of *Britain*, whose indubitable Right it is to petition against whatever they take to be a Grievance. You proceed next to a *false Fact*; you say, that this Corporation applies for the *Monopoly* of the *Assizes* in their County.—The very Reverse of this is true; instead of applying *for*, they apply *against* a *Monopoly*, for which you are an Advobate.—They desire the *Assizes* may be held *sometimes* at *Buckingham*; the Point you espouse is, that they should be *always* held at *Aylesbury*.—Which, dear Sir, looks most like a *Monopoly*?

After so happy a Beginning, you fall into a violent *Torrent* of *Abuse* upon a whole *Family*, founded on no Reason in the World, but because that Family is distinguished by the just *Rewards* of their *Services* to their King and Country, and in the Heat of your Resentment, you throw out things that are as unpardonably seditious, as they are palpably absurd. You take it for granted, that Men *force* themselves into a *Presence*, and into *Councils*, to which they have the Honour to be called, and into which our *Constitution* renders it impossible for any to *intrude*. In the same Breath, you make entering into a FATHER's Service, an Act of Ingratitude to a Son; and without so much as pretending to assign either Facts or Reasons, you bestow the most *low* and *infamous* Epithets upon Characters that all other Men mention with *Esteem*. In a Word, you forgot yourself to such a Degree, that you paint out Men of Birth and Fortune, and in high Stations, as if they were the most abandon'd and profligate Creatures in the Universe; without *Parts*, without *Morals*, without *Shame*, and who, if your Description had in it the least *Tittle* of *Truth*, instead of being M——s of P——t, or admitted to the P——y C——l, were fit only to be Members of a *Society*, once famous by the Name of the *Hell-fire Club*.

It would be in vain to follow you Step by Step, through that *Maze* of *Scurrility*, in which you delight to wander, and therefore I will keep to the Point in Question, and to what you would have pass'd upon the World for *Arguments*. You are pleased to say, that the *Precedents* that have been brought in support of this Bill, are few in Number, and that they have not been always successful. Why, that may be, and yet it does not at all answer the *Purpose* for which you bring it.—A single Bill of this Kind applied for and brought in, is a Precedent sufficient; that is, sufficient for the Purpose, as to which Precedents had been mentioned; as to the Usage of P——t, in hearing and determining Points of this Nature; for as to *what* they will upon the hearing determine, is another Point, and what must depend upon the *Merits* of this particular Cause. — But if ever the H—— of C——s received and examined, and afterwards *decided* upon a Case of this Nature, whether in *Favour* of those that brought in the Bill or *not*, it was a very good Argument for bringing this Point to be examined the same way; nor was there the least Probability that your little Sophism, of the *more* Precedents of *bringing in* so many *more* Precedents there were of *throwing out* such Bills, should prevail.

prevail. The Words jingle prettily enough, and no doubt but the *Witlings* of a Party may think this Manner of speaking *very fine*; but Men of Sense and Judgment will always distinguish between a *trite* Expression and a *sound* Reason.—A Bill of the *same Kind* brought in heretofore, is a good Precedent for bringing in one *now*, and *throwing* out that Bill afterwards is no Precedent at all, unless the *same Reasons* appear in this Case, that there did in *that*.—Now shew you but *these* Reasons, and no doubt the Bill will be thrown out. But in the mean time, what you have advanced is no Argument against *bringing it in*.

In the same arch Manner, you are for getting rid of the Argument drawn from its being a *County Town*.— That, you say, was to catch the Antiquaries; and pray, Sir, what was the Meaning of *your known Course of Law for appointing* Assizes *all over* England? Was not that thrown out to catch the *Lawyers?* But if you dispute its being the County Town, give me Leave to tell you, that there is an *Act of Parliament* in the Reign of *Henry* VII. by which it is enacted, *That the Standard of Weights and Measures shall be kept here*; and till that time you will give me Leave to say, that it was without Dispute the *County Town*, and that most of the *County* Business was done there.—Upon this fair State of the Case, it will appear that *Buckingham*'s being the County Town is no *Magic Term*, no Appellation grounded merely upon its giving Name to the County, but arising from an indisputable Matter of Fact, which therefore deserves to be well weighed and considered, notwithstanding your quaint Way of turning it into ridicule, more especially in a Place where, as you rightly say—*Jargon* is not their *Language*.

In the next Place, you are extreamly witty on the *prodigious Length* of Time, no less, say you, than *four and twenty* Years, that *Buckingham* has been in Possession of the Assizes; in which, give me Leave to say, that there is somewhat of Prevarication, tho' I must be so just to own, that you very possibly might not *intend* it.—For this prodigious Length of Time, with which you are so merry, does not really refer to the Possession of the Assizes, but to their being *restored* to *Buckingham*; and surely, if they had been deprived of them even for a *prodigious Length of Time* (to use that Term in its *proper* Sense) this, according to your own Manner of arguing, ought to be no Reason against *restoring* them, much less ought it to be urged as a just Cause for depriving them a *second* Time of what they had been, without any manifest Inconvenience, restored to in *Part*, that is, for the *Summer* Assizes only, for that is all that is contended for, and this for the Space of *four and twenty* Years.—Be so kind for once, Sir, as to let the Thing appear in its true Light: *Buckingham* was the *old* County Town where the Assizes were generally held: but by some Means or other, they were *taken away*, and by this Means this good old Borough *sunk* very much in its Credit. But after they had been long taken away altogether, and bestowed as a Favour on another Place, *Buckingham* had the good Fortune to recover the *Summer* Assizes, and found the Benefit of it. But by another *unlucky Accident*, they are deprived of their Turn of having the Assizes held there, without any Cause assign'd for inflicting this *Punishment*—and for this they ask *Relief*, which you and the Friends of *Aylesbury* say is *ridiculous*.—Other Folks think it *reasonable*, shall not the P——t be allowed to judge whether it is *reasonable* or *ridiculous*? Surely, Sir, all the Wit, and Spleen, and Prejudice, and Solicitation in the World, ought not to prevail in such a Case as *this*, to deny People a Hearing.

 The chief Argument upon which you seem to rely, and indeed it is the Argument upon which your Friends chuse

chuse to rest this Point, is the *Privileges* of the J-dg-s. *If the Bill passes,* say you, *the* J-dg-s *will no longer have the free Option which they have in other* Counties, *of appointing the* Assizes, *and there is no Cause why they should lose a* Privilege, *which it is not pretended they have* abused.—Immediately after, you are pleased to say, *that no Hardship is inflicted on* Buckingham, in *taking away the* Assizes, *the* original Hardship *was to* Aylesbury, *from whence they were* removed *by a* former Judge, to *cultivate* a Family-Interest *in the present petitioning Town.*—Now, Sir, all this to me is Mystery, Absurdity and Inconsistency: for I would be glad to know how you can reconcile the *not abusing* this Privilege to your *Assertion*, that the Assizes were *removed* (you should have said the *Summer* Assizes *restored*) to *Buckingham*, by a Judge, to *cultivate* a *Family-Interest*.—If there be any Truth in your *Insinuation*, what becomes of your *Argument*? Is *cultivating* a *Family-Interest* a sufficient Reason for transferring the Assizes from *one* Town to *another*? Surely not. If there be a Syllable of Truth in this *Insinuation*, a stronger Argument cannot be offered for preventing any Thing of the *like Sort* for the *future*. But, Sir, I beg Leave to say, you have advanced another Absurdity, as to the *original Injury* being offered to *Aylesbury*.———Pray when and how got they hither? was *Aylesbury* the *old* County Town? were they always *held there*, both Summer and Winter? If not, surely the *original* Injury was offered to the *Place* from whence the Assizes were *transferred* to *Aylesbury*.—By your Archness upon *Antiquaries*, I doubt you will not be able to answer this Question.—You will not *thank* me, perhaps, but I will answer it for you.—It happened once upon a Time, a *prodigious long* time ago, in the Reign, if I am rightly informed, of *Henry* VIII. that the Lord Chief Justice *Baldwyn*, who was a *Native* of the Town of *Aylesbury*, and who had purchased the *Lordship* of that Place, had Interest enough to carry the *Assizes, Sessions*, and all *County Business* thither.—My Author says, that this was out of *Partiality*; but let that pass, whatever his Motive was, certain it is, *that he did it*; and if there be any Strength in your *Logic*, this was the *original* Injury, and therefore *the Injury* that ought to be *repaired*.—You will forgive me, Sir, for demolishing your *Argument*, when you consider how much I have strengthened your *Insinuation*.

One Stroke more, and the Piece is finished. You seem to be mightily alarmed at the Inconveniencies that would follow upon granting the *Prayer* of the *Petition*.—Had there been any such *Inconveniencies* ever experienced when the Assizes were at *Buckingham*, no doubt they would have been removed some other way than they were.—In a Case of this Nature, it is the Benefit of the County in general, it is a fair and equal Distribution of *public Favours*, that ought to be considered, and not *Family-Interests*, or the *Conveniencies* of *particular Persons*, however dignified or distinguished. This, Sir, if I understand the cooler Parts of your Speech clearly, is what you mean, and I protest I mean *the very same Thing*.—You have shewn in *one* strong Instance, that for the sake of cultivating a *Family-Interest*, this great Point was slighted; I have mentioned another Instance, where on the Score of a *Purchase*, it was also slighted. How do we know, Sir, that in the ancient or modern Times, *other* Instances of the same Kind may not have occurred, and therefore that they may *never* occur *more*; why should not this Point be fairly and fully discussed before those who are not like to be biassed by any such Interests?—Here, Sir, lie the *true Merits* of the *Cause*, and by the *Merits* let it be determined. You are pleased indeed to be ludicrous, very ludicrous, in representing the Contest be-

twixt

'twixt the two *great States* of *Buckingham* and *Aylesbury;* but surely the Concerns of *two* Corporations deserve to be treated a little more *seriously;* especially when they come to be examined before so *august* an *Assembly.* If in itself this be such a trifling and ridiculous Affair, why do you make such a Point of it, and if it is otherwise, why would you represent it in that Light?—Alas! the *Reason* is but too *plain;* if it is considered in any *other,* all you have been saying must go for nothing. All your Eloquence is lost, all your Jokes are spoiled, all your Wit is thrown away; for all these, Sir, are employ'd to procure a *Decision* without a *Hearing.*—Yet you are so kind, and indeed so just, as to declare, that you are *impartial.* You are acquainted with the *County* some other way than by the *Map,* tho' it may be the Case of some of your *warmest Friends,* to be no otherways acquainted with it; and it seems, you are acquainted likewise with *Aylesbury,* very *well* acquainted with it, by the Character you bestow upon it.—*I never got a* Vote *there that I did not* pay for.— You are a *Man* of *Honour,* Sir, and no-body will doubt the *Truth* of what you say; perhaps this Method of procuring Votes may not be altogether *out* of *Fashion,* but it is to be hoped for the future, that *private Interests* will be supported by *private Purses;* for I dare say, Sir, even you will not think it reasonable to exchange that *Method* for *public Privileges.*

The SPEECH *of* Richard White-Liver, *Esq; in Behalf of himself and his Brethren. Spoken to the most* August Mob *at* Rag-Fair.

Hear *Us,* for *We* have been on both Sides.
A new Maxim of our Family.

Friends, Countrymen, Fellow-Labourers,

YOU must not expect that I should make you a very sensible Speech; for though *wise* Men sometimes give Speeches, yet we that are *otherwise* cannot always get them. Nor though I have the highest Reverence for this Assembly, must you expect that I should do more here than I do in S. St—s C—l. A certain M—r has been content to inlist us, because we have a Friend that speaks well; and we hope, that after his Example, you will excuse whatever Nonsense I or my Brothers may talk in Consideration that we have a Kinsman who is as fine-spoken a Gentleman as you would wish to hear. Oh! Neighbours, can you forget with what charming Language he used to tickle your Ears! how he railed against M—s and Pl—n, and how he used to shew you the Duty of R—n, and how some Folks deserved to be disposed for preferring H—r to O— E—d? And don't you remember how we used to whisper you whom he meant by *some Folks?* This was public Spirit, this was Patriotism! Nor did we deceive you; for there was not an Indecency which we vented before you *at this Hour of the Day,* which we did not afterwards hawk again in the H— of C—s, not considering how much we must *incur the Resentment of every Man of Honour, nor the dangerous Consequence of divulging such scurrilous Invectives amongst the licentious Populace;* for such, my my dear Friends, I muſt fairly own to you we think you; and if you had not been ſuch, we could never have made the Uſe of you that we have: If you had not been *twenty Degrees* below reaſonable Creatures, would you have been Tools to a Faction who are twenty Degrees below the moſt profligate Incendiaries that ever exiſted? Or if you were not twenty Degrees below Brutes, would you ſubmit to Men, who have impoſed upon you, duped you, betray'd you, and who now tyrannize and intend to tyrannize ſtill more over you?

But as M—s have *ſmarted ſufficiently by the Miſchiefs that have attended theſe Mob Declarations*, and as our Turn is ſerved by them, I ſhall tell you fairly and honeſtly, contrary to our Cuſtom, that we are determined not to ſuffer ourſelves by our own Weapons. We have a M—r at our Devotion, who though he frets, and fumes, and winces, and ſhews all the World how he is galled by being rid, and how little he dares attempt to throw his Riders, yet he muſt go on with our dirty Work. If we are abuſed and told of all our Villainies in the Senate, why our Orator ſhall abuſe again; or if that won't do, he ſhall clap his Hand on his Sword and hector. If we are abuſed in Print, we will take away the Liberty of the Preſs; and if there is any other Law or Liberty, any Sage of the Law or Champion of Liberty that riſes in their Defence, why we will make the whole Legiſlature interpoſe, and execute our Revenge and perſecute our Enemies; for I muſt tell you, my dear Friends, what you nor any Man living will believe, *that all Men mention us with Eſteem*, which is as true as any of the Profeſſions which we made when we were Patriots, or as our late Aſſertion that we are *diſtinguiſhed by the juſt Rewards of our Services to our King and Country*. What we did deſerve, the poor Wretches, whom our Example beguiled till they

they met with the just Rewards of *their* Services at *Kennington-Common,* can witness; what we *are distinguished* by, the rest of our Countrymen can testify; and what Truth there is, of *our Constitution's making it impossible for any Man to intrude into the Royal Presence and Councils,* let the World judge from the Truth of our other Assertion that we were ever called into either.

But, my good Friends, we are taxed with Ingratitude to the Son, as well as Insolence to the Father. I do assure you one is no truer than the other. The Ingratitude is on his Side, who would not co-operate with us in dethroning his Father. Indeed when we saw that, and that he was not in the same Haste to make us M———rs, as we were to make him K—, or as we were to be M———rs, why, it is true, we left him; and as he would not accept the Dignity when we offered it him, we are resolved to prevent his ever having it at all. And therefore whatever Indignities we put upon him, or whatever Lies we tell of him, are to be imputed not to Ingratitude, but to Self-Preservation, the primary Law of Nature and favorite Rule of our Family, *whom all Men mention with Esteem.*

Would you know for what all Men esteem us—Why for the whole Tenour of our Conduct: For our Virulence in Opposition, for our Insolence in Power; for the Courage with which we plunged into Treason during the former, and for the Intrepidity with which we left it, and for the astonishing Assurance with which we tax every body of Crimes of which we ourselves were only guilty: For our Art in maintaining the same Rank in Government, which we held in Sedition, and for our Steadiness of Character in being the same noisy, intriguing, buzzing, senseless Demagogues, in a Court Party, that we were in a Faction: For our good Fortune in meeting with another Party, who will lift with us, us, after our notorious Treachery to our old Friends, and for our Dexterity in ruling those to whom we acceded, not who came over to us.

You will perhaps be told, that I sent a most illegal, unwarrantable and threatening Message to *Aylesbury*, but upon my Honour it is not true. They will tell you, that an hundred and fifty creditable substantial Freeholders are ready to attest it — *but am I to be put in Competition with a Parcel of Aylesbury-Fellows?* If any Part of my Life has ever been guilty of Falshood, don't believe me now, but rather believe an hundred and fifty poor rascally honest Men, who never betray'd their Party and Friends, and who have not Spirit enough to deny a Truth with oratorical Assurance. They say, I threaten'd if they sign'd the Petition, to take away the Winter-Assizes, and Quarter-Sessions too, and appoint them where I pleased. Is it probable I would have *threaten'd* that, when I have such a Mule of a M——r at my Disposition, who will bear any Load we lay upon him? Should I not rather have done it than threaten'd it? And if I had a Mind, why could not I oblige the P———t to take away the Winter, as well as the Summer Assizes? The one would not have been a more insolent Act of *arbitrary Power* than the other, nor more repugnant to all Law and Justice, and Custom.

And now, my good Friends, for as such, however they may tax me with Ingratitude, I shall always own *you*, and confess that I owe the Preferments of my Family to you; it only remains, that I recommend our common Friend, the M——r, to your Notice. Our Friend the Orator has sufficiently celebrated, this Winter, the many great and shining Qualities of the elder Brother, whom he has bedaubed as much with his coarse Praise, as he used to do other M———s with his Invectives. Let it be my Part to bring you acquainted with the younger, who, I aſſure you, is as ready and well diſpoſed to violate any of the Laws, as you yourſelves can be in your moſt riotous Hours. He hates a J——e as much as you can do; and is ſo favourably diſpoſed to the brave and outlaw'd Part of the Community, that he has argued moſt warmly for paſſing this Bill, by which you will every Summer have an Opportunity of reſcuing your Friends, as they are tranſported from *A*——*y* to *B*———*m*. So great is the Sympathy of his Sentiments with yours, that he is the moſt avow'd Friend to Bribery in Elections, and has ſo great an Averſion to old formal Rules and Orders of P———t, that he not only infring'd them in his own Perſon, and in Company with his Brother in his own Country this Summer, but procured a Majority to juſtify his arbitrary Proceedings; and I leave you to judge what a fair Proſpect you have of Anarchy and Confuſion when the Orders of the H——e are ſet at nought, when the Privileges of the J——s are taken away, and the Countenance of the L——ſl——e withdrawn from them.

It was to acquaint you with theſe important Points that, my good Friends, I called you together this Day. We have formerly ſet you the Example of inſulting M———y, of propagating T——n, of defaming M——s; we now ſhew you the Way to inſult J——s, to aboliſh Cuſtoms, to puniſh Enemies.

Go ye and do likewiſe.

The SPEECH of Dick Green in the Lower House of the Gentlemen of the Cloth.

Come *Thomas* and *Peggy*, come *Robin* and *Phyllis*,
  Come all ye Thirteen,
  And pray for Dick Green,
  And sing the Renown-a
  Of *Buckingham* Town-a;
So faith my good worthy old Friend Master WILLIS.

Delivered March *the* 21st, 1747.

* SIR,

IT gives me great Concern to find, that this Bill is not like to go through our Assembly with as little Difficulty, as it passed the other. I do not say this because I would not have the Matter freely debated. For, as we have hitherto observed the greatest Impartiality in all our Proceedings; and as all our Actions are governed *here* by Justice and Equity, without any Regard to what hath been transacted in *another Place*, I would therefore have this Bill perfectly well understood before it passes into a Law. 'Tis on that Account I now rise up quite unprovoked (for no wise Man ought to speak in a Passion) to give my Reasons, for my Assent to it; not such flimsy cobweb Reasons, as have been offered by the Gentlemen over the Way; which, to confess the Truth, were not at all worth a single Pot of good Porter; but such solid and substantial Arguments, as I am convinced must necessarily have their due Weight with every Member of this Assembly. But before I come to my Point, I will endeavour to remove

---

* The Footmen, who attend their Masters during the Session of P——nt, chuse a S——r for themselves, and a Mock P———t.

the general Prejudices, which have been entertained against the Bill, especially by those Gentlemen among us who have heard the Matter canvassed in *Leicester-Fields*, or who are obliged to give their daily Attendance at the Tables of *Tories* and *Patriots*. All the Arguments made use of in those Places, as well as in the other Assembly, may be reduced to these Two, The inconvenient Situation of *Buckingham*; and, The Privilege which by this Means will be taken from the Judges. As to the First, the more inconvenient the Situation is, the worse the Roads are, and the further *Buckingham* may be from any Man's Habitation, whose Business shall call him to the Assizes, the better it must needs be for that Person. Change of Air, and Exercise, is universally allowed to be the best Preservative of Health. And if a Man be obliged to ride five Days in the Week instead of two, and to lie abroad in two Places instead of one, will he not be proportionably benefited by it? If his Expences are a little increased by this Means (which is a trifling Objection, and can only affect some poor Farmers, who may be subpœna'd as Witnesses, or summon'd upon a Jury) had he not better bestow his Money in good Eating and Driking, than give it to a Physician or an Apothecary? Then again, suppose the Man leaves at home a Wife, who is a Shrew, as it is ten to one if he does not, he gets three Days of Ease and Happiness extraodinary. And this one Consideration would, I am sure, induce many honest 'Squires, to whom I have the Honour to be known, to give their Assent to the Bill. But, Sir, I have still a more forcible Answer to make to all the Objections, which have been urged concerning the ill Situation of our County Town. The great Mr.———, one of our Burgesses, and whose Father was a Burgess before him, a most excellent Casuist, and a most profound

found Scholar, hath lately difcovered in an old Law Book, which was publifhed many hundred Years ago, that *Buckingham* is as conveniently fituated as *Aylefbury*; or, that whatever you have at *Aylefbury*, you may find at *Buckingham*; or in other Words, that whether the Affizes be held at *Aylefbury*, or at *Buckingham*, 'tis the very fame Thing. 'Tis well known, that in ancient Times the Laws were all written in *Latin*, and the Words of the Law I fpeak of are, *Quod petis hic eft*; *eft Ulubris*; which hath been interpreted as above by my learned Friend, and which of itfelf is fufficient to confound all the Cavils of your W—lles and P—tters, &c. But 3*dly*, Sir, I affirm, upon very good Grounds, that two or three Summers hence, *Buckingham* will be better fituated than any corporate Town in *England*, or perhaps than any City in *Europe*. For our noble V——t makes fuch a quick Progrefs, that it will not be long ere he takes it into his Gardens. What a grand Figure will it make then? or who will not rejoice to go the Affizes, when they are held at a Place, where he may have an Opportunity of feeing fo many fine Sights for *nothing*; Groves and Walks, and Boats and Bridges, and Canals and Pillars, and Temples and Heroes, and Aldermen and Kings, and Queens, and Gods and Goddefies of all Sorts, and of all Nations? If this Advantage were duly confidered, my Mafter and the Brotherhood, inftead of being infulted in fuch an outrageous Manner, would have the Thanks of the whole County for their Generofity and Condefcenfion.

It has been often faid, and ftrongly infifted on by fome Members, to prove the inconvenient Situation of *Buckingham* for the Purpofes in the Bill mentioned, that there is no Goal in that Town. But this is fo far from being an Objection, that in my Opinion it is the ftrongeft Argument we can produce in Favour of the Bill. 'Tis

well

well known, that the Goal-Sickness is always infectious, and generally mortal; and we have not only Instances in our History to prove, that half the People attending at an Assize, together with the Judges themselves, have been carried off by this Distemper; but the same Thing hath happened in our Memory, witness the unfortunate End of the Lord Chief Baron *Pengelly*, a few Years since at *Exeter*. Now, Sir, if the Prisoners are obliged to travel a Day's Journey, before they are try'd, as in the present Case, they will be so purified by the sweet Air on the Road, that there will be no Danger of their bringing any Infection with them into Court. And this is a sufficient Reason, why a Goal ought not to be ever built in *Buckingham*, and yet, why the Assizes ought to be held in that Town in Winter, as well as Summer.

The Objection drawn from the Map, which has been enforced with so much Vehemence to demonstrate the inconvenient Situation of our County Town, I had almost forgot, because 'tis so very absurd. For can any Thing be more erroneous, than a Map? Don't your Map-makers often put Lions, and Bears, and Hottentots, where there ought to be great Cities, and Kings Palaces, and Assemblies of fine Gentlemen and Ladies? Don't they often make a Sea, where there should be dry Land; and Land, where there should be a Sea? For this Reason some of our great Men have never been able to understand the Geography of their own Country, even when the Map hath been perfectly well coloured, and all the Counties properly distinguished.

The 2d Objection, that the fixing the Summer Assizes at *Buckingham* takes away a Privilege from the Judges, I do not deny, and therefore I propose, that a suitable Compensation should be made them for this Loss, by adding 500*l*. a Year to their respective Salaries;

ries; which in our prefent flourifhing Condition, and when we have fuch a Plenty of Money, is a mere Trifle. This, I make no Doubt, would fufficiently content them. At leaft, I can anfwer for a certain good Friend of mine, that if you will make him a Judge, he fhall agree to hold the Affizes in *Lucifer*'s-Hall for half that Sum.

Having thus, Sir, fully anfwered all the material Objections, which have been offered againft the Bill, I come now to fhew the great Benefit and Advantage, which will accrue to our Order, and the whole Footmanry of the County of *Bucks*, if it fhould pafs into a Law. And this I fhall do by Nineteen Arguments, every one of which is irrefragable. And firft it will be granted by all Gentlemen of the Cloth, both without Doors and within, that we never live more to our Satisfaction, or are fo much refpected, as when we accompany our Mafters on a Journey. In every Inn the Landlord and Landlady are our Companions; and all the Servants, from the Chamber-maid down to the Oftler, very diligently and exactly obey all our Commands. We are allowed Board-Wages and Drink-Money, which is all clear Gains. For we have no Occafion to fpend a Shilling, and we live high, and generally much better than our Mafters. Who can therefore be againft the Bill, (which is intended to keep us abroad three or four Days beyond our ufual Time) who is not either a Fool, or a Tool to Faction?——*Here he was called to Order, and obliged to fit down.*

ISIS. An ELEGY.

Written in the Year 1748, by Mr. MASON.

Ω ΔΥΣΤΗΝΟΣ
ΤΙ ΠΟΥ ΟΥ ΔΗ ΠΟΥ
ΣΕΓ ΑΠΙΣΤΟΥΣΑΝ ΤΟΙΣ ΒΑΣΙΛΕΙΟΙ
ΣΙΝ ΑΓΟΥΣΙΝ ΝΟΜΟΙΣ
ΚΑΙ ΕΝ ΑΦΡΟΣΥΝΗ ΚΑΘΕΛΟΝΤΕΣ.
SOPHOCLES in Antig.

FAR from her hallow'd Grot, where mildly bright
 The pointed Cryſtals ſhot their trembling Light,
From dripping Moſs where ſparkling Dew-drops fell,
Where Coral glow'd, where twin'd the wreathed Shell,
Pale *Iſis* lay; a Willow's lowly Shade
Spread its thin Foliage o'er the penſive Maid;
Clos'd was her Eye, and from her heaving Breaſt
In careleſs Folds looſe flow'd her zoneleſs Veſt;
While down her Neck her vagrant Treſſes flow
In all the aweful Negligence of Woe;
Her Urn ſuſtain'd her Arm, that ſculptur'd Vaſe
Where *Vulcan*'s Art had laviſh'd all its Grace;
Here, full with Life was Heav'n-taught Science ſeen,
Known by the Laurel Wreath and muſing Mien;
There cloud-crown'd Fame, here Peace ſedate and bland,
Swell'd the loud Trump, and wav'd the Olive Wand;
While ſolemn Domes, arch'd Shades, and Viſta's green
At well-mark'd Diſtance cloſe the ſacred Scene.
 On this the Goddeſs caſt an anxious Look,
Then dropt a tender Tear, and thus ſhe ſpoke:
Yes, I cou'd once with pleas'd Attention trace
The mimic Charms of this prophetic Vaſe;
Then lift my Head, and with enraptur'd Eyes
View on yon Plain the real Glories riſe.

Yes,

Yes, *Isis!* oft haft thou rejoic'd to lead
Thy liquid Treasures o'er yon fav'rite Mead,
Oft haft thou ftopt thy pearly Car to gaze,
While ev'ry Science nurs'd its growing Bays;
While ev'ry Youth with Fame's strong Impulse fir'd,
Preft to the Goal, and at the Goal untir'd,
Snatch'd each celestial Wreath to bind his Brow
The Muses, Graces, Virtues cou'd beftow.
   E'en now fond Fancy leads th' ideal Train,
And ranks her Troops on Mem'ry's ample Plain;
See! the firm Leaders of my patriot Line,
See! SIDNEY, RALEIGH, HAMBDEN, SOMERS shine.
See HOUGH superior to a Tyrant's Doom
Smile at the Menace of the Slave of *Rome*.
Each Soul whom Truth cou'd fire, or Virtue move,
Each Breast strong panting with its Country's Love,
All that to *Albion* gave the Heart or Head,
That wisely counfell'd, or that bravely bled,
All, all appear; on me they grateful smile,
The well-earn'd Prize of every virtuous Toil
To me with filial Reverence they bring,
And hang fresh Trophies o'er my honour'd Spring.
   Ah! I remember well yon beachen Spray,
There ADDISON first tun'd his polish'd Lay;
'Twas there great *Cato*'s Form first met his Eye,
In all the Pomp of fire-born Majesty.
" My Son, he cry'd, obferve this Mien with Awe,
" In folemn Lines the strong Refemblance draw;
" The piercing Notes shall strike each *British* Ear,
" Each *British* Eye shall drop the Patriot Tear;
" And rous'd to Glory by the nervous Strain,
" Each Youth shall spurn at Slav'ry's abject Reign,
" Shall guard with *Cato*'s Zeal *Britannia*'s Laws,
" And speak, and act, and bleed, in Freedom's Caufe."
   The Hero spoke, the Bard affenting bow'd,
The Lay to Liberty and *Cato* flow'd;

N° VI.   G   While

While Echo, as she rov'd the Vale along,
Join'd the strong Cadence of his *Roman* Song.
    But ah! how Stillness slept upon the Ground,
How mute Attention check'd each rising Sound;
Scarce stole a Breeze to wave the leafy Spray,
Scarce trill'd sweet *Philomel* her softest Lay,
When LOCKE walk'd musing forth; e'en now I view
Majestic Wisdom thron'd upon his Brow,
View Candour smile upon his modest Cheek,
And from his Eye all Judgment's Radiance break.
'Twas here the Sage his manly Zeal exprest,
Here stript vain Falshood of her gaudy Vest;
Here Truth's collected Beams first fill'd his Mind,
Ere long to burst in Blessings on Mankind;
Ere long to shew to Reason's purged Eye,
That " NATURE'S FIRST BEST GIFT WAS LIBERTY."
    Proud of this wond'rous Son, sublime I stood,
(While louder Surges swell'd my rapid Flood)
Then vain as *Niobe*, exulting cry'd,
Ilissus! roll thy fam'd *Athenian* Tide;
Tho' *Plato*'s Steps oft mark'd thy neighb'ring Glade,
Tho' fair *Lyceum* lent its aweful Shade,
Tho' ev'ry *Academic* Green imprest
Its Image full on thy reflecting Breast,
Yet my pure Stream shall boast as proud a Name,
And *Britain*'s *Isis* flow with *Attic* Fame.
    Alas! how chang'd! where now that *Attic* Boast?
See! *Gothic* Licence rage o'er all my Coast.
See! Hydra Faction spread its impious Reign,
Poison each Breast, and madden ev'ry Brain.
Hence frontless Crouds, that not content to fright
The blushing *Cynthia* from her Throne of Night,
Blast the fair Face of Day; and madly bold,
To Freedom's Foes infernal Orgies hold;
To Freedom's Foes, ah! see the Goblet crown'd,
Hear plausive Shouts to Freedom's Foes resound;
                                                  The

The horrid Notes my refluent Waters daunt,
The Echoes groan, the Dryads quit their Haunt;
Learning that once to all diffus'd her Beam,
Now sheds by Stealth a partial private Gleam,
In some lone Cloister's melancholy Shade
Where a firm few support her sickly Head;
Despis'd, insulted by the barb'rous Train,
Who scour like *Thracia*'s Moon-struck Rout the Plain,
Sworn Foes like them to all the Muse approves,
All *Phœbus* favours, or *Minerva* loves.

 Are these my Sons my fostering Breast must rear?
Grac'd with my Name, and nurtur'd by my Care,
Must these go forth from my maternal Hand
To deal their Insults tho' a peaceful Land,
And boast while Freedom bleeds, and Virtue groans,
That " *Isis* taught Rebellion to her Sons? "
Forbid it Heav'n! and let my rising Waves
Indignant swell, and whelm the recreant Slaves,
In *England*'s Cause their Patriot Floods employ,
As *Xanthus* deluged in the Cause of *Troy*.
Is this deny'd? then point some secret Way
Where far from hence these guiltless Streams may stray,
Some unknown Channel lend where Nature spreads
Inglorious Vales and unfrequented Meads,
There where a Hind scarce tunes his rustic Strain,
Where scarce a Pilgrim treads the pathless Plain,
Content I'll flow; forget that e'er my Tide
Saw yon majestic Structures crown its Side;
Forget that e'er my wrapt Attention hung
Or on the Sage's or the Poet's Tongue,
Calm and resign'd my humbler Lot embrace,
And pleas'd prefer Oblivion to Disgrace.

A CHARACTER of Baron MOUNTNEY.

A Friend to all whom Virtue may commend,
 A Foe to none but who deserve no Friend;
Guardian of Law, yet true to Virtue's Trust,
Mild without Weakness, without Rigour just.
Where Truth inclines, his Sentence pours its Weight,
And fixes Virtue firmer in her Seat:
Where Error loads, he makes the Burden light;
But Guilt, tho' titled, startles at his Sight.
 Great Man! was ev'ry Ermin'd Sire like thee,
Soon may the World as at the first be free.
Vain wou'd be Laws, no Vices to restrain,
And gen'ral Justice wou'd all Rights maintain:
Peace, Love, and Joy, and Freedom ever known
Their dear Companion, wou'd be all our own:
Each Rock a second Paradise wou'd dress,
And God's sole Work wou'd always be to bless.

A REFLECTION.

What in this World deserves a Moment's Thought?
 What's worth possessing after being sought?
Nothing but well-plac'd Love or Friendship can
Make blest, or merit the Regard of Man.
Increase of Wealth is but Increase of Pain,
To lose in such a Traffick is to gain.
What else mistaken Mortals Blessings call,
When duly weigh'd, to as low Value fall;
Except those Antidotes to earthly Ill,
Without whose Aid the Soul wou'd ne'er be still,
But fretted, tost, like Seas by ev'ry Wind,
Fly off and leave her heavy Load behind.
Mix Love and Friendship in the Cup with Pain,
Their soothing Pow'r will make its Fury vain.

What churlish Wretch wou'd brood alone o'er Joys,
And think the Man who shares them but destroys?
Wou'd you increase your Store, share with your Friend,
You're paid with Int'rest for the Joys you lend.
Not less the sacred Pow'r of soothing Love,
Pain to asswage, and ev'ry Joy improve.
Can I regard the Threats of loud Alarms,
Surrounded by my *Celia*'s shielding Arms?
There, Heav'n to prove thy Joys, oh! let me lie,
And when my Glass is out content I'll die:
Thy Pow'r, which gave me *Philon*, I adore,
Now grant me *Celia*, and I ask no more.

ADVICE to Mr. L—g—n, *the Dwarf* FAN-PAINTER, *at* Tunbridge-Wells.

PAinting aud Poetry, you know,
  Were Sisters many Years ago:
And every Critic must allow,
They have the same Connection now.
My little Dwarf, allow me then,
To guide my Pencil by my Pen:
Then let the Muse present a Plan,
To be the Subject of a Fan.
Receive, and from no Woman-Hater,
A well-intention'd honest Satire.
Thick, my Dwarf, lay thick enough on,
The Majesty of M—y T—n.
Nor yet forget, you little Varlet,
Th' eternal Frown of gloomy C—l—t.
Yet be their Colours nicely plac'd,
To give an Air of Sense and Taste.
But begin each frowning Feature
With Pride, Ill-Humour, and Ill-Nature.
Let ugly Scorn distort their Faces,
And frighten thence the Loves and Graces.

With

With Patience who can bear to think on
Th' imperious Airs of haughty *L——n*:
But give the Piece a little Merit;
Give it Senfe, Addrefs and Spirit.
Near her draw, but pray don't tell 'em,
The faucy Face of either *P—l—m*.
Shade, oh! Shade enough allow,
To bronze the Saffron Face of *H——e*:
But let her Drapery be flaring,
Loofely flaunting, wildly ftaring.
Draw three Fair Ones, finging, fhouting,
Clapping, dancing, hoyd'ning, routing;
Difturbing Concert, Walks, and Ball,
With Beau *Nafh* frowning on them all.
While *K——l* all alike derides,
Draw him holding both his Sides.
Contention and Confufion over,
This Quality Compartment Rover.
Hither fcreaming Scandal bring,
Let her flap her baleful Wing:
With hundred Tongues, and hundred Eyes,
Emblem of Female Talk, and Lies:
Pride and Envy ftalk among
This wretched, clam'rous, thoughtlefs Throng.
Let Riot feem to rule the Place,
And drive away Content and Peace:
Difcretion will no longer ftay,
But fpreads her Wings, and fleets away.
Then Lady *F——r*, but fpare, O Bard!
The youthful Spoufe of *E—r—d*;
Indulgent to her Youth advife,
Avoid, take Warning, and be wife.
Let there be a Fribble Groupe,
Of *B—l, S—n, P—l, S—.*
And in the midft confpicuous, fain I
Would fee the fimple *A——y*.

But

But rather draw the little Peer,
Gallanting with that pert thing *F—r*.
Here bring the happy Husband in,
Sneering a senseless ghastly Grin.
To raise the Price, and Fops to fleece,
Let pretty *L—s* grace the Piece.
But O be sure with strict Formality,
Bring her in among the Quality;
Or else she'll think you use her ill,
Sweet let her smile on Master *B——*;
And make the Youth receive the Grace
With open Mouth, and simple Face.
But, on my Life, I hardly mist her,
I think there is another Sister:
Draw her hearing, blith, and merry,
The blubb'ring Talk of *L—d—y*.
But now, my Genius, shift the Scene,
Draw a gaping Gulph between,
Mix the Colours, stretch the Line,
Be the Stroke and Pencil fine.
Great the Skill, and nice the Touches,
That can describe the decent Dutchess,
But say, what Pencil can express
Her faultiess, easy, free Address?
Now mingle Dignity with Ease,
And teach a Piece like her to please.
Decent, sensible, and cruel,
Draw the little Face of *N—l*.
Let the prudent *Yorkshire* Lasses *,   * Miss *A-l-bies.*
Exhibit here their sober Faces,
Bring them forth with Motion, Mien,
Steady Gait, and Look serene;
Much reserv'd, yet inoffensive,
Shy, demure, and somewhat pensive.
In brightest Colours let me see
The Ruby Lips of laughing *L—*.

And

And next, the Muse had almost past her,
The *J'en scay quoy* jaunty F—r.
V—l's opening Bloom adorn,
With Colour blushing like the Morn,
Such Innocence, and heav'nly Grace,
As smooth, as Youthful Cherub's Face.
But Colours now my Dwarf prepare,
Bright as the Fancy of my Fair;
And let the nice Design appear,
Like her own Judgment, fine and clear;
Let strictest Rules of Art direct,
And be your Taste, like her's, correct,
Find Expression soft and strong,
As any Poet's lofty Song;
To this lovely Piece annex,
Parts beyond her Years and Sex.
Temper more than manly Sense,
With softest Female Diffidence;
And to her blooming Looks impart
The Candour of her tender Heart.
But, cries the Painter, what d'ye call her?
Your Pardon, Sir, the Wits would maul her,
Her Face and Shape the Belles may mangle,
Or fluttering Fops for ever dangle:
I'll save her from the envious Rout,
I think you'd better leave her out.
You'll say, this is my Fancy's Baby,
Well such a one there is, or may be.
Hence flirting Fops, and flirting Belles,
A long Adieu to *Tunbridge-Wells*.
Farewell Jilt, Coquet, and Prude,
Welcome solemn Solitude.
Shady Walks, and sultry Hills,
Warbling Birds, and purling Rills.
Where free from Envy, Noise, and Strife,
I'll loll away a Laughing Life.

The

The following Bite upon the Publick is of so new and so extraordinary a Nature, that it deserves to be recorded, as it shews, that a foolish Credulity and ridiculous Curiosity seem to have banished common Sense from the Quality and Gentry of this great Metropolis. Towards the Middle of January, 1749, *the following Advertisement appeared in the News Papers.*

AT the *New Theatre* in the *Hay-Market*, on Monday next, the 16th instant, to be seen a Person who performs the several most surprizing Things following, *viz.* First, he takes a common Walking-Cane from any of the Spectators, and thereon plays the Musick of every Instrument now in Use, and likewise sings to surprizing Perfection. Secondly, he presents you with a common Wine-Bottle, which any of the Spectators may first examine; this Bottle is placed on a Table in the Middle of the Stage, and he (without any Equivocation) goes into it in Sight of all the Spectators, and sings in it; during his Stay in the Bottle, any Person may handle it, and see plainly that it does not exceed a common Tavern Bottle.

Those on the Stage or in the Boxes may come in masked Habits, (if agreeable to them) and the Performer (if desired) will inform them who they are.

Stage 7s. 6d. Boxes 5s. Pit 3s. Gallery 2s.

To begin at Half an Hour after Six o'Clock.

☞ Tickets to be had at the Theatre.

⁎⁎⁎ The Performance continues about two Hours and a Half.

N. B. If any Gentlemen or Ladies, after the above Performances (either singly or in Company, in or out of Mask) are desirous of seeing a Representation of any deceased Person, such as Husband or Wife, Sister or Brothre, or any intimate Friend of either Sex, (upon making a Gratuity to the Performer) shall be gratified seeing and conversing with them for some Minutes as if alive. Likewise (if desired) he will tell you your most secret Thoughts in your past Life; and give you a full View of Persons who have injured you whether dead or alive.

For those Gentlemen and Ladies who are desirous of seeing this last Part, there is a private Room provided.

These Performances have been seen by most of the crown'd Heads of *Asia*, *Africa*, and *Europe*, and never appear'd publick any where but once; but will wait of any at their Houses, and perform as above, for five Pounds each Time.

☞ There will be a proper Guard to keep the House in due Decorum.

This other Advertisement was also publish'd at the same Time, which, one would have thought, was sufficient to prevent the former's having any Effect.

Lately arriv'd from Italy,

SIG. *Cappitello Jumpedo*, a surprizing Dwarf, no taller than a common Tavern Tobacco-Pipe; who can perform a great many wonderful Equilibres, on the slack or tight Rope: Likewise he'll transform his Body in above ten thousand different Shapes and Postures; and after he has diverted the Spectators two Hours and a Half, he will open his Mouth wide, and jump down his own Throat. He being the most wonderfull'st Wonder of Wonders as ever the World wonder'd at, would be willing to join in Performance with that surprizing Musician on *Monday* next, in the *Hay-Market*.

He is to be spoke with at the *Black Raven* in *Golden-Lane* every Day from Seven till Twelve, and from Twelve all Day long.

Never-

Neverthelefs, the Contrivance took, and the Playhoufe was crouded with Dukes, Duchefses, Lords, Ladies, &c. the Confequence of which will appear from the following Paragraph.

Laft Night (viz. *Monday, Jan.* the 16th) the much expected Drama of the Bottle-Conjurer of the *New Theatre* in the *Hay-Market*, ended in the tragi-comical Manner following. Curiofity had drawn together prodigious Numbers. About 7 the Theatre being lighted up, but without fo much as a fingle Fiddle to keep the Audience in good Humour, many grew impatient. Immediately follow'd a Chorus of Catcalls, heighten'd by loud Vociferations, and beating with Sticks; when a Fellow came from behind the Curtain, and bowing, faid, that if the Performer did not appear, the Money fhould be return'd. At the fame Time a Wag crying out from the Pit, that if the Ladies and Gentlemen would give double Prices, the Conjurer would get into a Pint Bottle, prefently a young Gentleman in one of the Boxes feized a lighted Candle, and threw it on the Stage. This ferved as the Charge for founding to Battle. Upon this, the greateft Part of the Audience made the beft of their way out of the Theatre; fome lofing a Cloak, others a Hat, others a Wig, and others Hat, Wig, and Swords alfo. One Party however ftaid in the Houfe, in order to demolifh the Infide, when the Mob breaking in, they tore up the Benches, broke to Pieces the Scenes, pull'd down the Boxes, in fhort difmantled the Theatre entirely, carrying away the Particulars above-mentioned into the Street, where they made a mighty Bon-fire; the Curtain being hoifted on a Pole, by way of a Flag. A large Party of Guards were fent for, but came time enough only to warm themfelves round the Fire. We hear of no other Difafter than a young Nobleman's Chin being hurt, occafioned by his Fall into the Pit, with Part of one of the Boxes which he had forced out with his Foot. 'Tis thought the Conjurer vanish'd away with the Bank. Many Enemies to a late celebrated Book, concerning the ceasing of Miracles, are greatly disappointed by the Conjurer's non-appearance in the Bottle; they imagining, that his jumping into it would have been the most convincing Proof possible, that Miracles are not yet ceased.

Several Advertisements were printed afterwards, some serious, others comical, relating to this whimsical Affair; among the rest was the following, which, we hope, may be a Means of curing this Humour for the future.

This is to inform the Publick,

THAT notwithstanding the great Abuse that has been put upon the Gentry, there is now in Town a Man, who instead of creeping into a Quart or Pint Bottle, will change himself into a Rattle; which he hopes will please both young and old. If this Person meets with Encouragement to this Advertisement, he will then acquaint the Gentry where and when he performs.

The Reason assign'd, in another humourous Advertisement, of the Conjurer's not going into the *Quart Bottle,* was, that after searching all the Taverns, not one could be found.

On the above Action in the Hay-Market.

WHEN Conjurers the Quality can bubble,
And get their Gold with very little Trouble,
By putting giddy Lies in publick Papers,——
As jumping in Quart Botfles,——such like Vapours;
And further yet, if we the Matter strain,
Wou'd pipe a Tune upon a Walking-Cane:

Nay,

Nay, more surprizing Tricks! he swore he'd show
Grannums who dy'd a hundred Years ago:—
'Tis whimsical enough, what think ye, Sirs?
The Quality can ne'er be Conjurers,——
The De'el a bit;—no, let me speak in Brief,
The Audience Fools, the Conjurer a Thief.

E P I T A P H.

Beneath in the Dust, the mouldy old Crust
  Of *Moll Batchelor* lately was shoven,
Who was skill'd in the Arts of Pyes, Custards and Tarts,
  And every Device of the Oven.
When she'd liv'd long enough, she made her last Puff,
  A Puff by her Husband much prais'd;
And here she doth lie, and makes a Dirt Pye,
  In Hopes that her Crust may be rais'd.

To the I—d—t E—ɛl—rs of W———r.

GENTLEMEN,

AT the Recommendation of the late *Conclave* held at *Rome*, your *Votes* and *Interests* are desired for two Gentlemen, to be your Representatives in the ensuing Parliament; *you* are therefore requir'd to meet at Mr. POPE's, at the Sign of the *Cross*, in *Jeffery's-Street*, near *Bloody-Lane*; where *you'll* be entertain'd with the best of *Holy Water*, such as hereafter 'tis to be hop'd will, by this Canal, overflow the whole Land; also with *Golden Beads* to chain you down to *Arbitrary Power:* At which Place you'll be inform'd of the above *Candidates* Names, who *you* may be assur'd are well affected for the *Old Constitution* (as from 1684, to 1688.) as manifestly appear'd by their strenuously opposing the Associations and Subscriptions made towards suppressing the late Rebellion: And as your Welfare is what they have most at Heart, they will [if possible] at their own Expence, for the Good of your City, appoint a STUART to have the Management of both your private and publick Interest; and you may depend upon it, will do their utmost Endeavours to put an End to this dishonourable and unnecessary *French War*, by as glorious a Peace as that of *Utrecht*.

The noble Struggle lately made in *North Britain*, fomented and so well supported by I—d—p—y, will, we hope, very much add to the above Recommendation, for your readily voting for the said Patriots.

As independent Orations are absolutely necessary on so important an Occasion, *our* seraphic Orator H—— will give you a Lecture, in which he will, in his obscure Language, demonstrate, that Jacobitism, Popery, and *England*'s becoming a Province of *France*, should be the earnest Desire of every *English* Protestant, as the only Means to support our Liberties.

N. B. After the Election, each Voter shall be entitled to a *Jacobus*, to be received from Mr. *Judas French*, at the *Bloody Dagger*, in *Bondage-Street*, near *Wooden-Shoe-Lane*.

A SONG, *by a* LADY.

YOU say you love, and twenty more
    Have sigh'd and said the same before,
And yet I swear, I can't tell how,
I ne'er believ'd a Man till now,
          I ne'er believ'd, *&c.*
'Tis odd that I shou'd Credit give
To Words, who know that Words deceive,
And lay my better Judgment by,
To trust my partial Ear or Eye,
          To trust, *&c.*

'Tis Ten to One—I had deny'd
Your Suit—had you To-morrow try'd,
But faith unthinkingly To-day
My heedless Heart—has run astray,
    My heedless Heart, &c.
To bring it back—wou'd cost me Pain,
Perhaps the Struggle might be vain,
I'm indolent, and he that gains
My Heart—may keep it for his Pains.
   My Heart, &c.

An ODE to PEACE.

Downy Peace! extend thy Pinions
 O'er *Britannia*'s drooping Isle!
Bless our Sov'reign's wide Dominions,
 Make his faithful Subjects smile.

Banish F--ction, change the Tory,
 Make of him an honest Whig;
Chase Corruption, stain her Glory,
 Shame her Sons that look so big.

Calm the Hero, sooth his Anger,
 Stop the murd'ring Cannon's Roar;
Bid the Trumpet's solemn Clangor
 Kindle martial Rage no more.

Favour Commerce, Arts and Science,
 Sink our Taxes, hear our Moan!
Let not *Gallia* bid Defiance,
 While the Seas are all our own.

Industry to Temp'rance marry,
 That we may * *weave Truth with Trust*;
Hence let none our Fleeces carry,
 But be to their Country just.

          Stop

   * The Weaver's Motto.

Stop the Smuggler, and the Hawker,
   Who illicit Commerce drive;
Hang the Rogue and Midnight Walker—
   These are Drones that rob the Hive.

While we wait thy warm Caresses,
   Urge us on in loyal Ways;
Not in formal trite Addresses,
   Nor in Riot and Huzzas:

But in Acts of Love and Duty,
   To our KING and to his HEIR;
These confer a real Beauty,
   And our Principles declare.

Mix with Reason ev'ry Pleasure,
   Sparing, hand the giddy Bowl;
Deal us Liberty by Measure,
   Lest Excess should drown the Soul.

On the PEACE.

AT length the rude Alarms of War are o'er,
   All Parties very wise, and very poor;
No longer Nations against Nations rise,
Nor hostile Warriors meet with hateful Eyes.
Lo! *Peace*, angelic Maid, from Heav'n descends,
And bids contending Foes be mutual Friends.
   Come, then, fair Goddess! lovely Mildness, come!
Expel the Clouds of War's oppressive Gloom!
Come, *Peace*, more welcome than the dawning Light
To those, who dwell full half the Year in Night!
Come, heav'nly Charmer, chase our Cares away,
And bless *Britannia* with thy brightest Ray!
Hark! a glad Sound the lonely Desart chears,
Let Discord cease: the Nymph, the Nymph appears!
Joy, Love and Harmony attend her Train,
Earth joyous laughs, and smiles the rural Plain.

Now brazen Trumpets kindle Rage no more,
Nor dying Groans refound along the Shore:
Loud Cannons now in Gratulation play,
To hail the Glories of th' auspicious Day.
No longer now is heard the Din of Arms,
Of Hosts encount'ring, and the dread Alarms:
No flaming Weapons with effulgent Glare
Flash o'er the Field, and lighten in the Air;
Secure the Faulchion sleeps within its Sheath,
With all the murd'ring Implements of Death.
  Hail, blest *Saturnian* Times! again return!
Let *Europe* now no more your Absence mourn,
Propitious now your kindest Blessings shed
On *William*'s Labours and on *George*'s Head:
Let happy Days, by peaceful *George* restor'd,
Compleat the just Designs of *William*'s Sword.

An ODE to PEACE.

QUEEN of Plenty! Queen of Smiles!
  Welcome to thy fav'rite Isles!
Welcome! as refreshing Rains
Pour'd on *Afric*'s thirsty Plains!
To polar Regions as the Morning Ray!
  The Morning of a lasting Day,
    Period of tremendous Night;
      Night diffus'd thro' half the Year,
      Brooding Want, and Pain, and Fear;
Peace is Joy, and Life, and Light!

  See *Britannia* drown'd in Tears!
    Sooth her Sorrows, chafe her Fears;
Come, plume the Wings of Hope again,
    Industry's wither'd Strength restore,
Send busy Commerce o'er the Main,
    And bid her yet new Worlds explore.

Bid exil'd Arts return, and swell
 The Muse's long neglected Shell;
To Love attune the genial Song,
To Love the sweetest Strains belong,
 Sink the Trumpet to the Flute,
  The lessen'd Drums to Tabors turn,
 Bid the Cannon's Voice be mute,
 Let no Torch but Hymen's burn.

Already thro' my Breast I feel
 All thy pleasing Influence shed,
In Song my Raptures I reveal,
 And the Bay entwines my Head.
  O prolong the joyful Hour!
  Still, O still exert thy power!
Here fix at length thy lasting Throne,
And call my native Realms thy own,
 Here let thy Olive flourish high
A blissful Shade to latest Times supply,
And Friend to Nature, but with Nature die.

A RHAPSODY *on* PEACE.

WITH Whimsies perplex'd, t'other Day out of Spite,
Having nought else to do, I e'en sat down to write:
But, horrid to tell! my black Lines were not true,
My Paper so thin that the Ink went quite thro';
My Pens were so bad that I wish'd 'em at *Rome*;
For my Pen-knife I felt, but had left it at home.

Such Crosses what Mortal with Patience could bear?
 Yet, in Spite of them all, I determin'd to try,
With Ambition for Fame, and Contempt of Despair,
 How high my young Muse in Heroics could fly.
                                Come

Come then, my Muse, and sing of *Peace* with Joy,
What sweeter Subject can my Muse employ!
A Theme like this might animate a *Cope*;
A Theme like this make *Ogilby* a *Pope*.

   A Theme like this inspires spontaneous Lays,
Peace, and the bless'd Effects of *Peace* I praise.
Hoarse Voices now no longer shall amuse,
Or fright the Town with Sound of *bloody News*.
No longer now shall thund'ring Cannons roar,
And fright the Vessels from the hostile Shore;
But harmless Squibs in Air with Rockets play,
And Torches imitate the Blaze of Day.
The *Fribbles* now, an inoffensive Crew,
Shall, without Dread, their Fopperies pursue.
In *White*'s first Floor undaunted shall they meet,
And view, unhurt, th' Artillery of the Street:
There let them taste the Pleasures of Champaign,
Enough for me that, in a mirthful Vein,
My Voice, tho' harsh, tho' impotent my Song,
I chant the Pleasures that to *Peace* belong.

  Oxford, Nov. 16.   Car. Combes.

A SONG on the PEACE.

WHO see de Peace To-day proclaim-a?
    By wise Men made with *France* and *Spain*-a,
Where *Britain* quits what she did gain a,
            Doodle, doodle, doo.

When we at first began the War-a,
And brave Jack Tar, not fearing Scar-a,
To take *Cape Breton* went from far-a,
            Doodle, &c.

And brave *New-England* Men did fight-a,
To gain from *France* their Mother's Right-a,
Which she gave back to *France* in Spite-a,
            Doodle, &c.

From proud Monsieur, and eke from *Spain*-a
When many a *Frenchman* had been slain-a,
And we triumphant o'er the Main-a,
       Doodle, &c.

Tho' we at Mercy had the *French*-a,
Destroy'd their Fleets, their Commerce 'trencht-a,
They have all back for Soup and Drench-a,
       Doodle, &c.

We've spent Millions Three-times ten-a,
And brought our Soldiers back again-a,
Except the Thousands that were slain-a,
       Doodle, &c.

Such Negotiators ne'er were mix-a
Since good King *Harry*'s Reign the Six-a,
Whose Father conquer'd *France* for Nix-a,
       Doodle, &c.

Sure Men so wise 'n no Nation bore-a
The Burden of a State before-a,
Or none such liv'd in Days of Yore-a,
       Doodle, &c.

If *France* did not for Mercy call-a,
And Brothers were not 'fraid to fall-a,
Why did we give them Peace at all-a?
       Doodle, &c.

Our Hostages will soon come back-a,
And wise Men sure the Nation lack-a,
Red Ribbands should adorn their Neck-a,
       Doodle, &c.

Such *France* ne'er saw from before-a,
Tho' we from them have had some Score-a,
But dat be past Three Age or more-a,
       Doodle, &c.

Now if our Sportsmen shall think fit-a,
To ride their Steeds with *Pelham* Bit-a,
Ye Gods preserve them from a *Pitt*-a,
       Doodle, &c.

A Reduced OFFICER's *Complaint.*

CUrs'd on the Star, dear *Harry*, that betray'd
My Choice, from Law, Divinity, and Trade,
To turn a rambling Brother of the Blade.
Of all Professions, sure, the worst is War;
How whimsical our Fortunes, how bizarre!
This Week we shine in Scarlet and in Gold,
The next, the Sword is pawn'd, the Watch is sold;
This Day, familiar with my Lord, we dine,
The next his Grooms our Company decline.
Like Meteors, rais'd in a tempestuous sky,
A while we glitter, then obscurely die.
Of such Disgrace must Heroes still complain,
And curse an honourable Peace in vain?
I, who so lately pass'd my smiling Hours,
In witty Converse, and in soft Amours;
Who in rich Volwey, and Champaign cou'd toast
The reigning Beauty, and her Favours boast,
Must now retire, and languish out my Days,
Far from the Realms of Pleasure, and of Praise;
Quit dear *Hyde Park*, for dull provincial Air,
And change the Play-house for a Country Fair;
With sneaking Parsons beastly Bumpers quaff,
At low Conceits, and vile Conundrums laugh;
Toast to the Church, and that and this Divine,
And herd with Country Squires, a Swine with Swine.
Ye Gods, such foul Disgrace must Heroes bear?
Is this of honourable Peace their Share!
There was a time, oh! yes, there was a time,
Ere Poverty made Luxury a Crime;
Ere Broths, with Marygolds bestrew'd, were known;
When Soups made way for Dainties not our own.
When *French* Ragouts were orthodox and good,
And Truffles held no Heresy in Food.

Nor to eat Mackrill was adjudg'd high Treason,
Tho' Goosberry Sauce, as yet, was not in Season.
But under —— frugal Dispensation,
These splendid Sins submit to Reformation.
Scourg'd by his Wand, and humbled by his Sway,
I've learn'd to suit my Diet to my Pay.
And, now, even sanctify with solemn Face
A heavy Dumpling with a formal Grace.
In aukward Plenty slovenly I dine,
And nappy Ale supplies the want of Wine.
No nice Desarts my tutor'd Palate please,
To fill up Chinks, a Slice of *Suffolk* Cheese.
⎨ Must *British* Heroes thus like *Roman* live?
⎨ And is this all a glorious Peace can give?
  But, ah! the hardest part is still behind,
The fair, too, gentle *Harry*, prove unkind.
Think then how wretchedly my Time must pass,
For what's this World, my Friend, without a Lass?
Tho' pinch'd by Poverty, inglorious State!
Give me but Woman, I'll absolve my Fate.
But, ah! to those by Poverty deprest,
Not Fate itself can give a Female Guest.
The Sex, no Vows of needy Love will trust,
To pamper Pride they'll even starve their Lust,
And vain of Titles, Equipage and Show,
Quit the rough Soldier for the tainted Beau.
I, who so oft my forward Zeal have shew'd,
And in their Service spent my warmest Blood,
Am now reduc'd (hard Fate!) for want of Pelf,
To keep the worst of Company—myself.
⎨ Are Heroes banish'd, by the Peace they won,
⎨ To dwell with those whom all combine to shun?

Verses

Verses occasion'd by hearing certain grumbling *Coffee-House Politicians descanting on what the* KING's SPEECH *would be, before he went to the House.*

NOW, great with Expectation, looks each Man,
Able at once, his Sovereign's Speech to scan:
Whether too late his Royal Wrath did cease,
Or if too soon he has made up a Peace:
With doubting Shrug, uneasy they appear,
Whether he Peace proclaim, or War declare;
Just Judges still, to speak on either Side,
And, capable alike, they soon decide;
And, either Things might have been manag'd better!
Or, we in one Year more might *Europe* fetter!
Or, else the War was enterpriz'd too late!
Each Way, however, *wretched is the State!*
Always, too late, or soon, is each Design,
Of Peace, or War; and all, at once, combine
Against all Measure, and, from what they say,
'Tis wrong, you may be certain, either Way:
If War you carry on; Oh, what Expence!
If Peace is made; it is against all Sense!
Or Peace, or War, among such wretched Vermin,
Whatever is, is wrong, they first determine.

England's *ALARUM-BELL: or, Give not up* GIBRALTAR; *A new Ballad, The Tune,—Come listen to my Ditty*, &c.

> *The fatal Hour draweth on,*
> *The Winds and Tides agree;*
> *And now (sweet* ENGLAND*!) oversoon,*
> *I must* DEPART *from* THEE.
>   OLD BALLAD.

I.

PALE her Looks, and clad in Mourning,
 Smiting sore her aching Breast,
From Skies, *Albion*'s GENIUS frowning,
 Thus her injur'd Sons address'd:
How will *Britons* sink in Story!
 Dup'd alike in Peace and War!
Fled's our *Trade*, eclips'd our *Glory*,
 Shou'd we give up GIBRALTAR.

II.

This restor'd to a proud Nation,
 Groaning under *Bourbon* Sway,
French and *Spanish* Fleets united,
 Europe must their Flag obey.
These bold Fleets, in diff'rent Oceans,
 By the *Streights* late sever'd far,
May, combin'd, insult AUGUSTA*,
 Lost our darling GIBRALTAR.

* LONDON.

III.

Fix'd in *Italy* the *Bourbons* †
   Leghorn will our Ships exclude;
Scorn'd our various Manufactures,
   Frenchmen soon will theirs intrude.
Then the *Algerines*, who court us,
   Will no *English* Vessel spare;
Lost the Port, to vend their Prizes,
   Should we part with GIBRALTAR.

IV.

Yielded this important Harbour,
   All our *Turky* Trade, adieu!
Port-Mahon must change its Master;
   Gone th' *Italian* Traffick too!
Then will *French* and *Spanish* Vessels
   Safely either *India* dare,
The *Streights-Mouth* by us unguarded,
   Fool'd away our GIBRALTAR.

V.

Doubly blest, in Situation,
   Here a glorious *MART* would rise,
A free Port to ev'ry Nation,
   Monarchs might its Friendship prize.
Subject to the Laws of *Britain*,
   A new *Tyre*, 'twould shine a Star;
But vile Governors have curs'd It;
   Such wou'd give up GIBRALTAR.

VI.

Lo! the Tongue of foul Corruption,
   Greedy, licks up all Things round!
Soon the PRESS may want its Freedom;
   Writing Truth be dang'rous found.

† *Don Carlos* and *Don Philip*.

Rouze (brave *English!*) Check these Evils!
    Fam'd CAPE-BRETON's gone!--Beware!
Wooden Shoes you'll surely put on,
    If you give up GIBRALTAR.

VII.

See a geugaw *Pile* ascending
    Whence ten thousand Stars will blaze!
Dear-bought *Arts* Assistance lending;
    F—E-W—KS, play'd for Fools to gaze.
High in Air, whilst flock the Millions,
    Pallas whirls around her Car;
Laughing at a People's Frenzy,
    After losing GIBRALTAR.

VIII.

This fam'd Rock (the ancient *Calpe*,)
    Hercules did fiercely seize:
British Sailors, when reign'd *Anna* ||,
    Brav'd its Cliffs with equal Ease.
Lads! who form such matchless Conquests,
    (Hear me, ev'ry gen'rous Tar!)
Take your Clubs, beat down Their Houses,
    Who would give up GIBRALTAR.

IX.

See in *France* our Honour bleeding,
    As our Hostages appear!
Sure such mock *Negot--t--ns*
    Ne'er disgrac'd a crazy Year!
Shou'd our BLUND—RS § yield that Fortress,
    We completely ruin'd are.
Hang the *Wretch* who first proposes
    To give up fam'd GIBRALTAR.

|| GIBRALTAR was taken under Sir *George Rook*, in 1704.
§ Some Copies have it PLUND—RS.

A LETTER to Miss JENNY.

Would you know, my dear Miss,
   How your Brother *Ben* is,
Whether thriving, in Health, and good Humour?
   This our Letter will tell,
   How he is, and lives well,
And resolves not to quarrel with you more.

   When he opens his Eyes
   To the Window and Skies,
And perceives that the Morning looks gay;
   If he wakes in no Fret,
   Up in Haste he will get,
And undrest hurry down to his Play.

   But at first takes a Pill,
   With Intention to kill
Gnawing Worms, and remove a slight Fever,
   Having vow'd to obey
   All the Doctor should say
And his Mamma command him, for ever.

   Tho' a little he is sick
   By his taking of Physick,
Soon he laughs, sings, and halloos aloud;
   If he sets up a Cry,
   We discern the Cause why,
'Tis not minding to do as we shou'd.

   With the Dog and the Cat
   He'll play Tricks, and he'll chat,
But the Fiddle oft gives him most Pleasure;
   Then to Cards, or Bopeep,
   Whipping Top, smacking Whip,
A Variety strange without Measure.

When he talks broken *French*
To the Fellow or Wench,
Entertaining with innocent Prattle,
By his cracking of Jokes
Full as arch as old *Nokes*,
Not his Head, but his Tongue, proves a Rattle.

His Behaviour is good,
In his Manners not rude,
Whether fitting, or walking, or feeding;
In his Temper and Sense
Shines the bright Influence
Of his elegant Mamma's fine Breeding.

This our little plain House
Finds us Mirth and Repose,
With a Zeal for our Patrons so ready,
That as oft as we dine,
Tho' not tempted with Wine,
We remember my Lord and my Lady.

Little minding the Fears
Of those Commons and Peers,
Who suspect the *French* Faith in all Treaties;
But securely we live
In the Hopes we conceive
From the Wisdom of S—nd—ch, that great is.

The PETITION of *Justice* Boden's Horse to the Duke of Newcastle.

Quite worn to the Stump, in a piteous Condition,
I present to your Grace this my humble Petition.
Full twenty-five Stone, as all the World says,
(To me it seems more) my plump Master weighs,
A Load for a Team this, yet I all alone
To *Claremont* must draw him, for Help I have none.
O'er

O'er *Esher*'s hot Sands, in a dry Summer's Day,
How I sweat, and I pant, and curse all the Way.
But when I return, the Draft is increas'd
By what he has cram'd, a Stone at the least,
No single Horse can be in Conscience thought able
To draw both the Justice, and eke half your Table.
Thus my Case, gracious Duke, to your tender Com-
    passion,
I submit, and O take it into Consideration.
To drive with a Pair put the 'Squire in the Way,
Your Petitioner then, bound in Duty, shall Neigh.

On a DREAM.

Dreams are Monitions sent us from high Heav'n;
    But what avails the scanty Prescience given;
Unless the same kind Power wou'd reveal
How Man may shun the Ruin they foretell?

Epitaph *on* John Trotplaid, *alias* J— F—

Beneath this Stone
   Lies Trotplaid John,
His Length of Chin and Nose:
   His crazy Brain,
   Unhum'rous Vein
In Verse and eke in Prose.

   Some Plays he wrote,
   Sans Wit or Plot,
Adventures of Inferiors!
   Which, with his Lives
   Of Rogues and Thieves,
Supply the Town's Posteriors.

But

But ah, alack!
He broke his Back,
When Politics he try'd:
For like a Fart
He play'd his Part,
Crack'd loudly, ftunk, and dy'd.

On the late M——rt——l Bills.

OUR Ifland's Guardian, LIBERTY,
　In all her Charms confeft,
Perufing the two Mart——l Bills,
　Her Anger thus expreft.

O *Britons!* once my darling Sons,
　The Envy of Mankind,
How are you fall'n from what you were,
　To all but *Inter'ft* blind.

Thus grov'ling had your Sires behav'd,
　(They who for Freedom dy'd)
Beneath the hated *Gallic* Yoke
　In Chains you now had figh'd.

A FABLE.

To the Earl of GR——NV——LE.

DID Pow'r and Liberty agree,
　That all might act and fpeak as free
As Confcience bids, as Reafon guides;
Then Hate wou'd ceafe on both the Sides;
But let *Corruption* have the Sway,
Let Truth and Juftice both give way,
'Tis mean of thofe who then obey.
If Money gives a St——n Pow'r
To ruin, wafte, confound, devour;

If no Resentment check his Hand,
If absolute be his Command;
What Insults will approach a Th—ne,
When Thousands are by him undone?

    Whether bestow'd on Age or Youth,
Remark 'tis plac'd in Worth and Truth;
Then let my Meaning borrow Shape,
And quote *Horse*, Monkey, Bear, and Ape.

    A noble *Steed*, of Birth and Fame,
By Fortune's Smiles had rais'd a Name;
Had liv'd in Credit and in Trust,
And was esteem'd extreamly just.
At length to Height of Pow'r he rose;
From thence began his secret Foes.

    A *Monkey* pert, of Modes and Airs,
Was chose to rule in St—e Affairs,
Whose ready Wit cou'd quickly bribe
The Vices of the fawning Tribe;
Cou'd act the Lion's, Spaniel's Part,
And still profess the Friend at Heart.
His greatest Talents always lay,
The cunning Honest to betray:
Whate'er resolv'd was surely done,
Either by Gold or Flatt'ry won.
By this he gain'd the M——ch's Ear;
Nor had he any pop'lar Fear,
'Till vex'd with Murmurs, Cares, and Toils,
He quits, retiring with his Spoils.

    The *Bear*, who stood the next in Station,
Was glad that he might serve the Nation;
For Worth and Truth were his Profession,
And Genius was his own Possession;
Not did he value others Spite,
For what he did was just and right.
His principal Design was set,
To bring the Nation out of Debt;

To judge aright, correct Abuses;
Nor spend the Gold for private Uses.'
   This stung the fawning Tribe too much,
Who, quite unlike him, envy'd such.
Besides, their Pensions now grew short,
And surely they must *live* at C—t.
But Ways they did ere long contrive
To ruin him for them to thrive.
Thus they with Bluster, and with Rout,
Compell'd the Steed to turn him out.
   Next came in Turn the sneaking *Ape*,
More to be shun'd for Vice than Shape:
He studied all the Monkey's Ways;
His Vanity was fed with Praise;
His whole Intent was fix'd on Wealth,
Which soon he got by Fraud and Stealth.
What might advance the publick Weal,
For private Int'rest he'd conceal;
By diff'rent Projects, Ways wou'd try,
To drain the Nation's Money dry.
   A *Brother Ape* this S——n had,
In Sense as short, as Morals bad;
This was enough to recommend
Him, as a publick trusty Friend.
   Oppression, Want, and Fear began,
To grow from their united Plan:
Whatever Good to Trade was meant,
Was plainly known by *Five per Cent.*
The Beasts but murmur'd for a Time,
Then loudly told the Brothers' Crime.
   The Steed enrag'd, cries, ' Hence ye Crew,
' What Punishment is justly due
' To such Offence?——At length I find,
' Whatever Evils you design'd,
' Has, by your base Administration,
' Been charg'd on me, who gave you Station.

(73)

The Inner Temple Gate, London, *being lately repaired, and curiously decorated, the following* INSCRIPTION, *in Honour of both the Temples, is intended to be put over it.*

AS by the Templar's Holds you go,
　　The *Horse* and *Lamb,* display'd
In emblematic Figures shew
　　The Merits of their Trade.
That Clients may infer from thence
　　How just is their Profession,
The *Lamb* sets forth their *Innocence,*
　　The *Horse* their *Expedition.*
O happy *Britons!* happy Isle!
　　Let foreign Nations say,
Where you get Justice without Guile,
　　And Law without Delay.

Written in Answer to the above.

DEluded Men, these Holds forego,
　　Nor trust such cunning Elves;
These artful Emblems tend to shew
　　Their Clients, not themselves.
'Tis all a Trick; these all are Shams,
　　By which they mean to cheat you;
But have a care, for you're the *Lambs,*
　　And they the *W—l—s* that eat you.
Nor let the Thoughts of *no Delay*
　　To these their Courts misguide you;
'Tis you're the *shewey Horse,* and they
　　The *Jockeys* that will ride you.

FILCH *at the* GALLOWS.

*B*Ackwards rode FILCH, who *Pockets* us'd to rifle,
　　And thought it hard to *hang* for such a *Trifle:*

Nº VI.　　　　　L　　　　　Under

Under the Tree his *Scruples* he declar'd,
Repeating still, ' 'Tis *hard*, 'tis *very hard:*
' Were RACKIT with me, I *the less* should grieve:
' 'Till wrong'd by *Him*, I never took to *thieve.*'
  Poor FILCH, I pity thee, the *Parson* cry'd:
But by thy *Country*, Lad, thou hast been *try'd:*
Thy *Crime* was evident, and just thy *Sentence;*
And nothing now remains—but *short Repentance.*
Thy *poor* Petition had no Friends to *back it.*——
Forgive the *World*, and to his *Guilt* leave RACKIT.
' *Leave to his Guilt!* quoth FILCH: ah, Sir, that's *fine!*
' All I would ask, is—to be *left to mine.*
' But here I come to make a *dying Speech:*———
Poh! Thou art *poor*, I say, and RACKIT's *rich;*
The *Fates* decree (and who *their Doom* can alter?)
To Him an *Equipage*, to Thee—a *Halter.*
True, *Law* condemns the *Rich*, as well as *Poor:*
But *Wealth* from Law can find a *secret Door.*
Tho' here so many *Smugglers* have harangu'd,
The *richest* of them, doubtless, are *unhang'd.*
The *Guinea-filers* spent so ill their Time,
That GAHAGAN had Nothing left but—*Rhime;*
But *Great* Sir R————*t* knew the *Use of Pelf;*
He stripp'd the *Tr****y*, and sav'd *Himself.*———
Others, of *equal Rank*, have *learn'd* as much:
They come not here, who *properly* can TOUCH.

An EPIGRAM, *on a disconsolate* TUTOR.

TUTOR *B*——, they say
   Is in Dumps and Dismay,
 Offended at generous Satire;
And, while under the Lash,
He condemns the late Trash
 He vented against *Alma-Mater.*

Thus

Thus Teddy (no Slur)
The pert Village Cur
  That attacks a poor innocent Stranger;
That is noisy to seize him,
And with Snarling to teaze him,
  Must find itself often in Danger.

The Whip it provokes,
And gall'd with its Strokes,
  (A Lesson worth each *Puppy*'s Knowledge)
It limps, howls and begs,
With its Tail 'twixt its Legs,
  Unpitied, as you are in College.

Miss L—TT—R, *to Cornet* F—R, *on his falling down and breaking his Nose, sent with a Nose of Clay.*

IN Scripture, Sir, 'tis said, we must,
  As Dust we are, return to Dust,
Then why should you your *Nose* bemoan,
Since 'tis but just before you gone?
And surely, ev'ry Booby knows
That wheresoe'er a Person goes,
He can but follow his own *Nose*.
But, since your *Nose* has naughty Tricks,
Not caring in your Face to fix,
And (Villain like) is *run away*,
I've sent, you, Sir, *a Nose of Clay*;
Undoubting that you'll take it kind,
I bear your *Nose* so much in Mind,
And, really Sir, I think you ought
To thank me for the happy Thought,
That, when y' had lost your Nose in *Pother*,
I sent y' again *just such another*:
For, tho' a Man may meet his Foes
In *Battle*, when he's lost his Nose;
Yet, *Ladies* often take Aversion,
And think *no Nose* a great Aspersion:

But any Fool, you know, will pass,
If he has but a *Nose* in's *Face*.
Then stick on this, when with *your Love*,
'Twill keep as close as Hand and Glove,
And I defy *both great and small*,
To say—*you've got no Nose at all.*
   Reading, Jan. 2.

On the REPORT *of a* BRITISH FLEET *being to be sent to the* BALTICK.

WHEN *War* subsided in the *South*,
   BELLONA seem'd to *close her Mouth*;
Her *Cheeks* were smooth, her *Arms* were flung,
And down her *Trumpet* careless hung;
She look'd so *tranquil* on the Nations,
They all appear'd like near *Relations*.
   But see! *already* she goes forth,
And sounds a *Prelude* through the *North*:
The *military Bands* prepare,
And *glow* beneath the *Frozen Bear*.
   Unhappy BRITAIN! plac'd between
The *Southern* and the *Northern* Scene;
Thy *Sons*, of *various Nations* mix'd,
Thy *Line* to *ev'ry Movement* fix'd;
Whoever *leads* the *martial Dance*,
From SWEDEN *upwards, down* to FRANCE;
'Tis thine to *join* some *purchas'd* Friend,
And *pay the* MUSICK—in the *End*.

On the Report that Sir PETER WARREN, *Sir* EDWARD HAWKE, *and* EDWARD VERNON, *Esq; are to be created Peers.*

IF true these *Hearsay* Writers tell,
   'Twill please the People wondrous well.
A brave *Triumvirate* of Tars,
Ennobled *more* than by their Scars,
                              Would

Would *grace* a Century that bears
A Crop so large of *Common* ————*rs.*
But *Doubts*, as yet, perplex the Spirit,
Doubts, rising merely from *their Merit.*
Shall ————M's Voice call *Honours* forth
To crown *acknowledg'd British Worth?*
Will not th' *ill-natur'd* World reflect,
That VERNON long lay in *Neglect*;
That when *the Knights* triumphant reign'd,
Peace soon was made, and they *restrain'd?*
Why give ye then (*this World* will ask)
Th' *Award*, yet keep back *Half the Task?*
Is it, that ALL *your Acts*, alike,
By their ABSURDITY————should *strike?*

PROLOGUE and EPILOGUE, *spoken by his Royal Highness the Prince of* WALES's CHILDREN, *on their performing the* TRAGEDY *of* CATO, *at* Leicester-House *.

PROLOGUE.

Spoken by Prince GEORGE.

TO speak with Freedom, Dignity and Ease,
  To learn those Arts, which may hereafter please;
Wise Authors say—let Youth in earliest Age,
Rehearse the Poet's Labours on the Stage.
Nay more! a nobler End is still behind,
The Poet's Labours elevate the Mind;
Teach our young Hearts with generous Fire to burn,
And feel the virtuous Sentiments we learn.
  T' attain these glorious Ends, what Play so fit,
As that! where all the Powers of human Wit

* *The Parts were,* Portius, *by Prince* George; Juba, *Prince* Edward; Cato, *Master* Nugent; Sempronius, *Master* Evelyn; Lucius, *Master* Montague; Decius, *Lord* Milsington; Syphax, *Lord* North's Son; *and* Marcus, *Master* Maddan; Marcia, *Princess* Augusta; *and* Lucia, *Princess* Elizabeth.

Combine,

Combine, to dignify great *Cato*'s Name,
To deck his Tomb, and confecrate his Fame;
Where Liberty—O Name for ever dear!
Breathes forth in ev'ry Line, and bids us fear
Nor Pains, nor Death, to guard our sacred Laws,
But bravely perish in our Country's Caufe.
Patriots indeed! worthy that honeft Name,
Thro' every Time and Station ftill the fame.
Shou'd this fuperior to my Years be thought,
Know—'tis the firft great Leffon I was taught.
What, though a Boy, it may with Pride be faid,
A Boy, in *England* born, in *England* bred:
Where Freedom well becomes the earlieft State,
For there the Love of Liberty's innate.
Yet more—before my Eyes thofe Heroes ftand,
Whom the great *William* brought to blefs this Land;
To guard with pious Care, that generous Plan,
Of Power well founded,—which he firft began.

But while my great Fore-fathers fire my Mind,
The Friends, the Joy, the Glory of Mankind;
Can I forget, that there is one more dear?
But he is prefent—and I muft forbear.

EPILOGUE.

Lady AUGUSTA.

THE Prologue's fill'd with fuch fine Phrafes,
George will alone have all the Praifes,
Unlefs we can (to get in Vogue)
Contrive to fpeak an Epilogue.

Prince EDWARD.

George has, 'tis true, vouchfaf'd to mention
His future gracious Intention;
In fuch heroic Strains, that no Man
Will e'er deny his Soul is *Roman.*
But what have you or I to fay to
The pompous Sentiments of *Cato?*

George

George is to have imperial Sway;
Our Task is only to obey.
And trust me, I'll not thwart his Will,
But be his faithful *Juba* still.
—Tho', Sister! now the Play is over,
I wish you'd get a better Lover.

Lady Augusta.

Why,—not to under-rate your Merit,
Others would court with different Spirit:
And I,—perhaps,—might like another,
A little better than a Brother,
Could I have one of *England*'s Breeding;—
But 'tis a Point they're all agreed in,
That I must wed a Foreigner,
And cross the Sea—the Lord knows where;
—Yet let me go where'er I will,
England shall have my Wishes still,

Prince Edward.

In *England* born, my Inclination,
Like yours, is wedded to the Nation:
And future Times, I hope, will see
Me General in Reality.
——Indeed! I wish to serve this Land,
It is my Father's strict Command;
And none he ever gave, will be
More chearfully obey'd by me.

CATO to PORTIUS.

While I, exalted by my Prince's Grace,
In borrow'd Pomp assume old *Cato*'s Place,
'Tho' ill may suit his Form with beardless Youth,
Yet shall his Soul beam forth in honest Truth:
And thou, indulgent to my real Part,
Accept this Tribute from a faithful Heart.
Whether some Angel plan'd the Poet's Page,
And *Addison* foretold thy rising Age;
Or whether, prompted by a Kindred Flame,
Thy early Virtues wear an Hero's Name;

Still greater Glories wait approaching Years,
When *George* shall be, what *Portius* now appears;
When filial Piety shall guard the Throne,
And Love paternal make thy Fame its own.
Then shall great *Cato* from the Heavens incline
His raptur'd Eyes, to view his mended Line.
Well may a brighter *Marcia* shine on Earth,
When such she shines who gave our *Marcia* Birth;
While, fraught with *British* Worth and *Roman* Fire,
A second *Juba* emulates his Sire;
And Nature's Gifts, by liberal Care refin'd,
Stampt in *Elizabeth* a *Lucia*'s Mind.
Nor nameless thou, our younger Hope, repine,
The godlike *William*'s deathless Name is thine.
Should fell Ambition wasteful Torrents spread,
Or motley Faction raise his frantick Head,
Millions with *George* shall own his sacred Cause
Of Power, Freedom, Monarchy and Laws.
Thy Virtues then shall claim a better Fate
Than his, who fell beneath a falling State:
Our Throne shall rise more glorious than his Grave,
And *George* preserve, what *Cato* could not save.
Thus while thy Arm the Banner shall display,
While *Edward* learns to conquer and obey,
O! *Eton*, may this be thy boasted Pride,
Thy Sons shall combat near their Prince's Side.
Cheer'd by his Smiles, and honour'd by his Choice,
Thy Towers resound.—I hear th' inspiring Voice:
" Never shall Treason stain this bless'd Retreat,
" Nor barbarous Riot shake the *Muses* Seat:
" Pure shall the hallowed Stream of Learning flow,
" And the chaste Fires thro' spotless Bosoms glow.
" For these the *Roman* pour'd his Patriot Blood,
" For these, unmov'd, the royal *Spartan* stood:
" But *Rome* hath bled, and *Greece* has fought, in vain
" For those, who bend the Neck, and court the Chain.

An Account of the famous Sieur ROCQUET, Surgeon; *just arrived from* Paris. *Neceſſary for all* Gentlemen *and* Ladies, *that attend the* FIRE-WORKS.

E flammâ cibum petere poſſe hunc arbitror. TER.

THIS is to give Notice, That the *Sieur* ROCQUET, *Surgeon*, is lately arrived from *Paris*, and hath brought over with him fifty *Aſſiſtant Surgeons*, who will attend at the enſuing ROYAL FIRE-WORKS, as near to the ſeveral Scaffolds as can be done with Safety; where they will be ready to aſſiſt all Perſons of Quality and Diſtinction; and to prevent Impoſition, he engages to perform the following Chirurgical Operations, at the loweſt Prices, *viz.*

	£.	s.	d.
For carrying off and bleeding a dead Corpſe (he reſerving the Corpſe for Anatomical Lectures)	0	5	0
For ditto, returning the Corpſe to the Relations	0	2	6
Cutting off a Thigh, (Leg included)	1	1	0
Ditto, Leg below the Knee	0	10	6
An Arm cloſe to the Shoulder (Wriſt, Hand, Fingers, and Thumb included)	1	1	0
Hand, Foot, Thumb, Toe, or Finger, each	0	5	0
For clearing out a bruis'd Eye, and replacing a right *Paris* brilliant black, blue, or ſquinting one, in the Socket. *N. B.* To be put in red hot without Loſs of Time or Blood.	1	1	0

	£.	s.	d.
For repairing the Bridge of a broken Nose, with a right *French* enamell'd Case of any Complexion	0	10	6
Ditto, beautifully inoculated, with an artificial Small Pox	0	10	6
Teeth *per* Dozen	1	1	0
Ditto, single	0	2	6

He hath also brought over with him, a Quantity of *Kevenhuller* Cotton for the Ears, which will entirely prevent any ill Consequences which may otherwise arise from the Noise of the Cannon; absolutely necessary for Ladies, Gentlemen, and Officers of the Fleet and Army, not used to sudden and frightful Explosions. He also sells a most agreeable volatile Salt, highly useful for such Gentlemen of the Train, as cannot bear the offensive Smell of Gun-Powder. And he will extract Grains of Gun-Powder out of Ladies Faces, Necks, Arms, and other Parts of the Body, at the most reasonable Rates.

N. B. The said *Sieur* Rocquet sells, Wholesale or Retail, all Sorts of Legs, Arms, Eyes, Noses, or Teeth, made in the genteelest Manner, and as now worn by Persons of Rank in *France:* He repairs and beautifies, in a surprizing Manner, any old, decayed, or lost Parts of Human Bodies; fills up the Wrinkles and Furrows of old Age, as well as the Marks of the Small-Pox, with a new invented Paste; and sells artificial Breasts for Ladies, either *German Plumps, French Tetonettes,* or *English Primikins,* equal, if not superior for Complexion, Softness, and Elasticity, to Natural Ones. He rectifies all bad Shapes, by a new Method of making a *gentle* Incision to the Bone; and filing off the protuberant Parts. He also cures effectually the most stinking Breaths, by drawing out, and eradicating all decayed Teeth and Stumps, and burning the Gums to the Jaw-bone, without the least Pain or Confinement; and putting in their stead, an entire Set of right *African Ivory Teeth*, set in Rose-colour'd *Enamel*, so nicely fitted to the Jaws, that People of the First Fashion may eat, drink, swear, talk Scandal, quarrel, and shew their Teeth, without the least Indecency, Inconvenience, or Hesitation whatever. He deals only for ready Money with the Quality and Members of Parliament, but will give reasonable Credit to Citizens, Tradesmen, and Gentlemen of the Inns of Court.

Enquire for the said *Sieur* ROCQUET, *Surgeon*, at the Bar of *Old Slaughter's* Coffee-House.

Vivat REX.

No PEACE *for the Wicked: Or Wars broke out in the* CITY.

To the Tune of, *Under the Greenwood Tree.*

I.

DRAW near, ye sober Citizens,
   Who dwell in *London* City;
And if I can from Tears refrain,
   I'll sing a dol'rous Ditty:
But, oh! my Soul the Tale abhors,
   Alack! what Pity 'tis,
That Aldermen should rage in Wars,
   And Gen'rals rust in Peace?

II.

'Twas at a Feaſt, our Lord-Mayor gave
    To Lords, and Aldermen,
Where a moſt bloody War broke out
    'Twixt *W——r*, and *B——n*:
W——r was——I don't know what;
    B——n's Trade was boiling Soap;
And, if he minds no other Trade,
    He may eſcape a Rope.

III.

But he, to State-Affairs, alas!
    Muſt turn his Soap-ſud Brains;
And ſo, as Chains now hang on him,
    May he ne'er hang in Chains:
But ſay my Muſe, what Devil, or God,
    Could raiſe this mighty Pother;
Make peaceful Souls boil o'er with Rage,
    And Brother baffle Brother.

IV.

The noiſy God of Drunkenneſs
    Jump'd into *B——n*'s tenth Bottle;
And thence, with *Harlequin*'s Addreſs,
    Jump'd into *B——n*'s poor Noddle:
And then, and there, perſuade did he,
    Dull *B——n* for to be witty;
And to oppoſe ſome *Cocoa Tree*-
    Healths, in the Loyal City.

V.

" Let's drink," says he, " the brave Prince C——,
  " And d——n each H——r——n:
" The Rascal that will not pledge me,
  " By G—d's a *Presbyterian.*"
" O B——n, O B——n," cries W——r;
  " A Shame it is most burning;
" To name such treach'rous Healths, thou art mad;
  " *But, not with too much Learning.*"

VI.

In harmless Words they parlied first;
  As, " *You lie, Sir; and you lie:*
" *Thou art a Scoundrel,* W——r :
  " B——n, *thou art a meer Bully.*"
Then wanting Words to vent their Rage,
  They're forc'd to come to Blows;
W——r lugg'd B——n Ass's Ears,
  B——n tweak'd W——r's Nose.

VII.

Mars now let loose the Dogs of War,
  " To Arms," the Furies sound:
Earth to its very Center shook,
  When B——n fell to the Ground:
Oh! could blind *Homer* * but have seen,
  And sung, this mighty Battle,
How City Heads broke City Stones!
  How Chains of Gold did rattle!

VIII

How *W—r*'s pale Nose grew red,
    And spouted Streams of Blood;
How from the Breeches Knees of *B—n*
    Down rush'd a tawny Flood!
The Hero smil'd 'midst all his Fears,
    To find out by the Smell;
And by the Colour to discern,
    It was not Blood that fell.

IX.

And now, ye sober Citizens,
    Be warn'd by *B—n*'s sad Fate;
Observe *King Charles the Martyr*'s Rule,
    And *drink no Healths of State*:
But, if you needs must drink a Health,
    Then be advis'd by me,
Leave out the dangerous Words *brave Prince*,
    And only drink plain C———†.

X

And so God bless our good Lord-Mayor,
    A worthy Citizen;
And grant his Chair may ne'er be fill'd
    With such a F———l as *B———*:
May Men of Decency and Sense
    Our City Feasts still guide well;
And crazy Sots sent to preside
    At *Bedlam*, or at *Bridewell* ‖.

† By which is meant *Church, Con-stitution*, &c.
‖ The worthy Mr. Al—d—n *B—n* is President of both these Hospitals; famous for the sound Sense and good Morals of their Govenors, as well as Inhabitants.

On seeing the Workmen employed upon the Preparations for the FIRE-WORKS *in the* Green-Park, *on* SUNDAY *last.*

—— *Dies Solis, non Sabbati.* ——

FREED from the Toils of War, and long Distress,
Her Bliss increasing, tho' her Merit less,
Ungrateful *Britain!* scarce the Tempest o'er,
But of the Hand that still'd it thinks no more.
From her once fav'rite Isle Religion's fled,
And we again in Heathen Footsteps tread;
Like the poor *Persians*, we no more aspire,
Sunk from the God of Heav'n to serve the God of Fire.

On opposing the late Mutiny and Desertion Bill.

WHY has Lord E—— against this Bill
His whole declamatory Skill
So tediously exerted?
The Reason's plain—for t'other Day
He mutiny'd himself, for Pay,
And he has twice deserted.

EPIGRAM, *occasion'd by a Religious Dispute at* BATH.

ON Reason, Faith, and Mystery high,
Two Wits harangue the Table;
B——y believes he knows not why,
N—— swears 'tis all a Fable.

Peace, Coxcombs, Peace; and both agree,
    N— kils thy empty Brother;
Religion laughs at Foes like thee,
    And dreads a Friend like t'other.

PANTINE. *In Part an Imitation of the 8th Satire of the First Book of* HORACE.

FROM Rags to Paper, then to Pasteboard chang'd,
    From Toy to Toy the Artist's Fancy rang'd,
Whether to make me *Card,* or spruce *Pantine;*
Implements form'd to please, and go between:
The beaten Road no longer he'll pursue,
But for the Ladies strike out something new:
Hence a *Pantine* egregious I arose,
Silent Interpreter 'twixt *Belles* and *Beaux;*
Worn out almost in Service of the Fair,
At length a *Statesman* took me to his Care.
    Here dang'rous Secrets might *Pantine* unfold;
What snarling Patriots fawn'd, and took the Gold;
How *Two* fam'd *B———rs* (who the Publick plunder'd)
Sunk and emerg'd, and strain'd, and flounc'd and blun-
    der'd;
Ev'n 'midst the *War* made Opposition cease,
And bound our Fleets and Armies to the *Peace;*
Were disconcerted if our Foes we beat,
Laugh'd at our *Loss,* and join'd in our *Defeat.*
But when the *elder B———r* cross'd the Water,
Then I became their *prime Neg—ti—or.*
    As such, when first I launch'd from *E———n*'s Shore,
A Fortress strong upon my Back I bore,
On which *C. B.* in Letters plain appear'd:
But *homewards* when again my Course I steer'd,
To *D.* they varied shifting like the Wind;
Seas wav'd before, and Works were rais'd behind.
                            Again

Again I failed like proud *Don* PHILIP crown'd;
But home return'd like wretched *Hostage* bound,
With *H.* indors'd, and *Ninety thousand Pound.*
In short, *their* Boasts let envious Statesmen cease,
Know all—— *Pantine* procur'd your glorious P——e.

   FLACCUS, in arch Satyrick Strain, relates
How fell CANIDIA poisons those she hates;
How SAGANA consumes poor Infants Gizzards,
Vile Witches: But my Patrons were no *Wizzards*:
Yet, NERO like, could strip their Mother bare,
And ev'n her Vitals from her Bosom tear.
But ere again I'd act the Courtier's Tool,
I'd Refuge seek, in p—k—y Beau's Closestool.

   Last Night, intent, th' illustrious *B—rs* fate;
To give the *Coup-de-Grace* to *B—n's* Fate;
Quoth HAL, ' My B—r dear, let's e'en agree,
' The Fort surrender'd, to give up the Key.'——
' Agreed, (the other cries) with all my Heart;
' Let's give up All, 'tis mean to keep a Part.'

   Amaz'd I heard upon a Peg elate,
Our All surrender'd, e'en without Debate:
And shudd'ring down I tumbled from on High,
Like HERMES swift descending from the Sky.

   Aghast they cry, while Conscience yerks the Lash,
' Our Doom's at hand; What means that sudden
   ' Crash?'
But when their poor *Pantine* they prostrate see
' Strange Pow'r of Guilt! what Coward Slaves are
   ' we!
' Schock'd at the Fall of Pasteboard or a Card,
' While *Br——n* sinks without our least Regard.'

On admitting SOLDIERS, *under Arms, into St.* PAUL'*s
on the* Thanksgiving-Day.

HIS G—— of —— begun this Union,
    To guard our *Protestant* Communion:
He join'd the *Crosier* and the *Sword*,
Prov'd a *Red H—rr—g* on Record.
And *well rewarded* was his Labour,
To CANT. *translated* since, from EBOR.
If LONDON'*s* D——n improves the Hint,
What *Crime* or *Wonder* is there in't?
For since the *Army*, as no Stranger,
Receiv'd the *Church* in Time of *Danger*;
Is it unjust, or can it harm ye,
That now the *Church* admits the *Army?*

On the THANKSGIVING, *and the* JUBILEE-BALL
that is to follow it.

WHether inspir'd by *Heav'n*, or mov'd by *H—*,
    They made this *P—*, what Conjurer can tell?
'Twould puzzle *Britain*'s deepest MACHIAVEL.
If from *Above* the *gen'ral Blessing* flow,
(Since *Peace* is CHRIST'*s Beautitude*, we know)
At least, might not the *Terms* be hatch'd *Below?*
Superior Praise is rational and true:
But in the *doubtful Case*, which we pursue,
The Proverb says, *Let* SATAN *have his Due.*
Embarrass'd thus betwixt the *Good* and *Evil*,
The *B——rs* give, with Complaisance most civil,
This Day to God, *To-morrow* to the D———.

A PINDARICK ODE* *upon* ODDITIES. Extempore.

THE *Thansgiving-Day!* the *Jubilee-Ball!*
    The *Fireworks Fair!*   O rare! O rare!

  * *Irr*egularity of Numbers *be the chief Characteristick of a Pin-
*dar*ic*k*, *we must own our Correspondent has very happily succeeded.*

Changed

Chang'd Darkness to Light, made Fools to be wise,
   And lighten'd the Air.   O rare! &c.
The Fire of the *Green-Park* dispell'd all the Clouds,
   Made the *Ether* full *bright*:
The Crouds who resorted, the numberless Mob, did drink and carouse,
   And laugh at the Sight!   O rare! &c.
Such a Meeting of Hotch-potch, and Mongrels,
   Sure never was seen;
Who all flock'd together to ask but one Question?
   ' Sirs, What does it mean?'
The Cuckow aloft did answer the Thousands,
   ' 'Tis *April* Cajole,
' When Dukes are a Sporting, and Fools go a Nutting,
   ' The whole is a Droll.
Ye *Frenchmen*, I charge you, grin not nor laugh,
At Folly and Nonsense, nor Fireworks on Fire!
   It's merry enough
To see our *Green-Park* made the Net to catch Fools,
Who now fume and fret, and rail in high Pet,
   Because they are Tools.   O rare! &c.
To heap the Fools Pence into other Mens Pockets,
   And empty their own;
This was a strange Farce, which catch'd Great and Small,
   Tho' hatch'd in the Moon.
Ye Women and Fools, ye Children,
   And all who were there,
Be sure you remember the Wonders of *April*,
   And the Fireworks Fair!   O rare! &c.
The Laughter of Nations, the Sport of the Cunning,
   Full forty good Thousands
      Blown up in the Air.   O rare! O rare!

F I N I S.

www.ingramcontent.com/pod-product-compliance
Lightning Source LLC
Chambersburg PA
CBHW051738300426
44115CB00007B/611